The Singapore Story by the History-makers – Volume 1

SPEAKING
TRUTH TO POWER
SINGAPORE'S PIONEER PUBLIC SERVANTS

The Singapore Story by the History-makers

Print ISSN: 2661-4871
Online ISSN: 2661-488X

Series Editor: Loke Hoe Yeong

This book series showcases Singapore's history, through the words of the key figures themselves. Drawing on the records of the Oral History Centre at the National Archives of Singapore, this series presents transcripts of interviews with leaders from the fields of public service, politics, business, among others, with extensive annotations on biographical and historical background that make for easy reading. The series aims to serve as a valuable resource for future research, while also making the material accessible to a wider audience.

Published:

Vol. 1   *Speaking Truth to Power: Singapore's Pioneer Public Servants*
         by Loke Hoe Yeong

The Singapore Story by the History-makers – Volume 1

SPEAKING TRUTH TO POWER

SINGAPORE'S PIONEER PUBLIC SERVANTS

EDITED BY

LOKE HOE YEONG

NEW JERSEY · LONDON · SINGAPORE · BEIJING · SHANGHAI · HONG KONG · TAIPEI · CHENNAI · TOKYO

Published by

World Scientific Publishing Co. Pte. Ltd.
5 Toh Tuck Link, Singapore 596224
USA office: 27 Warren Street, Suite 401-402, Hackensack, NJ 07601
UK office: 57 Shelton Street, Covent Garden, London WC2H 9HE

British Library Cataloguing-in-Publication Data
A catalogue record for this book is available from the British Library.

The Singapore Story by the History-makers — Vol. 1
SPEAKING TRUTH TO POWER
Singapore's Pioneer Public Servants

Copyright © 2020 by World Scientific Publishing Co. Pte. Ltd.

All rights reserved. This book, or parts thereof, may not be reproduced in any form or by any means, electronic or mechanical, including photocopying, recording or any information storage and retrieval system now known or to be invented, without written permission from the publisher.

For photocopying of material in this volume, please pay a copying fee through the Copyright Clearance Center, Inc., 222 Rosewood Drive, Danvers, MA 01923, USA. In this case permission to photocopy is not required from the publisher.

ISBN 978-981-121-151-5
ISBN 978-981-121-212-3 (pbk)

For any available supplementary material, please visit
https://www.worldscientific.com/worldscibooks/10.1142/11586t=suppl

Desk Editors: Daniele Lee/Jiang Yulin

Typeset by Stallion Press
Email: enquiries@stallionpress.com

About the Book

It is said that the duty of public servants is to "speak truth to power" — to give honest, sound and sometimes unpopular advice to political leaders. Underneath the narrative of the Singapore story, as personified by Lee Kuan Yew and the first-generation leaders, lie the lesser-known tales of dedicated public servants in the nation-building process. Singapore's development cannot be fully understood without considering the role of those in public service during the transition to independence from the 1950s to 60s.

Featuring oral history interviews from the National Archives of Singapore with 11 pioneer public servants, *Speaking Truth to Power: Singapore's Pioneer Public Servants* reveals first-hand, personal accounts of the civil service's transition from the colonial era, their relationship with the political leaders, and how Singapore's economic development was driven by sound public administration in those critical years. The annotated interviews make for an easily readable format for researchers and general audiences alike.

About the Editor

Loke Hoe Yeong is a London-based analyst and researcher on politics and international affairs. Formerly an Associate Fellow at the European Union Centre in Singapore, National University of Singapore, he has published widely in academic journals and the media on a range of subjects from Europe-Asia relations to Southeast Asian politics and public policy, besides being a guest commentator on international affairs for TV.

He is the author of *Let The People Have Him – Chiam See Tong, The Early Years*, a biography of one of Singapore's longest-serving politicians which was shortlisted for the 2016 Singapore Literature Prize, and *The First Wave*, a history of the opposition in post-independence Singapore. He holds an MSc in Comparative Politics from the London School of Economics and Political Science.

Contents

About the Book	v
About the Editor	vii
Editor's Note	xi
Photo Credits	xiii
Introduction	xv

Wee Chong Jin — 1
The first local Chief Justice

Goh Koh Pui — 35
Chairman of the Port of Singapore Authority

Abdul Wahab Ghows — 75
Solicitor-General and High Court Judge

Hedwig Anuar — 101
Director of the National Library

Kwa Soon Bee — 117
Pioneer of Singapore's healthcare system

Alan Choe — 133
The Housing and Development Board's first architect-planner, and founder of the Urban Redevelopment Authority

Chan Chin Bock — 153
Chairman of the Economic Development Board

J. Y. Pillay — 167
The man behind Singapore Airlines

Ngiam Tong Dow — 199
The maverick Perm Sec

Tommy Koh — 239
Singapore's representative at the United Nations

Winston Choo — 267
The first Chief of Defence Force

Editor's Note

The transcripts in the book have been edited for grammar and for easier reading, while preserving the interviewees' personal speaking styles as far as possible in order to avoid misrepresentation. This largely adheres to the principles of editing oral history transcripts as in the Chicago Manual of Style. The original transcripts may be viewed at the Oral History Interviews @ Archives Online website of the National Archives of Singapore.

The transcripts have been arranged in the order of the interviewees' date of birth, so that there is a more chronological presentation of the various aspects of Singapore's history which they discuss.

While we respect the narratives recounted by our interviewees, we recognise that all oral history accounts, by their very nature, are personal, experiential and interpretive. They are founded on the memories, perceptions and viewpoints of individuals. While all reasonable attempts have been taken to avoid inaccuracies, the excerpts of the interviews found in this book should not be understood as statements of fact endorsed by the National Archives of Singapore, an institution of the National Library Board; the publisher; or the editor.

Photo Credits

The publisher acknowledges the following for their kind permission to reproduce photos in this book:

- Ministry of Information and the Arts Collection, courtesy of National Archives of Singapore

  p. 1

  p. 35

  p. 75

  p. 101

  p. 117

  p. 133

  p. 199

- The ACS Echo

  p. 153

- J. Y. Pillay

  p. 167

- Tommy Koh

  p. 239

- Winston Choo

  p. 267

Introduction

The figure of Lee Kuan Yew has been so dominant and so closely associated with Singapore that "it is tempting to credit him with all that is good or bad about Singapore," as Lam Peng Er and Kevin Tan observed in their edited volume *Lee's Lieutenants*. They added that "Singapore's economic development, political depoliticisation, the emergence of PAP's one-party dominance and the eventual paramount leadership of Lee cannot be understood without analysing the central role of his lieutenants," by which they refer to the Old Guard of the People's Action Party (PAP).[1]

By extension, Singapore's development cannot be fully understood without considering the role of the batch of public servants who served during Singapore's transition to independence from the 1950s to the 1960s.

The public policy successes of Singapore have made it of outsized interest to governments, policymakers, academics and the general public around the world. There are many publications on the current state of Singapore's civil service, including publications from the Lee Kuan Yew School of Public Policy, National University of Singapore. However, there is much less material on the evolution of the Singapore civil service as we know it today, especially in comparison to that on Singapore's political leaders around the time of independence. Perhaps this is to be attributed in part to the famed qualities of reticence and impartiality among civil servants in many national traditions, who have always preferred to serve quietly in the background than to upstage their ministers in public view. (That said, a number of the PAP Old Guard had a background in the colonial-era civil service before entering politics, most notably Goh Keng Swee, and their stories are better known than those who remained in the civil service for the entirety of their careers.)

This volume aims to contribute towards that fuller understanding and appreciation of the role of the so-called pioneer batch of public servants.

Most of our interviewees spoke of being fresh and lacking in experience when being approached to take on rather senior positions in public service, even as they went into those roles bursting with enthusiasm and a clear sense of purpose.

Of the Economic Development Board's (EDB) early efforts, J. Y. Pillay commented that "it would appear that we were a bunch of amateurs going about this process of industrial development in an amateurish manner." Pillay explained that "we tried our best to figure out what was the most appropriate course, given the limited resources at our disposal."

When Goh Keng Swee told a 30-year-old Winston Choo that he would be groomed to become the Director of General Staff — the highest position in the SAF that is now known

---

[1] Lam and Tan, 1999, vii–viii.

as the Chief of Defence Force — Choo said he was too young. Similarly, when Lee Kuan Yew approached a 30-year-old Tommy Koh to be Singapore's Permanent Representative to the United Nations (UN), Koh responded in disbelief: "It cannot be." Koh recalled that the Ministry of Foreign Affairs at that time consisted of just a few officers housed in a suite of a few rooms, and did not have a UN division nor even a desk officer in charge of the UN. In fact, there was not even a career foreign service to speak of, and it was Koh who convinced the prime minister to start one, because of the specialised skills and training required to be a foreign service officer.

Was the civil service then so bereft of local talent, or was this a sign of humility on the part of the pioneer public servants? The 1958 report of the Public Service Commission, which noted the difficulties of finding suitably qualified and experienced local candidates for posts vacated by the expatriate British officers, suggested that it is the former.

In this introduction, we explore three main themes around which the interviews with the public servants featured in this volume have revolved, relating to the transition from colonial rule to merger with Malaysia to independence in 1965. The historical context for their accounts is also provided here.

Malayanisation

In speaking of the featured interviewees as "pioneers", we do not in any way suggest that Singapore's civil service started from a blank slate upon independence. There had been a civil service operating almost continuously since Stamford Raffles founded modern Singapore in 1819 as a trading emporium. It continued even during the Japanese occupation of Singapore from 1942 to 1945, although it was an unsystemic form of government subordinate to a military administration — one that bred some of the worst forms of corruption Singapore had known.

For sure, the civil service of the British colonial era had often been derided for discriminating against local officers in matters of salaries and promotional prospects. On the eve of independence, it was blamed particularly for its inadequate responses towards the urban housing crisis in Singapore, among other issues.

But comparisons with the administrative bureaucracies that developed in other countries like Thailand, the only nation in Southeast Asia that was never colonised, are instructive. By the time of King Chulalongkorn's reign in the late 19th century, it was recognised that the problems of the traditional Thai public bureaucracy — its feudalistic, hierarchical nature — was in dire need of modernisation and reform. Accordingly, European government advisors were employed by the monarchy towards that end.[2]

---

[2] Quah, 1978, 19–23.

More importantly perhaps, the new PAP leaders of an independent Singapore must have deemed many aspects of the British civil service structures fine enough to have kept them largely intact. The chief among this were the Public Service Commission (PSC), the elite Administrative Service, and schemes such as the Central Provident Fund (CPF).

Already in 1946, the British colonial administration had begun the process of Malayanisation — of gradually staffing more and more service positions with local officers, with the view that self-government for Singapore was only realisable if more locals took up the reins of administration. It tabled a white paper entitled "Organisation of the Colonial Service" which stated that progress towards self-government for Singapore could only be realised if the civil service was staffed as far as possible by local officers.

Nevertheless in 1955, the incoming Labour Front government of David Marshall, Singapore's first Chief Minister, felt the Malayanisation process to be unsatisfactorily slow, and therefore set up the Malayanisation Commission to speed things up. That commission recommended further measures such as mandating the PSC with executive control over the appointments and promotions of civil servants, where it had previously been merely an advisory body.

The interviewees in this volume discussed the issues and circumstances behind this protracted "handover" process from the British. Goh Koh Pui was one of the earliest recipients of a scholarship from the civil service — specifically the Labour Department — to study law in London, the intent of which was to specifically cultivate local talent in the upper echelons of the Singapore civil service.

Attitudes towards the departing British administrators were mixed among our interviewees. On the Malayanisation process of handover, Goh Koh Pui said the British were "gentlemanly" and "did it very gracefully without any sign of grudge or resentment," while Abdul Wahab Ghows regarded his head of department at the Official Assignee as "a very good superior," with reference to that superior's mentorship in preparation for Malayanisation.

On the other hand, Ngiam Tong Dow noted a stark difference between the hierarchical nature of the British civil service and the collegial atmosphere fostered by Goh Keng Swee and Hon Sui Sen, the finance minister and permanent secretary of the Ministry of Finance respectively, despite Ngiam being a very junior officer in that ministry then. Yet others like Alan Choe were scathing in their assessment of the shortcomings of the colonial administrators and the Singapore Improvement Trust (SIT) in their housing policies, while Kwa Soon Bee's worldview was coloured by his experiences of racial discrimination when studying in Edinburgh (in another part of his interview transcript that is not reproduced in this volume, Kwa said rather unambivalently: "I have no love for the British").

After coming to power in 1959, the PAP government initiated the Political Study Centre, located at 4 Goodwood Hill, as a means of socialising civil servants to the local conditions in Singapore. There had already been a Staff Training School established by the British for the skills and vocational training of public servants, but the PAP had felt that they still held a "colonial mentality" that was not attuned to the needs of the local population.[3] Unsurprisingly, the Political Study Centre had a reputation for being an institution for "brainwashing", not least because of the choice of its rather loaded name.[4] Furthermore, Lee Kuan Yew and Goh Keng Swee had themselves given lectures at the centre on occasion, and the centre's curriculum was drawn up by a committee led by S. Rajaratnam, then the Minister for Culture. Hedwig Anuar was one of the civil servants given the responsibility of giving lectures at the Political Study Centre, while Ngiam Tong Dow recalled his times studying there.

The PAP leaders were probably fearful of the hostility of the civil service towards them, as they were aware of their reputation then of being pro-Communist and "anti-civil service", as Goh Koh Pui put it. The PAP government closed the centre in 1969, explaining that it had achieved its mission when all senior members of the civil service had passed through its doors — but probably also because the PAP had felt confident about having consolidated political power, including their control over the civil service.

Like the civil service, the Singapore Armed Forces was not formed from an empty slate either. It has its origins in the Singapore Volunteer Rifle Corps, which was formed in 1854, comprising mainly of the European residents of Singapore, and was one of the first such volunteer forces in the British Empire. Through several rounds of reorganisation over the years, the group played a role in quelling riots between the Chinese secret societies, in the Sepoy Mutiny of 1915, and in the defence of Singapore against the Japanese in World War II.

The group was renamed the People's Defence Force in 1965, the year Singapore separated from Malaysia, by which time it was already part of a military force that would be eventually known as the Singapore Armed Forces (SAF). The 1st Battalion, Singapore Infantry Regiment (1 SIR), which Winston Choo joined in 1961 after becoming a commissioned officer, was part of the SAF's predecessor.

Relationship between civil servants and political leaders

The working relationship between civil servants and political leaders is a subject of fascination. The Northcote-Trevelyan Report of 1854, prepared by a cabinet minister and a civil servant in the United Kingdom, was the seminal document that established two key principles of the British civil service — of recruitment on the basis of merit, and of political impartiality. The recommendations of the report were met with resistance from several quarters, and some of them were not even implemented until the early years of the 20th century.

---

[3] Quah, 1978, 18.
[4] Low, 2018, 36.

Rather than being a natural order of things, the British-bequeathed civil service and the qualities it stood for were born of a struggle of sorts that continued into the era of Singapore's self-government. In the last days of colonial rule in the Singapore of the 1950s and 1960s, the civil servant-politician relationship took on a heightened tension, in the context of the political battles between the right-wing Labour Front government of Lim Yew Hock and the left-wing PAP which was in the ascendancy.

Goh Koh Pui shared shared his memories on the sentiments of civil servants towards Chief Ministers David Marshall and Lim Yew Hock, and their suspicions of Lee Kuan Yew's PAP, regarded by them then as pro-Chinese and pro-Communist in the 1950s. Things proceeded on a collision course when in 1959, the incoming PAP government removed the cost of living allowance payable to civil servants in the middle to upper salary brackets.

It was considered a drastic move which was met with "very great bitterness" by civil servants, as Goh Koh Pui recalled. Goh Keng Swee, then the Minister for Finance, explained that his government was anticipating a $14 million budget deficit inherited from the previous Labour Front government, and needed to make major cuts in public expenditures. Nevertheless, the allowances were restored in 1961. It was only after the Harvey Report of 1968 on public sector salaries that the PAP government began to raise civil service pay, as a means of competing for talent.

We observe a variety of experiences some of our interviewees had in working with Lee Kuan Yew that, ranging from the young Tommy Koh's relatively collegial, lawyer-to-lawyer relationship with the prime minister, compared to Alan Choe's awe and fear of Lee during Choe's time in the Housing and Development Board (HDB). Winston Choo spoke at length about his working relationship through meetings, discussions and study trips with the no-nonsense Goh Keng Swee, whom he regarded with a mix of trepidation and admiration. J. Y. Pillay gave a flavour of the more recent working relationship between permanent secretaries and their ministers, including his frank insights on how the former dislike ministers who "would not accept the consequences of ministerial responsibility" or who are "a bit wobbly in that respect."

One well-known example where different ministers and civil servants were genuinely at odds with each other was on building the Mass Rapid Transit (MRT) system for Singapore. Robust discussions ensued because of the huge expenditure required, which led some heavyweight ministers such as Goh Keng Swee and Tony Tan to doggedly call for an all-bus transport system instead, against Ong Teng Cheong's, then the Minister for Communications, and Ngiam Tong Dow's push for the MRT ("He nearly torpedoed it," Ngiam recalled about Goh Keng Swee's stance towards the MRT). We learn that Lee Kuan Yew did not take a clear stance on the divisive issue ("He was sitting on the fence," Ngiam said). We also learn of how Goh and Ngiam tested their arguments with each other — Goh made Ngiam quantify the benefits of the MRT system in per citizen terms, while Ngiam argued that an all-bus system would lead to congested roads as Singapore's population grew. It was Ngiam, the loyal but outspoken civil servant, who won that argument of the day.

The gold standard of the impartiality of the civil service would ultimately be tested in the government's relation with the judiciary. Here, Chief Justice Wee Chong Jin explained how he "didn't like to have to go and see" Lee Kuan Yew, because Wee wanted to disassociate the judiciary from the ruling PAP as much as possible. We also learn about the arrangement where Lee would strictly have had to make an appointment in order to speak to Wee, and how Wee would decline to meet Lee during court hours.

Abdul Wahab Ghows related how Lee Kuan Yew was fuming when it was brought to his attention that Singapore had no specific law to tackle aircraft hijacking — a hijacked Vietnam Airlines flight had landed in Seletar Airport in 1977. The hijackers were eventually arrested under the Criminal Law Temporary Provisions, and within two weeks, Ghows drafted the Hijacking and Protection of Aircraft Act.

The neutrality of civil servants perhaps reaches its ultimate test in matters of controversial policies that may deeply conflict with their personal beliefs. Here, Kwa Soon Bee discussed the controversial government policies on abortion and family planning in the 1970s — while Kwa's own views were largely aligned with the government's, as he explained, he had the task of handling with delicate care the government's exchanges with groups such as the Roman Catholic Church and with Muslims on the matter.

Economic development

Singapore has flourished since its modern founding in 1819 because of its role in the entrepôt trade for the region — a trading hub to which goods are brought for re-export. In the course of the 1950s however, that role was in steep decline, because many countries and territories in the region became independent and their new governments were implementing protectionist economic policies.

In 1960, the Singapore government invited a team from the United Nations Development Programme (UNDP) to conduct an industrial survey mission, in a bid to kickstart industrialisation as a solution to Singapore's economic challenges. Albert Winsemius, the government's long-time economic advisor, first came to Singapore as part of that UNDP team, as did Tang I-Fang, a Chinese-born engineer and consultant who later played a key role in the EDB. The resultant UNDP report recommended a 10-year industrialisation programme for Singapore, and identified a core role for the EDB in trade promotion.

The report also made the recommendation for a common market to be formed between Singapore and Malaysia. Given the small size of Singapore's market, Winsemius thought it imperative that its goods be able to move in and out of Malaysia without duties and tariffs. Political merger with Malaysia took place in 1963 before the common market was established, and indeed, negotiations towards a common market carried on throughout Singapore's two years in Malaysia. In his interview here, Ngiam Tong Dow gave an account of the fraught discussions with Malaysia over the common market as well as on the common currency problem.

In any case, neither the common market nor political merger, which ended with Singapore's separation from Malaysia on 9 August 1965, succeeded. This forced Singapore onto a route of trading with the world at large rather than narrowly within Southeast Asia. Chan Chin Bock characterised the failure of merger and the common market as a "blessing in disguise," setting Singapore on a path of "first mover's advantage in globalisation," long before globalisation became a catchword in the 1990s.

Oral history, and Singapore's Oral History Centre

There are a number of challenges in working with oral history. Human memory can be imperfect, and different accounts of the same historical event by different persons could show up contradictions. There could be further contradictions with the written record. Even where no contradictions are apparent, the memories of an interviewee are inherently coloured by their biases and other personal experiences.

Nevertheless, there is also the false assumption that written documents are necessarily superior to an oral history record. In fact, oral history interviews provide the chance for the interviewee to be interrogated on their recollections of the past, whereas a diary, an autobiography or other historical documents cannot be. Oral history has thus become an established sub-discipline of history and an accepted category in the humanities and social sciences today.

The Oral History Centre was established in 1979, at a time when the country's anxieties of economic survival were giving way to a new-found confidence about its future. The establishment of the centre was an initiative of Goh Keng Swee, then Deputy Prime Minister, who said that "its first task was to collect information on the power struggle waged between the leaders of the People's Action Party (PAP) and the underground Singapore City Committee of the Malayan Communist Party."[5]

Nevertheless for Kwa Chong Guan, the former Director of the Oral History Centre, the centre also provided a medium for the PAP leaders as well as the PAP's opponents to record their role in history, and more broadly also to locate that political history "within a wider and longer historical context and explore its ramifications on our social and economic history."[6] In 1983, the first exhibition held by the National Archives, before the Oral History Centre was merged with it, made an attempt to extend the "Road to Nationhood" narrative back to 1819. Its other

---

[5] Kwa, 2008, 624.
[6] Kwa, 2005.

exhibitions also tried to explore Singapore's history in a bottom-up approach, such as in giving a voice to lightermen, stevedores and boatmen in an oral history project on the history of the Singapore River.

The selection of featured interviewees

The interviewees selected to be featured in this volume played a key role in their respective areas of the public service in the immediate years after Singapore's independence in 1965. The exception perhaps is Kwa Soon Bee, who was the Permanent Secretary for Health in the early 1980s — because that was when the most extensive reforms on health care policy in Singapore took place, with regard to the restructuring of hospitals, MediSave and MediFund. A conscious effort was made to ensure a broad enough representation of different policy areas in which our interviewees worked. In the crucial realm of economic development, for which there are more than one representative interviewees, effort was also made to ensure a diversity of areas and issues was covered within that.

Invariably, there are notable omissions from the pantheon of Singapore's "pioneer public servants." First and foremost, that is simply because not all of them have done oral history interviews with the National Archives. Even when they had, the resultant transcripts were sometimes classified and their release restricted; and when they were marked for open access, they were sometimes too brief and superficial for the purposes of our book series. Finally, there are prominent figures who had straddled the realms of civil service and politics, but whom are chiefly remembered today in the latter realm — Goh Keng Swee being the most notable example.

Nevertheless, there is scope and material for possible future volumes to feature pioneer civil servants missed out here.

Bibliography

Chua Mui Hoong [with additional interviews by Ken Kwek]. *Pioneers Once More: The Singapore Public Service, 1959–2009.* Singapore: Straits Times Press and Public Service Division, 2010.

Haque, M. Shamsul. "Public Administration and Public Governance in Singapore." In: Pan Suk Kim, ed., *Public Administration and Public Governance in ASEAN Member Countries and Korea.* Seoul: Daeyoung Moonhwasa Publishing Company, 2009: 246–271.

Kwa Chong Guan. "Desultory Reflections on the Oral History Centre at Twenty-Five." In: Oral History Centre, *Reflections and Interpretations, Oral History Centre 25th Anniversary Publication.* Singapore: Oral History Centre, National Archives of Singapore, National Heritage Board, 2005.

Kwa Chong Guan. "Oral Histories in the Making of Our Memories and Heritage." *Asian Journal of Social Science,* Vol. 36, No. 3/4 (2008).

Lam Peng Er and Kevin Y. L. Tan, eds. *Lee's Lieutenants: Singapore's Old Guard*. St Leonards: Allen & Unwin, 1999.

Lim, Patricia Pui Huen, James H. Morrison, and Kwa Chong Guan, eds. *Oral History in Southeast Asia: Theory and Method*. Singapore: Institute of Southeast Asian Studies, 2000.

Low, James. "Milestone Programs for the Administrative Service in the Singapore Public Service." In: Andrew Podger and John Wanna, eds. *Sharpening the Sword of State: Building Executive Capacities in the Public Services of the Asia-Pacific*. Acton: ANU Press, 2016.

Low, James. *Inception Point: The Use of Learning and Development to Reform the Singapore Public Service*. Singapore: World Scientific, 2018.

Ngiam Tong Dow and Simon Tay, eds. *A Mandarin and the Making of Public Policy: Reflections by Ngiam Tong Dow*. Singapore: NUS Press, 2006.

Public Service Division, Prime Minister's Office, Singapore. *Heart of Public Service: Our Institutions*. Singapore: Public Service Division, Prime Minister's Office, 2015.

Public Service Division, Prime Minister's Office, Singapore. *Heart of Public Service: Our People*. Singapore: Public Service Division, Prime Minister's Office, 2015.

Quah, Jon S. T. *The Origins of the Public Bureaucracies in the ASEAN Countries*. Singapore: Chopmen Enterprises, 1978.

Quah, Jon S. T. *Public Administration Singapore-Style*. Bingley, UK: Emerald Group Publishing, 2010.

UNDP Global Centre for Public Service Excellence. *UNDP and the Making of Singapore's Public Service Lessons from Albert Winsemius*. Singapore: UNDP Global Centre for Public Service Excellence, 2015.

Wee Chong Jin

The first local Chief Justice

Date of interview: November 1994
Interviewer: Elisabeth Eber-Chan

Wee Chong Jin (1917–2005) was the first Singaporean and the first Asian to be the Chief Justice of Singapore, a position that had existed since the Straits Settlements was officially transferred to the Colonial Office in London in 1867.

Born in Penang, Malaysia, Wee studied law at the University of Cambridge. He returned first to Penang in 1940, and then moved to Singapore the following year to join the law firm of Allen & Gledhill. During the Japanese Occupation, he stayed in Penang.

In 1957, he became the first local member of the Singapore Bar to be appointed as a high court judge, as well as the youngest. In 1963, he became the first local Chief Justice of Singapore.

In 1966, after Singapore separated from Malaysia, Wee chaired the Constitutional Commission that was formed to recommend measures to be included in the Constitution of Singapore to protect racial and religious minorities. The Presidential Council for Minority Rights, one of the outcomes of the Constitutional Commission, was established in 1973, and Wee was appointed its inaugural chairman.

At his retirement from the judiciary in 1990, Wee was the longest serving Chief Justice in Singapore and in the Commonwealth. In 1991, he was appointed the inaugural chairman of the Presidential Council for Religious Harmony.

In this interview, Wee shared about the events surrounding his appointment as a high court judge and as the first local Chief Justice of Singapore. In doing so, he also discussed matters on the separation of powers between the judiciary and the executive, and his relationship with the PAP government over the years.

Becoming a judge

EEC **Chief, can you start with the last couple of years before you became a Judge. You had changed practice in a sense. Mr Walters[1] had died and you had joined Wee Swee Teow & Company. What work did you do then?**

WCJ I was doing general work and very little conveyancing. More general work and litigation, although there was not much litigation. So it was a comparatively quiet time for me. At that time, maybe three or four or five years before I went on the Bench, the Chief Justice was Sir John Whyatt. He was the Attorney-General in Kenya. When the Mau Mau[2] was at its height, he was the Attorney-General. But I think for what he did in Kenya, he was then promoted to be the Chief Justice of Singapore, which was a big promotion then. But he had one characteristic which none of those who were before him had. He had no colour bar. In fact, he was very anxious to lead locals to take the place in the running of Singapore. He used to say: "The time is coming very soon when locals should be on the Bench."

EEC **Was he the only one of the expatriate judges who had this view at that time you think, Chief?**

WCJ I am sure he was. When I went on the Bench, Ah Tah had come in 1954. That was during Whyatt's time. He was the first. Then Freddy had come in just a few months before I came in. In the same year.[3]

EEC **That is correct. In March 1957. Your elevation was September 1957?**

WCJ August 1957.

---

[1] David Keri Walters was the senior partner of the law firm of which Wee Chong Jin was junior partner. Walters died suddenly in 1950.

[2] An anti-colonial armed rebel group in Kenya active in the 1950s.

[3] In reference to Tan Ah Tah and Frederick Arthur Chua ("Freddy") — Wee's fellow high court judges.

EEC It was reported in the MLJ [Malayan Law Journal] of September. That's why I recall the date September.

WCJ I think C. C. Tan was the one who spoke.[4]

EEC He was the Chairman of the Bar Council at that time. Who made the approach to you, Chief? Tell us, did you have to think about it?

WCJ Let's see if my recollection is a hundred per cent accurate. It was John Whyatt, the Chief Justice, who sent for me. He came straight to the point, saying that we had never had a Judge of the Supreme Court from the local Bar. He had been asked to sound me out whether I would accept the appointment to the Supreme Court Bench. My first answer to him was: "But I'm far too young." It had been brought up in the tradition that when you go on to the Supreme Court Bench, you should be in your 50s.

EEC You were then about 46.

WCJ No, I was under 40.

EEC You were under 40. In 1957, you were 40.

WCJ I was under 40. And that's what I said. Well, he said, "No. Somebody has got to start, to lead by accepting an appointment to the Bench. Because the time will come when you will be self-governing and you'll have your independence. Singapore should have its own local judges. Local conditions and all that."

So I said, "Yes, I'll have to think about it. I have to consult my wife. I'm just starting a family."

The Governor was then Sir Robert Black. "The Governor would see you." So an appointment was made and I went. The Governor repeated what John Whyatt had

---

[4] Tan Chye Cheng ("C. C. Tan"), a lawyer and politician who was one of the founders of the Progressive Party.

said. And he said, "Well, you know, we have already sent your name to London, to whatever it is, to the Ministry that appoints colonial judges. And I can tell you that they have already looked at your record. If you'll accept, it's not a conditional subject for London's approval. The approval has been pre-given."

So I said, "Well, that's very kind of them. But I must consult my wife."

I knew from what John Whyatt told me that John Eber (old man Eber)[5] was one of the ones who were consulted, and he had very strongly recommended me. He seemed to like me. I was very much younger. I could be his son. He liked me a lot, my practising days. So I decided, well, if something has got to be done, we'll do it. But I don't know. It will be a sacrifice. But she was keen. She said, "Well, if you've got to do something and you think you are suited for it, I think you should accept."

I then told John Whyatt: "I'll accept. But you give me a month or so to find out everything in your office."

So I spoke to Eng Lock.[6] And, of course, he said, "Yes, you must do what you like I think you're probably suited for the Bench. You'll like it."

So I said, "Okay."

EEC **From the point of view of financial rewards which are very much talked about nowadays, Chief, was there a great difference in salary then?**

WCJ I'm saying it, but few people would believe it, I expect. I never asked what my salary was. I just never asked. Well, it was I think $1,700 or $1,800 or $1,900 a month.

EEC **Was there a discrepancy in salary between a locally recruited Judge and a colonial one?**

WCJ I wouldn't know. They had the perks and all that. Every two years they'll go on a boat for home leave for six months. Six months every two years. But that problem surfaced not very soon after. For me, it was a big drop in income. By then in the final year, I was getting about $5,000 a month which is a big difference.

---

[5] John Eber, a Eurasian Singaporean lawyer and one of the leaders of the left-wing Malayan Democratic Union. He was detained for two years in the 1950s under the Emergency Regulations.

[6] Wee Eng Lock, the lawyer who ran the firm of his father Wee Swee Teow, where Wee Chong Jin worked at that time.

So I started work. Apart from my start on the Bench, the problem of remuneration surfaced in 1959. First of all, I had to continue to live in the house.

EEC **Where were you living then, Chief?**

WCJ I was living in Cable Road off Jervois Road. But I think after a while, because of the fact that the income had dropped so much, I couldn't afford to pay rent.

EEC **Did you have children by then?**

WCJ I had Veronica who was born in 1956, and Lawrence who was born two months after I went on the Bench. Two months after I was on the bench, I had two children.

And who was there? Ah Tah was there, Freddy was there. In the service you are entitled to quarters. In the Straits Settlements Service, there were quarters. I asked John Whyatt: "Look, I can't afford it." So I was allowed to choose quarters. I stayed in Goodwood Hill. All the bungalows were government and they were all expats. I was the only local. Stanley Stewart[7] had one at the bottom of the hill. So I paid five per cent or whatever per cent of the salary or whatever is deducted.

EEC **It was a great help I suppose.**

WCJ Yes. Well, it cost much less than the rent. The leave and all that was in accordance with the locals. I worked very hard because I was young and new. I worked very, very hard the first couple of years. In early 1959, I wasn't feeling well. So I went to see Monteiro, Professor Monteiro.[8] He said, "I recommend that you take a month's leave."

Then I asked for leave. I was entitled to leave. Three weeks or whatever it is, 39 days or 30 days or what. And he recommended I should take a break and go off because I overworked. I was getting something which was stress related. And he said, "When you go there, you go and see a specialist in Harley Street,[9] one of the government ones."

---

[7] Stanley Stewart, a Penang-born Eurasian, was one of the first locals to hold senior positions in the colonial civil service, having been Permanent Secretary for Home Affairs in the late 1950s among other positions.

[8] Ernest Monteiro, a well-known doctor in Singapore in the 1950s and 60s.

[9] A street in London known for its large number of private specialists in medicine and surgery.

So I said okay. Then my wife and I took a slow cargo boat. I said, "Am I not entitled to a period of leave as a Supreme Court Judge and the government will pay my salary?"

"No, no, no. You are on local terms, as far as your leave entitlements and your perks are. One of the terms is that you must have done 10 years before you are entitled to paid leave out of Singapore."

Stanley Stewart was then in Empress Place. But he was not the one obviously responsible. I said: "It's not possible. I didn't start as a civil servant at the age of 18 or 19 or 20. I started as a Judge of the Supreme Court. What do you expect me to be? You expect me to wait until 10 or whatever number of years before I could be entitled to leave?"

"No, I'm sorry. That's it."

"Then what about my pension?" Then I started to ask all those things.

"You count. You will get your full pension at the end of 33-and-one-third years."

The retirement age then was 60 for civil servants.

EEC **So you would never have qualified for full pension.**

WCJ Do you mean to tell me that when I came on to the Supreme Court Bench, my perks and all that, except for my salary, there was no increment, flat rate? And I was the longest-serving civil servant who joined after 1951. Well, that's it. There was nothing one could do about it. So I was very, very disappointed.

So when I went to London, I was given whatever it was, the amount of leave I had which I could take. I said, "No, no, no."

"It's alright. You need another month."

"Alright, if you say I need another month, you'll have to arrange it. Then I shan't go back."

"Yes, it's alright. You go back."

He gave me a date. What he said in London carried in Singapore. I was really astounded.

EEC **You never thought to ask all these things before.**

WCJ I never, never. Because they'll take it as something you should do. That's why I think when I hear what this exercise about this is, when you go in, you don't think about it. You just accept it. And if you don't accept it, you get out.

EEC It doesn't seem right to enquire about your terms.

WCJ If I got out, I wouldn't be allowed to practise. The answer was: "I'm sorry. These are the terms of service which apply to everyone." That's colonial. I couldn't practise if I got out because as a Judge, you are barred by the Legal Profession Act. That was a tremendous blow to me.

But jumping the gun. By the time I became Chief Justice, say about 10 or 15 years, in the late seventies, I took up the question again with SM [Senior Minister at the time of interview, Lee Kuan Yew], not about my salary but about my pension. "I'm speaking not for myself, but I don't think it is right. You're going to get people into the Bench from the Bar. They could never, never, never get the full pension in the civil service because they couldn't do 33 years. You can't step onto the Bench from the Bar at the age of 30."

So the answer was: "I'm sorry. I can't upset the service structure. I can't upset." Now, as I'm talking to you, you see what's happening?

EEC There is a great change.

WCJ But I said, "That's really not fair." Perhaps it was silly of me not to have asked all these things before I accepted. And then people in practice were doing very well and all that. Look at me. Instead of being able to raise a family, I have got to use a bit of my savings. Then at the end of retirement, what do I have? Look at what people are earning at the Bar. I wished I had not accepted.

EEC You might have considered differently.

WCJ You accepted because you are suited for the Bench, rather than the hurly burly of the practice.

EEC It's hard to come back to anything like that, isn't it?

WCJ So I said, "Okay, alright."

8 • SPEAKING TRUTH TO POWER

EEC **When you came back, you came back to the High Court. And you did the same sort of work, Chief? Did you do everything that was given to you?**

WCJ Everything. There was no question of specialisation. It's just like the English judges. In England, a Judge who is top in the criminal Bar, once he goes there, he is never sent to the King's Bench Division of the Criminal Bench. He is sent to probate or something. He is sent there, you see. They expect you to be able to handle, because it's the Bar that puts the matter before you. Whatever that is put to you, you must be sufficient in the law be able to deal with it. You've got to. If you have got a case which is something you know nothing about the law, you really have not any experience, then you've got to do your homework first.

That's why I think the Bar didn't like me. When I left, they were still very hesitant about me because I used to tell them: "From my own experience, thinking that if you get into the Bench, your life is very easy. I spent more time than you spent looking at it to try and put your case before me. I think that's not good. You must all spend time on it."

EEC **That has been the subject of your remarks at the opening of the Legal Year, Chief.**

WCJ I was speaking from experience, not because I liked to tell them. I am not a teacher. So I just told them. Well, now the feedback is: "Oh, I wish you are still here."

I said, "Well, your wish is too late. You think I have the time."

Transition to the first local Chief Justice

EEC **In 1957, if we can go back to your elevation, to put it in perspective in relation to other people. Winslow[10] was then the Solicitor-General; Mr Eber, Chairman of the Bar Committee. And they said very nice things about you, Chief, when you came up on the Bench. So between 1957 and 1963, you must have worked**

---

[10] Alfred Victor (A. V.) Winslow.

terribly, terribly hard. We know that. Who made the approach to you about the Chief Justiceship?

WCJ   John Whyatt must have liked me because he was the one who initiated it, put my name up, and went through all the process of even getting everything from London through, before I was even sounded. When he left, Alan Rose succeeded him.

EEC   **That's 1960, Chief.**

WCJ   1960. The PAP had come into power in the 1959 Election. SM [Senior Minister at the time, Lee Kuan Yew], what was he called? Was he called Prime Minister or Premier?

EEC   **Yes, Prime Minister.**

WCJ   He was the one. The Governor was Sir William Goode. He was the Governor. Of course, it was the present SM — I didn't know then — who had the final say as to who was to become Chief Justice. Alan Rose was only on a two-year term.

EEC   **That's right. He had come from Ceylon.[11]**

WCJ   He had come from Ceylon. He was a very, very nice man, very intelligent. He had been Attorney-General in Ceylon and they liked him very much. When they had independence, he was there. They kept him as Attorney-General and they made him Chief Justice. He was very much liked in Ceylon. The old people from Ceylon ... So they sent him here. I was already there for three years. Whyatt told us (the judges) that Rose was going to be next CJ [Chief Justice] on a contractual term. Whyatt didn't like it. Whyatt was fighting for us, the locals. There were only Ah Tah, myself, Freddy and Ambrose.[12] You see, there were four of us already. Ah Tah had been there a long time already. Since we are already self-governing, you had a local Prime Minister already, surely the Bench had somebody who is qualified.

---

[11] As Sri Lanka was known before 1972.

[12] In reference to James Walter Davy (J. W. D.) Ambrose — Wee's fellow high court judge.

EEC **He was the most senior of them all.**

WCJ He was the most senior and he was popular. He was very nice and popular. He had whatever faults there were, but be that as it may, that's really nothing ... In fact, we went, Whyatt and all of us, the locals. Whyatt demanded a meeting with Goode, the Governor, for the judges. And so Whyatt said, "Are you all prepared to go?"

I said, "Of course, I am. I don't think it's right to get anybody other than a local."

We didn't knew it was Ah Tah. Whyatt had recommended Ah Tah. So we went to Goode. They had a tiff when they were arguing for who it was.

EEC **The whole lot of you went.**

WCJ We went. But the result was nonetheless unsuccessful. I discovered that it was SM. He didn't choose him. He put his foot down. So far as Ah Tah was concerned. Not that he had a choice. The Colonial Office still had the choice. Of course, politics-wise, they would consult. And they would accept if he felt strongly about it. I think he felt very strongly about it. My personal judgement was, over some actual decision of his. Nothing to do with politics at all. Nothing to do with politics. You know what sort of a person he is. Now you know. He just says no. And he got his way.

EEC **In fact, the field had narrowed down to the three remaining local Judges.**

WCJ No, no, no. There was no narrowing down. After that, when Rose came in and if the PAP continued in power, then of course it narrowed down. I felt very, very unhappy over those few years.

EEC **Was the fact that Rose came in on a contract a concession?**

WCJ By whom?

EEC Colonial Office perhaps.

WCJ No, no, no.

EEC So Alan Rose came in.

WJC Alan Rose came in. Life is a series of ... Just one's luck. He took to me in the sense that he liked cricket and I was a cricketer. He played bridge and I played bridge. Common interest, you see. With the other judges, he didn't have this.

EEC The other judges at that time, if we can go through it, in addition to the three local judges that we had, plus yourself ...

WCJ We had Buttrose, we had Clifford Knight. Thorogood had come and gone. I think that was it. Rose and the four of us, and Buttrose.

EEC When Alan Rose came, it was 1960 to 1963. In fact, his tenure was till the end of 1962 because you became Chief Justice in January of 1963.

WCJ He had two years, and then they extended him for one more year.

EEC Because I was aware that he was Chief Justice in 1960. So 1961, 1962 till the end.

WCJ And then they gave him an extension for another year. Now, strangely enough, as I've told you, we hit it off in the sense that we could talk and discuss things. So towards the end of 1962, he said, "You may be the next Chief Justice."

I laughed. "No," I said, "Ah Tah should be the one." Although I thought to have him come in before ... I didn't know it was just a question of principle. "No," I said, "Ah Tah should be the one."

"No," he said, "I don't think so. You are in the running."

So I said, "I'm far too young. Absurd. I'll be 45. Far too young. I don't think it's good too."

But be that as it may, end of 1962, he told me, "Well, you are going to be."

So I asked him: "Who decided?"

He said, "The Prime Minister."

EEC **At this time we were negotiating to enter Malaysia as well.**

WCJ Was the PAP represented in the Malaysian Parliament?

EEC **Not yet, not yet. But it was just before we entered Malaysia, Chief. We entered Malaysia in September of 1963.**

WCJ We were a colony by ourselves. No more a Straits Settlement. Penang had gone into Malaya or Malaysia. Malacca had gone. We were just the sole Colony instead of three Straits Settlements.

EEC **Semi self-governing from 1959 to 1963. The Battle for Merger, as it was then called, was beginning and going on throughout this time, and we had the Referendum to decide that. Now, the appointment of yourself as Chief Justice had to take place I think before we went into Malaysia.**

WCJ We went into Malaysia. It was September 1963. We became part of Malaysia in September 1963.

EEC **You were already Chief Justice. So I think your appointment was rather crucial. It had to be done before we entered Malaysia.**

WCJ I knew that when I was appointed.

EEC Prime Minister at that time had approved, agreed and chosen you in fact. Did you have an interview with Mr Lee Kuan Yew at the time? Can you recall it?

WCJ No, to the best of my recollection.

EEC How did you know officially that you were going to be Chief Justice, Chief?

WCJ Well, at least Rose told me. If I had an interview ... Probably I must have. But it was such a short interview. I was told: "You will be Chief Justice (CJ)." No question do you accept. You accept. I mean, you are a Judge. I was told. I'll try to remember. When I was told I would be CJ, I was asking myself: "Look, if anything, my friends' and my background was all with the Lib-Socs."[13] Although I'm not in politics and all that, they were the people I moved about, not with anybody else.

I was asking myself: "Why did he choose me?" I knew that he wouldn't choose Ah Tah.

EEC You knew by then he wouldn't choose Ah Tah.

WCJ Because Rose had told me earlier.

EEC But of the other two, only one (Freddy) was senior to you.

WCJ Freddy was senior. Ambrose also. I suppose it's difficult to say. I suppose, if I may guess, my academic background, the fact that I was on a scholarship and I got a studentship, this and that, and the fact that he had appeared before me once or twice or whatever it was, and from what Rose recommended, those things, I suppose he thought I had the presence to be accepted not by the Bar probably, but by the public at large.

---

[13] The Liberal Socialist Party, formed from the merger of the Progressive Party and the Democratic Party in 1956, which included the lawyers John Laycock and C. C. Tan. The party was dissolved by the mid-1960s.

EEC   **Also he felt that you were from the Bar, Chief. Your exposure is wider and a Judge should come through the Civil Service.**

WCJ   Right. All those little things counted. I knew the wife better than I knew him.

EEC   **So you were installed as Chief Justice in January.**

WCJ   The interesting part about it was that Malaysia was already coming. So I told him, the first time I advised him for something, I said, "Look, Malaysia is coming."

He said, "Yes, sometime this year. We are going to be federal and not state anymore." The Judiciary, you see.

So I told him: "Look, I am not a politician. But I would like you to consider appointing two more judges before we go into Malaysia. Because once we get into Malaysia and we are short, you will have no say, I will have no say. It will be the UMNO, whoever is the government. I'd much rather have somebody ..."

So he said, "Who?"

"Well, no one from the Bar will come in."

EEC   **What made you so sure of that, Chief? What made you so sure no one would come in?**

WCJ   At $1,900! Look at the time when he came and he slashed salaries. I was tempted really to have John Whyatt again. I said, "Look, you must never touch the Judges' salaries. That's the principle." I think maybe I did it, whatever it is. Look at England, when they were in the Bench, the Judges themselves agreed to reduce their salaries to that level. And I said, "You must leave it to the Judges." I said something like that to him.

"Any? Who?"

I said, "Well, it's Kula and Choor Singh."[14]

---

[14] Thilliampalam (T.) Kulasekaram and Choor Singh — high court judges in the 1960s to 80s.

EEC So they came up in August of 1963.

WCJ Just before.

EEC Before. Just before Malaysia.

WCJ I knew that if they were intelligent enough, UMNO[15] will know that it was a deliberate filling of the post to make sure that we had a choice as to who our judges were, rather than somebody outside Singapore. I didn't want political appointments.

EEC Kulasekaram and Justice Choor Singh, they were not the most senior people in the legal service at the time.

WCJ Ahmad Ibrahim was.[16] But I knew he couldn't be spared because he was the one who was doing all the legal work.

The judiciary during merger with Malaysia

EEC We go back to the appointments to the Judiciary. By the time we entered Malaysia, we had raised our Bench to local people, except for Buttrose who remained the only expatriate in 1963. Now we come to this Malaysian era, Chief. After we entered Malaysia, we became part of Federal Court set-up. You and Justice Tan Ah Tah were members of the Federal Court. How did you get along

---

[15] United Malays National Organisation (UMNO), the Malaysian political party which dominated the country's politics from independence to 2018.

[16] Ahmad Mohamed Ibrahim, who later became the first Attorney-General of the Republic of Singapore (1965–1967).

with Thomson[17] because the rumour and the stories are, of course, that he was an extremely difficult man, and there was friction between you? Thomson had remained after Merdeka.

WCJ   He remained after Merdeka and when Malaysia came in, when Singapore joined, he was made Lord President. I stand on principle. I said, "If we are going to have Malaysia and Singapore comes in, the head of the Judiciary of Malaysia should never be an expatriate. Look at blooming Hong Kong. By 1997 it shouldn't be. Whoever is on the Bench. Anyone would be capable anyway. Because Thomson will have to go and then the next person still has to be appointed.

EEC   **That's right. He would be there anyway.**

WCJ   He would be there. Having felt that way, I couldn't even sort of take it up with anybody because we were already in Malaysia. That's why I did nothing. Then I sensed that he was trying to, when he came to Singapore, to lord it over me, let's put it this way. I never like being lorded over. In terms of the Judiciary, he was the Federal Court; mine is the Supreme Court. Our cases may go up to you for you to decide. You are one level above us in terms of decision-making. But we should be independent. When he came, he wanted this, he wanted that. I just ignored what his wishes were. When I went up there, he just ignored me. You see the picture there? Right, sitting there.

EEC   **You all had to sit together. But when you actually sat together, did you ever consult with each other? Not at all?**

WCJ   We would just speak. "What do you think?"
         I said, "Well, I've made up my mind."

---

[17] Sir James Beveridge Thomson, a barrister and judge who was the first Lord President of the Federal Court of Malaysia (the former title of the Chief Justice of Malaysia until 1994). Thomson was Scottish, hence the references to him as the "Celtic paramount Judicial Chief."

EEC **But you decided on the law only.**

WCJ Because we were in their Federal Court. It's an appeal. I said, "Well, I won't allow that appeal. When I finished, then we'll decide who is right." More often than not, he was right.

EEC **Was he a strong Judge?**

WCJ I think he was. But I may be unfair to him. He pays regard to what he thinks would be the wishes of the government. He was very friendly with the Tunku.

EEC **This possible friction between you and him was so well known that Mr C. C. Tan remarked upon it at one stage in your farewell address. Mr C. C. Tan, in his address on the occasion of your final appearance in court, Chief, said: "During the 27 years of your Lordship's tenure, the administration of justice in Singapore has undergone many stresses and strains. In the early part of your presidency, your Lordship had the unfortunate task of having to contend with a rather overbearing Mahatkim" (I suppose he means Maha Hakim[18]) "who was holding sway in Kuala Lumpur and whose attitude towards Singapore, and particularly the Singapore Bar, left a lot to be desired. Friction between him and the Singapore Bar resulted in the Bar taking the unusual course of passing a vote of no confidence against this Celtic paramount Judicial Chief from the North. Fortunately, your Lordship, with your tact and diplomacy, was able to bring about a period of peace and reconciliation which lasted until Singapore was separated from the Federation of Malaysia." Can you remember this, Chief? Against this Celtic paramount Judicial Chief, I presume, was a reference to Thomson. Can you remember anything, particularly about this matter?**

WCJ I can't remember the Bar did this so strongly. Their feelings were my own feelings. I felt that he somehow didn't like Singapore. And also, Malaysia could be manipulated

---

[18] Literally "Great Judge" in Malay.

easily because they were nice. But Singapore was a thriving place. So he somehow didn't like. I didn't accord him; I refused to accord him the number one place when he was in Singapore. I just ignored him. He ignored me and I ignored him. He didn't put me on the Federal Court Bench. I can't remember. I went only once during that period to East Malaysia.

EEC **Chief, I've just checked the MLJs [Malayan Law Journals]. I take 1964 because that was the full year when we were in Malaysia. 1963 we went in towards the end and we left in August 1965. In 1964, you did rather a lot of work in the Federal Court, Chief. You sat in, altogether, 15 Federal Court appeals. 15 reported in 1964. You delivered two judgements in Kuching.**

WCJ At the same time.

EEC **No, in the same year. Certainly in the same year. And one in Kuala Lumpur. You sat in Kuala Lumpur, but the judgement was delivered by somebody else.**

WCJ I always sat in Singapore appeals. My recollection was, I sat in the Federal Bench, once in Malaya and once in Sabah and Sarawak. That is my recollection.

EEC **You sat in Jesselton once and twice in Kuching. Jesselton is now Kota Kinabalu. Kuching twice because there are two reported judgements.**

WCJ I made one trip. You go to Kuching and then go to Jesselton. Just one. You couldn't bring separate judges. If I went there, then I would have to sit all round. I don't even remember sitting in Penang.

EEC **Well, it's a case of *Ibrahim v. Abdullah* [1965] MLJ.**

WCJ Was it? Probably in Kuala Lumpur.

EEC May well have been the case arising out of Penang. Is it true, Chief, that there were some difficulty (these are rumours again) that when you went to East Malaysia, they insisted that you have a passport? There's a story going about that they insisted you have a passport to go to East Malaysia to sit. Do you recall anything like this? Because it was quite a strong rumour.

WCJ But if they insisted on me having a passport, they would have to insist on everyone, all the judges. East Malaysia was a bit separate. In any case, there was no difficulty. I would carry a passport and it can be shown.

EEC Apparently, your point was that you were a Federal Court Judge and you should not have to carry a passport to go to East Malaysia. You can't recall this instance?

WCJ I don't recall it.

EEC You worked awfully hard, Chief. There were 15 reported Federal Court judgements where you sat. Tan Ah Tah travelled a lot more than you.

WCJ Yes, because he was the sole Federal Judge. The Federal Court consisted of three: Chief Justice of East Malaysia, Chief Justice of West Malaysia …

EEC It was Wylie at that time, Chief Justice Wylie.[19]

WCJ Yes, Wylie. And the third member of the Federal Court was Chief Justice of Singapore, The Lord President. There were five of us. Ah Tah was appointed Federal Judge.

---

[19] Sir William Campbell Wylie, the New Zealand-born judge who was the last Chief Justice of Sarawak, North Borneo and Brunei (until 1963, when the Sultan of Brunei decided not to join the Federation of Malaysia as a response to the Brunei revolt), and the first Chief Justice of Borneo (a position known as Chief Judge of Sabah and Sarawak since 1994).

EEC So Tan Ah Tah, in the law reports, sat quite a lot in Kuala Lumpur.

WCJ Most of the time he sat in Kuala Lumpur.

EEC You don't recall travelling all that much?

WCJ I don't.

EEC Well, we have 15 cases. Quite a lot of them, of course, were Singapore cases. But some in Malaysia as well.

WCJ I rather encouraged this. I wanted to be the CJ of Singapore and do the Singapore work. Not as a Federal Judge but as a Judge of the Supreme Court. That was, to me, my responsibility to Singapore, although I was a Federal Judge.

EEC You could have sat in any one of the Federal Courts.

WCJ I could have sat. To me, whether it's right or wrong, my loyalty was with Singapore, not to the whole of Malaysia in that sense in terms of the work I had to do. As Chief Justice of the State of Singapore, my loyalty, in terms of the Judiciary, was to Singapore. Whereas I was just a member of the Federal Court. So I was just one of three Appellate Judges. So in that sense, I probably contributed to it.

Relationship with the PAP

WCJ Those were the days [around 1964, before Singapore's separation from Malaysia] when I knew the happenings in the PAP. But I was outside it. There were people who were decent people. I got a bit of knowledge of the goings-on.

EEC I think it helps to know what is going on.

WCJ But I was never kept interested. I decided when we were going into Malaysia and I was made Chief Justice, that the only way was to stick strictly to what the English system was, completely separated, and I would be responsible, and that if there's anything, who would defend me in Parliament? It will be the Prime Minister. He would be the spokesman for the Judiciary. And expecting that he, as a lawyer, would protect us.

EEC Yes, he would understand what you were doing.

WCJ But Eddie [Barker][20] wasn't there. Eddie came in later. And so my relationship with the Prime Minister from the very start was "I am not your man" without saying so, although he knew I knew that he appointed me. I think it gave me a little bit of courage in spite of the fact that I was not anywhere ... I think in those days, a lot of the people who were in politics knew that I didn't like the way PAP did things, whatever their policies. I just wasn't ...

EEC But this is your personal view.

WCJ Personal view which I never said about the way PAP did things. When he chose me, I said, "Well, he must know we are not pals, we are not friends. You must know that I don't agree with the policies of PAP purely as an individual, a Singaporean."

But he chose me, so I gave him credit for that. Because of that, I decided, well, since it's that, I would be exactly what the English Chief Justice would be because our system is English, not the old days when the Colonial Secretary was boss over the Chief Justice. No more. I had enough of the problems with my leave. I must have 10 years in the service in order to have certain perks, not what the expats have, but the locals have.

---

[20] Edmund William (E. W.) Barker, Singapore's Minister for Law from 1964 to 1988.

EEC   **Yes, very unjust terms.**

WCJ   Right. In that sense, it just hurt to think of that. They'd ask you to sacrifice. They would say, "Oh, you must do something for the locals. You need the local men. You must bring up. If no one starts, then others won't come in, this and that." Yet when you are in, they will say, "Well, those are the rules and regulations."

So with Lee Kuan Yew, I decided from the very start. And take it from me, he stuck to it. It was never spoken, it was unspoken, an understanding. I didn't like to have to go and see him. Because knowing what the public would say, they would associate me with the PAP and associate the Judiciary with the PAP in any decisions. So as much as possible, I wanted to disassociate with them. When he wants to speak to me, I would go. But he would make an appointment. If it's during court hours, I would say, "No. I am in Court." Every civil servant would just drop everything. I would always say, "Never say yes unless it was true."

EEC   **You retain your independence.**

WCJ   In that sense. What I wanted was for the Civil Service, the ministers and the people to see that I was perhaps the only one who didn't sort of ...

EEC   **... toe the line. Well, that's not quite the word. To retain your independence as a Judge.**

WCJ   To let the public feel that in my sphere, what I decide is what the judges decide according to law. They were not political considerations. In the end the public believes it. That doesn't matter anymore. But I think it helped in that sense because I could see it everytime I go there.

EEC   **Did you see him a lot more after we left Malaysia? During Malaysia he was rather busy. He was going up there all the time. So it was relatively peaceful here from the judicial point of view.**

WCJ   Yes, it was peaceful. He knew, he sensed because of the fact when I told him, "Look, would you appoint Kula and so and so, because I think it is wise not to?" So he knew that I was pro-Singaporean whatever my background was.

EEC Yes, that's right, having come from Penang as well.

WCJ He sensed in me somebody who just doesn't think that way. Because we are in Malaysia, we will be there forever. Make friends there with the top people. At least I think he came to that conclusion. So he had a bit more faith in me. During those periods, I acted as Yang di-Pertuan Negara.[21] But the problem started the few days when Tunku was going to kick them out.

After separation from Malaysia: The Constitutional Commission of 1966

EEC This [the separation of Singapore from Malaysia] was 1965, in August.

WCJ In August. Two days …

EEC Did you know about this, Chief?

WCJ I knew because he rang me up to my house on the night before we left Malaysia.

EEC That must have been the 8th of August.

WCJ It was I think the night before that he rang me up. I sensed that he was feeling very sad, emotional and all that. Tunku and he were now drafting this separation. He rang me up. He was very emotional. So I knew beforehand. I'll say this for him. He let me know.

EEC Yes. The whole of Singapore did not know until morning.

WCJ Until morning, until he went on TV. I had been invited to the Commonwealth Law Conference in Australia. They made it a very, very big thing. So I went. Then he sent

---

[21] The formal title of the Head of State of Singapore, the position held by Yusof Ishak who later became President of Singapore. Wee stood in for Yusof Ishak when latter was away or indisposed.

24 • SPEAKING TRUTH TO POWER

for me just a few days before. He said, "CJ [Chief Justice], are you going to Sydney to this conference?"

I said, "Well, I will go."

"Why don't you go earlier? Go earlier. The press ... Will you handle whatever it is, the separation, this and that?"

I said, "Certainly. If I go, normally I'll just ignore the press. I'll just walk away. I'll say 'I'm a Judge. I don't give press conferences."

"No," he said, "Will you?"

Sure enough when I arrived in Adelaide …

EEC **Was this shortly after we left?**

WCJ Shortly after. The press was there. I sort of just generalised. Eddie also went as Law Minister. Throughout he never laid down what should be done for which I respect him for it. It was very difficult for him, I'm sure. I'm sure very difficult for me. But I never encouraged it. In fact, by my way of handling it, he knew I wouldn't want to, would not like it at all. I discouraged it.

EEC **You believed in the separation of powers.**

WCJ I believed. I'm glad that there was nothing of any importance. The only thing of importance was the Jeyaretnam thing later on.[22] But even so, he knew where to draw the line and he never stepped across the line.

EEC **Of course, in that case you were fortunate in one sense, Chief, that he at that time did not take so much interest in the law and the legal profession as he does now.**

---

[22] In 1986, a Commission of Inquiry was convened as a result of allegations, from J. B. Jeyaretnam, the leader of the Workers' Party and the Member of Parliament for Anson, of executive interference in the Subordinate Courts related to the transfer of a senior district judge. The Commission concluded that the allegations were "wholly unfounded and scandalous."

WCJ Although he was so concerned with the economics of Singapore, in terms of administration, there was nothing very, very startling. His mind wasn't thinking of doing this and doing that. Not at all.

EEC **It was running smoothly.**

WCJ He must have been satisfied because it was running alright.

EEC **After we left Malaysia, we reached some difficult times. What happened is that they set up a Constitutional Commission in 1966 of which you were the Chairman. Can you give us some background about this, Chief? The Deputy Chairman was A. P. Rajah.[23]**

WCJ You remember, in 1965, was it the riots?

EEC **1964 we had riots. When we were in Malaysia, we had riots in July and September of that year rather seriously.**

WCJ It spread over here. This was politics of course. I think it was politics because his mind was thinking that this can never end. He was afraid it could never end the UMNO and ... because they hated him. Who was this chap, the present Law Minister's father?

EEC **Jaffar Albar.**

WCJ He hated him because there was a case here. He brought Lord Desmond Ackner who became a very good friend. And I knew Desmond because Desmond was a very good friend of my sister's husband Lamb, he was a solicitor. And Desmond was acting for him.

---

[23] Arumugam Ponnu (A. P.) Rajah, a high court judge who was also the first Speaker of Parliament of independent Singapore.

EEC Who heard this case, Chief? I can't recall this.

WCJ It was in the Subordinate Court, in the District Court.

EEC It must have been the first DJ [District Judge] in that case. Cheow Chye maybe?

WCJ No, no, no, I can't remember. Jaffar surrendered. They somehow or other came to some agreement. That was the time. He was thinking of setting up a Commission to make sure that minority rights are protected, to show that politically he was going to still treat Malays according to the old Constitution. There are some special rights in the Constitution itself. He was a very astute politician. He knew the problems he had to face with Malaysia all the time. All the time his thinking was about what the Malaysians could do to us. He was thinking about it all the time.

So he said, "Will you head the Commission?"

I said, "Well, of course, I will."

Then he suggested names and he asked me to suggest names. That was the time when I saw him. But I saw him for a reason which has nothing to do with the Judiciary. It was my duty to be able to help in terms of our relationship with Malaysia. Maybe, we don't know. But the time may well come when we come together again. I think it's wise to do nothing to antagonise them.

EEC That's a sensible thing to do.

WCJ We are in no position. That was even before the British walked out of us in 1970. That was the worst time for us economically too.

EEC The members of the Commission — did you choose them or did he? I will run through them. In addition to yourself, there was then Mr A. P. Rajah, the Speaker, who was the Deputy Chairman. The members were Cuthbert Ess ...

WCJ Each representation was all properly represented.

EEC   **Mr Namazie,[24] Mr C. C. Tan, Mr Simon Elias, Tan Sri Syed Esa Almenoar, Geoffrey Abisheganaden, Graham Starforth Hill, Manaf Ghows, Kirpal Singh, and the Secretary was Mr Naranaswamy Iyer of the Public Service Commission.**

WCJ   He gave me a list and asked me about my views. I saw that the names he chose was to give representation to all the minorities.

EEC   **Every one of these people is a lawyer, including the Secretary.**

WCJ   They had to amend the Constitution. I suggested Graham Starforth Hill because he would be a useful man of the legal side, the constitutional side. Just one expat out of the lot. David Marshall ...[25]

EEC   **No, he's not. Elias represented persumably the Jewish community.**

WCJ   David Marshall was one of the names I suggested.

EEC   **But the interesting one is Tan Sri Syed Esa Syed Hassan Almenoar who died recently. Tan Sri Syed Esa was an UMNO man.**

WCJ   Yes. Marshall's name cropped up. Marshall was a firebrand. I wanted the Commission to be smooth so that if we recommended anything, hopefully there wasn't anything which he would not like. I knew that our recommendation would not. But with Marshall, it could be difficult. In fact, Marshall wrote me a very, very complimentary letter after the Commission came out with its report.

---

[24] Mohamed Javad Namazie.

[25] David Marshall, the first Chief Minister of Singapore.

EEC   **You regarded this very seriously, Chief. It's a very long report.**

WCJ   We had a lot of meetings. I decided that we better have a recommendation that was strictly, purely, legally, politically and obviously acceptable. I think they accepted a few recommendations. They altered a bit here and there but not the substance of the recommendation. Again, one thing. He never tried to influence. He never spoke about it to me in terms of what he would like. He just left it. They drew up the terms of reference. He consulted me on it. So I had a hand in it from the very beginning.

EEC   **So out of this came the Presidential Council for Minority Rights.**

WCJ   That's politically ... That I had no say in it. There were certain things we recommended which he didn't like. I think he didn't incorporate them into the Presidential Council for Minority Rights.

EEC   **Those are matters for the Cabinet presumably.**

WCJ   Marshall — was he one of those appointed to the Presidential Council for Minority Rights?

EEC   **Yes.**

WCJ   Yes, he was. The first few meetings, what I did not like ...

EEC   **You were the Chairman.**

WCJ   Yes, I was the Chairman. But in the end when they had the Presidential Council for Minority Rights, I wasn't consulted. The Constitution provided that the Prime Minister will be there for life, Keng Swee will be there for life, Rajaratnam will be there for life.

That I didn't think was good. Well, they had the votes. It will go through. There was no point in saying. But what happened was, at the first few meetings of the Council, Marshall was quite a firebrand. He was there.

EEC **I see. Very critical.**

WCJ Whatever it was, Marshall wanted to go into details of each. So I took the point of view that so long as whatever is part of the amended Constitution, we would have to decide whether or not the proposed legislation was contrary to the provisions of the Constitution. But I never found anything. Again, that would require us to say no, and go back to Parliament to override us by a two-thirds majority. Never cropped up. In fact, it was a very, very smooth Commission.

Then he realised, of course, in the end. There was nothing for him and he was far too busy. He never turned up afterwards. Being a member for life, he doesn't have to turn up at all. He couldn't be removed. [Goh] Keng Swee never turned up. Rajaratnam was the one who made it a point to come. The other member was Othman Wok.

EEC **Yes, he's still there.**

WCJ Yes, for life. He is for life, you see. He's there. They never changed.

EEC **Do you think this Presidential Council for Minority Rights is actually worthwhile since nothing has happened that it has to put its foot down or make recommendations about?**

WCJ Like all Articles in the Constitution, to me, in legislation the test of the government is whether or not they try to slip in something which would differentiate our rights. To give credit to them (the Attorney-General's Department), they drafted the laws, they took the trouble to do it in case the Council will say, "Well, that's discriminating."

EEC **So you think the Presidential Council is a success.**

WCJ Yes, it's a success simply because nothing was ever introduced during my time that I personally thought it's a discriminatory measure. Which is the same now, with this Council that I am heading, the Presidential Council for Religious Harmony. What I told Jayakumar[26] was: "Well, we will meet for the first time officially and then we will never have to meet I'm sure." Because if we have got to meet, then there is something very, very wrong. There is a possibility of religious disharmony. Everything is tranquil.

I think insofar as they are concerned, they know that certain things they have got to adjust, ensure that minorities are never, never discriminated against.

EEC **Religious minorities as well as racial ones. There is one interesting paragraph in the Constitutional Commission's Report, and that concerns the Judiciary. There is one paragraph: "If the public is to have full confidence in the administration of justice, we think it is necessary to safeguard against political appointments of what maybe to be so of superior Judges. We therefore recommend a provision in the Constitution vesting the power of appointment of the Judges of the High Court and other superior Judges in the President acting on the advice of a body comprising the superior Judges and presided over by the holder of the highest judicial office in the Republic." Now, they didn't take this recommendation?**

WCJ That is one of the things they didn't accept. Again, he wanted to be exactly what the English Constitution was.

EEC **This would have been a more judicially democratic way, chosen by your peers in fact.**

WCJ I have great respect for his brain and his acumen. He would leave whatever the British approach to the Judiciary as it is. Whereas with the British, the control was always in the hands of the government of the day, the Lord Chancellor. In terms of the rest of the world, they wouldn't criticise him. The Prime Minister is the one who chooses the Judges. As a politician, he never wanted to give that out, I think. He would never want

---

[26] S. Jayakumar, the Minister for Law at the time of this interview with Wee (1994).

to let the control be in the hands of a judicial body. In many other Constitutions under the Westminster model, they changed it.

EEC **Theoretically speaking, if it's in the hands of a politician, they can do like what is in America, packing the courts.**

WCJ Fortunately for us, the American system was never applied here.

EEC **Of course, in the American system, the Judges go through a gruelling Senate hearing which may or may not be a good thing. Of course, every President incumbent packs the court just in case he doesn't come in again.**

WCJ Simply because there are two opposite parties with completely different views of how things should be run.

Keeping the Privy Council, abolishing the jury system

WCJ Again, as Chief Justice, I could never have anything to do with the Attorney-General's Chambers. Because the moment it shows that we are close, then the public will think: "What is this? They are the prosecution, you are the Judge." The fact that we are sitting in the same Commission is alright. But apart from that, I would like to separate the government side from the judiciary side because the Attorney-General is the government's top legal man. And then he is a public prosecutor. So I wanted as much as possible.

Right from the very beginning when we had this Indonesian trouble and the Malaysian trouble and seeing in Africa what they were doing, I said, "I don't care what happens. I am going to make sure that at least Singapore has a reputation of the Judiciary as being completely separate from the rest of government, whatever it is." The thinking public would see what's happening all over. They would sense that we are something like the others who have gone down and down, the newly independent countries. It's terrible. We could never succeed. At least if we succeed in having the public believing that they can get justice, it is a step in the right direction.

It's confidence in the Judiciary. And I was in favour of retaining the Privy Council[27] simply because I said, "We have not yet reached the stage when we can decide. We will have to have the Privy Council."

I used to see the Australian and New Zealand Chief Justices. They go to the Privy Council regularly. They go to put in my words and say, "Well, you must take into account local conditions, this and that." To that extent, they were not the Privy Council of pre-World War II judges. They know the conditions here. I said, "If you think the Australian business community here has no faith in us, they may have no faith in the politicians. But if they have no faith in the judges, the Judiciary also is terrible. Who is going to ever come in?"

So I said, "Well, I think we keep the Privy Council for as long as possible until such time we got a Judiciary that can really be decisive." But now we have got a Court of Appeal which says: "Oh, if you don't agree with the previous decision of two months' ago, we can change it." Then where is the finality? How do you advise? Have a try? Different judges different decisions. That is the thing which I am afraid of.

EEC **That bothers you a bit. In fact, it took place after you left the Judiciary, the abolition of the Privy Council. In the Sixties, the biggest event in the judicial system was the abolition of the jury. What were your views on this, Chief? Were you in favour?**

WCJ Again, it's very much a personal approach. The jury may well be ideal or suitable for the British Isles. A jury of my peers. But having known the jury system here ever since, first of all, I ask myself: "They listen to everything that is going on in front of them. Do they understand? Do they know how to appreciate what is evidence?" Difficult at least to be confident that each one of them understands and then they arrive at a decision. And I said to myself: "Secondly, you choose a foreman. If the foreman is a personality, he will influence the others." Not that the others want to be influenced, but they really don't understand what's going on.

---

[27] The Judicial Committee of the Privy Council was the highest court of appeal for Singapore until the Singapore government abolished its role in stages between 1989 and 1994. It continues to be the highest court of appeal for some Commonwealth countries such as Jamaica, Mauritius and — to a limited extent — Brunei, and for British territories and dependencies such as the British Virgin Islands.

EEC It's an unconscious process.

WCJ I mean there is nothing deliberate. They don't understand what is going on, and then they decide. Is that justice to the person in the dock? It may well be his life; it may well be years and years and years of imprisonment, or whatever it is. And I ask myself: "I sit as a Judge. I have got a jury there. If I am a proper Judge in the sense of the system, knowing what it is, and I listen, isn't what I decide the fairest decision to the man, rather than what the jury decides?"

Goh Koh Pui
Chairman of the Port of Singapore Authority

Date of interviews: June–July 1983
Interviewer: Dr Daniel Chew

Goh Koh Pui (b. 1919) was the first local Chairman of the Port of Singapore Authority (PSA). He also played an important role in the development of Singapore's labour laws in the 1950s, when he was the Commissioner for Labour.

In 1950, when Goh was an officer in the Labour Department, he was awarded a scholarship by the British colonial government to study law at Exeter College (today the University of Exeter). He was one of the first few local civil servants to be sent to the United Kingdom to prepare for the eventual Malayanisation of the Singapore civil service. Upon his return to Singapore in 1954, he was made the Assistant Commissioner for Labour, and then the Commissioner for Labour. He became Acting Permanent Secretary to Deputy Prime Minister Toh Chin Chye in 1961, where he dealt with the communications portfolio that was part of Toh's office, in the days before the Ministry of Communications was created. In that capacity, Goh oversaw of the construction of the passenger terminal of Paya Lebar Airport, which opened in 1964 to become Singapore's gateway to the world.

Later in 1964, he was transferred to the PSA to become its Chairman and General Manager, as part of Prime Minister Lee Kuan Yew's plans to Malayanise the senior posts there.

Goh retired from government service at the age of 50 and joined the Overseas Union Bank (OUB) as General Manager for 11 years, before retiring in 1981.

In these interviews, Goh shared about his dealings with the left- and right-wing trade unions in the 1950s, when he was the Commissioner for Labour, as well as the sentiments of civil servants towards Lim Yew Hock's Labour Front government and Lee Kuan Yew's PAP government, which came to power in 1959. He also discussed his role in transforming the PSA into an autonomous body, where it had been previously run by the government, and how that gave him the latitude to introduce the idea of a container port in Singapore early on, so as to capture a role for Singapore in the transshipment of cargo from Japan to Europe.

Joining the civil service

DC So when did you return to Singapore upon completion of your law degree?

GKP 1954.

DC And did you go back to your previous job in the Labour Department?

GKP No. I was made the Assistant Commissioner for Labour.

DC Was that immediately?

GKP Some time after.

DC After how many months?

GKP Not very long. Then I was made Commissioner for Labour for a few years.

DC How did your overseas education and experience help you in your work?

GKP Well, I didn't make full use of my knowledge of law in the administration of labour matters. I assisted in the drafting of the various labour laws like the Labour Ordinance. I drafted the Workmen's Compensation Ordinance, then later, the Employment Ordinance. And I put them into practice. And the most memorable thing I did in the Labour Department was when there was turmoil, political and union turmoil.

DC **In 1955.**

GKP Yes, 1955 onwards, starting with the Hock Lee strike and all that.

DC **Were you Assistant Commissioner at that time, during the outbreak of the Hock Lee Bus strike?**

GKP Well, I was appointed to the Administrative Service in July 1955. And I think the Hock Lee strike started in 1956 ...

DC **April 1955.**

GKP Yes, about that time. And I had joined the labour service in 1950.

DC **So how were you personally involved in the handling of the Hock Lee Bus strike?**

GKP Not much, because there were some seniors before me. And that was a very bad period. Of course, at the back of it, it was the Communist elements who made use of the labour unions and the schools to stir up political discontent, agitating for independence against the colonial masters.

DC **So what was your own attitude towards these agitators as a civil servant?**

GKP In a way, we felt that they were unjustified in taking the law into their own hands. But on the other hand, those with revolutionary ideas felt that these were processes which were indispensable in the fight for freedom from the colonial masters. So, it was a conflict of ideas.

DC   **And how did you see your own role as a public servant?**

GKP   Of course our duty was to maintain law and order. We could not be seen to agitate with the strikers and throw law and order to the wind.

DC   **But did you take a personal part in the handling and the arbitration of the dispute?**

GKP   No.

DC   **The first general election under the new Singapore Constitution was held in April 1955 and David Marshall was sworn in as Chief Minister, heading a coalition government — the Labour Front and the UMNO-MCA [United Malays National Organisation-Malayan Chinese Association] Alliance. How did you see Marshall as Chief Minister?**

GKP   Well, we thought very well of him because of his fervour for gaining complete independence for Singapore. Although he was a bit too drastic in his approach and was a very impatient man, the underlying motive was that he was a patriot.

DC   **So did you see it as inevitable that he would step down because of his lack of patience and other personal qualities?**

GKP   No, it was a sudden shock that he resigned when he failed to obtain complete independence during his negotiation with the British government. I think that was typical of David Marshall.

DC   **What was his attitude towards the civil servants?**

GKP   Not very much impressed by him as far as the civil servants were concerned.

He was more a politician. And at that time, the civil servants played very little role in the cause for independence.

DC **Could you enlighten me on that?**

GKP Civil servants were not supposed to be participating in any political movement. Much less did they entertain any serious political opinions and thoughts of independence, although the more educated group would have liked to see independence come earlier than expected, because that would have affected their status and their positions in the government. But the general class of civil servants was quite indifferent.

DC **Senior civil servants like Goh Keng Swee and Kenny Byrne were very much involved with the Council for Joint Action.[1] Would that be considered as some kind of politicised activity, especially in their struggle for Malayanisation?**

GKP Well, they did it, I think, quite discreetly without coming out into the open.

DC **So were you involved in any of the discussions or forums that were taking place around this time?**

GKP No. Actually, they abstained as far as possible from participating in any political forums and discussions.

---

[1] A committee that was formed in July 1952 to demand fairer terms of service for local officers in the civil service, after the British colonial government granted allowances to expatriate officers but not to local officers, who felt discriminated against. They were led by K. M. Byrne, Goh Keng Swee and S. Rajaratnam, with Lee Kuan Yew as the secretary — men who later founded the People's Action Party (PAP).

Dealing with the trade unions

DC   **Mr Goh, you were talking about the labour turmoil just now. As Assistant Commissioner, were you aware of the subversive activities of the trade unions?**

GKP   Yes, to a certain extent.

DC   **Where did you develop that awareness, or how did you develop that awareness?**

GKP   I had the information from various sources.

DC   **For example, were you aware of the relationship between the Chinese Middle School students and the pro-Communist trade unions?**

GKP   Yes. But I was not so much interested in the activities of the schoolchildren vis-à-vis the Communist Party's activities. But they were inter-related to a certain extent, the common objective of making things unpleasant for the government.

DC   **Can you remember any examples of student-worker solidarity in the staging of strikes?**

GKP   Well, the student population was mainly, I think, connected with the Communist-sponsored unions, and they helped each other. And many of the leftist trade unions recruited the top people from the Chinese schools. Why the Chinese schools were picked by the Communists was very simple — the Chinese-educated were not in such a good position as the English-educated were, as far as jobs and opportunities were concerned. So, they were a discontented lot and very easily fell prey to Communist propaganda. And, of course, in the English schools, you would have had more of what we called the colonial education element in that curriculum. And then the students in the English schools were less patriotic than the Chinese-educated.

On the other hand, from my contacts with those Chinese-educated trade unionists, I discovered one thing — that they had very strong character and were willing to wield power to achieve their aims, and also prepared to sacrifice heavily for certain causes.

DC   **How did you get into contact with these trade union leaders?**

GKP   Well, they used to come to my office for negotiations on labour matters, and they were also my clients on labour laws. And invariably, they were very fiery, outspoken and seemed to have a grudge against the government, namely the colonial government. And, of course, they did not show their left-wing tendencies very obviously. And their actions were anti-capitalist and anti-colonialist. But not the English-educated students.

DC   **The English schools students were more contented with their lot?**

GKP   More contented, and they lacked the fire and enthusiasm of the Chinese students.

DC   **Can you remember any instances of strikes that you personally handled?**

GKP   There were numerous. In one year, there were about 300 strikes which I had to handle several myself, the big ones.

DC   **Can you give some examples and illustrate your point?**

GKP   Well, I don't think examples are good enough. I will just give you a coverage of the strikes and the tactics of the left-wing trade unions at that time. They would pick industry by industry — they would pick on the bank workers' union, clerical workers' union, postal workers' union, white collar union, then the industrial workers like those working in shipyards, working in motor factories, in manufacturing. That would have been done one by one.

DC   **How did they go about doing it?**

GKP   It was a very cunning process. The so-called trade union leaders within the industries agitated and helped them to demand better wages and better conditions of service. Of course, the employers would react very strongly, and disputes would arise. And there were big disputes involving the Singapore Traction Company, Shell (the oil company), Caltex, Mobil. These were very big disputes. And, of course, some were very nasty ones where military force or police force had to be employed to disperse the strikers and picketers. And so then, they moved on to the transport section, the workers on ships and sampans, truck workers, lighter workers. There were many nasty incidents.

DC   **When the notice of a strike came to your attention, how did you respond to it?**

GKP   I would call the union first to find out from their leaders what the nature of their complaints was. Then I would ask them how far they had gone in their negotiations. Usually they came to us when there were breakdowns.

DC   **In negotiations with the employers?**

GKP   Employers. I must say the employers were not very well-organised. They were in disarray because of these sudden attacks and uprisings here and there.

DC   **Would you be able to describe for me a typical working day during your tenure of office as Assistant Commissioner of Labour?**

GKP   Well, I was mainly in charge of disputes and negotiations. And when any disputes arose, I would send for the party, trying to settle them amicably, without allowing them to deteriorate into those strikes. But of course, not every time would be successful. And perhaps the unions felt that unless they showed their force of strength, they would never obtain their demands. And it depended on the bargaining power of two parties. At that time, the arbitration ordinance was not yet introduced. It was a bit difficult to settle because most of the disputes had to go through the process of their own discussions, then negotiations before the Labour Department, and then if the things could be settled, it would be alright. But sometimes it could not be settled, then there would be nasty scenes of strikes and lockouts.

DC **So when the strikes took place, what was your personal response when there was a breakdown in the negotiations?**

GKP Well, I took it as a natural course of events. I couldn't do very much to stop them. And sometimes I felt that strikes — before the arbitration ordinance came into force — were necessary to force the employers to come to their senses, because some of the employers were really obstinate and very conservative in their outlook. So, by this gradual process of hard education, most employers became enlightened. Then there evolved a pattern of wage rates, condition of service, which were applicable to each industry. And the agreements of some of the companies were taken as examples for negotiations.

DC **When did this come into effect?**

GKP This happened between 1956, 1957, 1959. At that stage, most of the unions were supported by left-wing elements with, of course, independence as their primary objective. And the unions were only used as a tool in their cause. I am unable to give you exactly the progress, year by year, because I do not have the records with me. I have burnt all of them.

The main trend was first, there was a struggle between the left-wing unions and the right-wing unions. Then when the Lim Yew Hock government was formed, or when David Marshall was Chief Minister, Lim Yew Hock's unions were mostly right-wing and he used them to fight the left-wing unions. And as an independent civil servant, I had to deal with both the left-wing unions and the right-wing unions. And I managed to win the confidence of both by remaining neutral, without requiring to take sides, even with Lim Yew Hock's unions.

44 • SPEAKING TRUTH TO POWER

DC **What was the nature of the struggle between the right-wing and left-wing unions? How was that manifested?**

GKP The left-wing unions were more vociferous and aggressive in their demands, as well as in their attitudes towards the authorities. They would not hesitate to fight the police or create some riots to capture the attention of the public.

As the right-wing unions were milder, they would resort to negotiations, and would not disturb the peace as far as possible, because they were supporting the government. It was a phase where the left-wing unions were very, very aggressive. And the employers really were frightened of them.

DC **So who had the upper hand — the right-wing unions or the left-wing unions?**

GKP Well, the irony of it was that both unions tried to get the upper hand to win the support of the majority of workers. So, the better the demands were met, they would feel that they had fought for the unions supporting them. Of course, there were rivalries, underground fights between the two factions.

One thing I would like to drive home is the underlining force — which added to the confusion of the disputes, apart from the political factor — was that some of the unions had the support of the secret societies.

DC **How did this connection come about?**

GKP In certain trades and industries, the workers at that time were also members of secret societies. And whenever they could not win their demands or satisfy themselves, they would resort to force by soliciting the help of the secret societies.

Malayanisation

DC   **I want to ask you about the Malayanisation process during the time when you were Assistant Commissioner of Labour. What were the attitudes of British officers towards the Malayanisation process, which was gradually picking up pace by the mid-1950s?**

GKP   From those with whom I came into contact, I had the impression that it was a voluntary effort on their part to transfer the civil service to the local people. And they did send batch after batch of our qualified young students to go for higher studies. I had further training in England for various fields of service.

DC   **Were there any dissenting voices among the expatriates towards the replacement process?**

GKP   I did not feel it at all. In fact, they helped a lot in our efforts. Well, I wouldn't say efforts in the replacement process.

DC   **What were the attitudes of the local senior servants who were gradually replacing the expatriates at the senior level?**

GKP   There were not many as far as I remember, at the beginning. And they were usually promotions from the upper sector of the civil service. Direct recruitment was not very extensive, probably because of the lack of candidates. Of course, their demands were very high. They always insisted on higher degrees, honours degrees for the senior positions, comparable to what they themselves had done for their own Administrative Service.

DC What was the relationship between local and expatriate officers in the Labour Department?

GKP It was very cordial.

DC What was the ratio of British officers to local officers at the very top level?

GKP At the beginning, of course the local element was very small. Then gradually the British civil service dwindled and transferred their positions to the local civil servants. But they did it very gracefully, without any sign of grudge or resentment.

Communist agitation and labour legislation of the 1950s and 60s

DC You were responsible for drawing up several pieces of labour legislation.

GKP Yes.

DC What were they and what was the background and rationale for each of these pieces of legislation?

GKP I can only give you a general idea of the thinking of the government at that time. You see, there was no specific stipulation on various conditions of service. And that led to wild demands presented by the trade unions, sometimes very unreasonable, sometimes quite rational. And on the other hand, the employers also didn't know what their rights were, or what they should have given the employees as reasonable remuneration for their contributions in production and service. So, the government decided that the whole thing had to be put in proper order. So various labour codes were enacted like the Workmen's Compensation Ordinance, the Clerks and Payment Ordinance. The Labour Ordinance was revised to bring it up to date. And many of these ordinances, I think, were based on the ILO [International Labour Organization] conventions at that time. Singapore was a member of the International Labour Organization of the United Nations at Geneva. And they had these conventions giving basic rights to the unions, which were supposed to be observed by the government. So, in order to give effect to some of these conventions, there had to be some code of law to govern the relationship.

DC   **When were these ordinances enforced, gradually or in phases?**

GKP   Now, without any reference to record, I would say, during that period ...

DC   **Of turmoil.**

GKP   ... of turmoil, it was felt that there was more reason that such codes ought to be revised and brought up to date.

DC   **How effective were these codes, for example, the Workmen's Compensation?**

GKP   Very effective, I should say, because it had the force of law; and if there were any complaints regarding the infringement of the codes by the employers, the workers had a right to bring them up to the Labour Department, which would enforce the ordinance and impose penalties on employers who did not observe them. So those were the bases of the present labour codes.

DC   **Did the Labour Department have the manpower and resources to enforce the codes?**

GKP   Yes. We had inspectors, labour officers to hear these complaints, either on the spot and at work sites, or when the cases were brought to the Labour Department. There would be some officers to deal with these cases.

So, that established a certain law and order in the field of labour and industrial relations. And that also served as a guide to agreements and contracts between employers and employees. On the other hand, the unions were not entirely restricted by the stipulation of the law. They could ask for more, and if the employers were generous, they could give more than what were required by the law. For example, bonuses in many cases — the banks and some commercial firms would give more than enough or higher than what was expected by the workers, according to their profits.

DC **But what if the employers refused to give more?**

GKP Well, there would of course have been hagglers and stragglers and all that. Then someone had to bring the unions to their senses that the basic requirement of the law was less than what they had asked for. And the employers had every right to stick to the law. Unless they showed the strength by going into strikes. And that finally led to the introduction of the Arbitration Ordinance.

DC **When was that?**

GKP That was after the PAP [People's Action Party] came into power. The left-wing unions which were supporting the PAP suddenly turned hostile. And the government felt that unless they were controlled by certain code in their disputes, the situation would be chaotic as before. So the Arbitration Ordinance was introduced, stipulating that the disputes, which cannot be settled amicably by negotiations, could be brought before the Arbitration Court. And that would have been the end of the disputes.

DC **So before the Arbitration Ordinance was enforced, how was arbitration carried out?**

GKP There was no question of arbitration, in the sense that most of the disputes were just settled by negotiations. But there were decisions made by the Commissioner for

Labour, which were not binding on both parties. It was only a recommendation for them to abide by them. But after the Arbitration Ordinance came into force, they were obliged to comply with the orders of the court. So that itself had a calming effect on the industrial situation in Singapore.

DC **You mean the working of the Arbitration Ordinance?**

GKP Yes. It reduced the opportunities to go on strikes and reduced nasty scenes between the employers and employees. The Singapore Arbitration Ordinance was based mainly on the Australian Arbitration Ordinance. And that time, we invited an Australian expert on this matter, to help us in drafting the ordinance. I can't remember his name. The English system was also something akin to this arbitration system. But it had not had such a binding effect as the Singapore ordinance. That was what I could recall, I think, as the most interesting events in the Labour Department.

DC **Going back in time to June 1956, when Lim Yew Hock took over from David Marshall as Chief Minister, what were the reactions of senior public servants like yourself, towards Lim Yew Hock's government?**

GKP We had no choice but to accept him as Chief Minister. And at that time, he was also Minister for Labour concurrently, because of his connection with the trade unions before. He had very strong support from the right-wing unions.

DC **So what were his attitudes towards the public service?**

GKP Well, I should say, quite amicable. He was too much involved in the political element to think of the improvements for the public service. Anyway, the public service was a service which could only improve in a very gradual manner. That could not be any revolutionary events leading to improvement, like the unions.

50 • SPEAKING TRUTH TO POWER

DC **Lim Yew Hock's government was of the view that its ability to maintain a certain measure of political stability was the yardstick by which the British assessed the colony's political maturity. He carried out anti-Communist arrests and dissolved the Chinese Middle School Students' Union in September 1956. This led to the school riots in October of the same year in the Chinese High School and Chung Cheng High School. How did you then view the actions of Lim Yew Hock's government towards Communist elements in the schools and trade unions?**

GKP Well, as civil servants, we did not feel very strongly about the actions of the government. And to a certain extent, we agreed that the actions were necessary for the maintenance of law and order. I would say that the civil service was a very cowardly service; the less problems there were in the country, the less they had to crack their brains. That was the tradition of the British colonial service — very conservative, not very revolutionary in their outlook. And they were very contented.

DC **Did public servants feel that Lim Yew Hock did a right and proper thing in purging Communist elements in the unions and schools?**

GKP At that time, I think the sentiments were against the disturbances brought on by the Communist elements.

DC **During the course of the anti-Communist purges and the student/worker riots, Lee Kuan Yew criticised the government in the Legislative Assembly. How did you then see Lee Kuan Yew as an opposition leader in the Legislative Assembly, as a champion of the underdogs of the working class?**

GKP Well, he appeared to be so.

DC **How did you see him then in that context?**

GKP It was very difficult to assess him at that time, because he appeared to be a champion for the workers. And most of these workers belonged to the left-wing groups. Of course, he had to seek their support to gain power. Whereas the Lim Yew Hock government had commanded the support of the right-wing group. So naturally, any political opposition would have had to take up the challenge against the right-wing by getting the support of the left-wing. Or else, you would have had no means at all to establish a footing in the political arena. So, the Chinese students, the left-wing unions were backing Mr Lee Kuan Yew.

DC   **What was the civil service view towards the PAP in its association with the left-wing trade unions?**

GKP   Well, the main bulk of the civil service were indifferent to the political developments, knowing full well that as soon as the British left, there would be some turmoil politically and socially, until time itself would tell when this would settle down. And nobody had the foresight to know when that would come. And as far as the civil service was concerned, I think the majority of them were afraid that a left-wing government would come into power, and their interests would be jeopardised. It was a general feeling.

DC   **Was that the feeling among your colleagues or civil servants in general?**

GKP   Most of the civil servants.

DC   **They were afraid of the power of the different trade unions?**

GKP   They were, I think to a certain extent, worried about the aggressiveness and their violent attitudes towards society in a general way. And again, the civil service was a very conservative group of people, who rather preferred to maintain the status quo in their own interests.

DC   **So did they have any fears of the PAP coming into power?**

GKP   Not exactly fears. The mentality was they would rather prefer the right-wing to remain in government.

DC There was a purge of Communist elements in the PAP in August 1957 when five out of six pro-Communist Central Executive Committee members were arrested. According to the Prime Minister, Mr Lee Kuan Yew, the arrests took place because Lim Yew Hock's government was afraid of the Communist capture of the Singapore Trade Union Congress. Why did you think the raid took place?

GKP Of course Lim Yew Hock at that time was afraid of the growing strength of the left-wing trade unionists, and the strong infiltration of the Communist elements into trade unions and high schools. So, they were trying their best as the government to eliminate that threat to their existence. It was nothing but a fight for survival.

DC What were your views of Lim Yew Hock's tough measures against the PAP?

GKP We did not, as civil service, have very strong views. But quite a number of them felt that the actions were justified in the interest of law and order.

The civil service after the PAP's coming to power, 1959

DC When the PAP won 43 out of 51 seats in the May 1959 General Elections. What were your attitudes and expectations of the PAP leaders like Lee Kuan Yew, Toh Chin Chye, Rajaratnam and Goh Keng Swee?

GKP Well, the public servants in general did not know much about them, mainly because the civil servants were under British rule for too long, and they fought shy of coming too close to any political faction. So, they were quite aloof in the political sense and were not very much interested in these changes, except that they had a fear that their privileges — whatever they had — could be taken away or reduced. Because there were threats by the PAP leaders, who said that the English-educated had been pampered and had enjoyed the best out of Singapore. And that the Chinese-educated were the underdogs. And that was why they took away the cost of living allowance that was granted by the British.[2]

---

[2] The incoming PAP government insisted that the removal of the cost of living allowance for civil servants was a necessary measure to plug the deficit which they inherited from the previous government.

DC   **How substantial was the cost of living allowance?**

GKP   Not very much, if my memory does not fail me, about $150 each. Of course, $150 at that time was big money. And that was received with very great bitterness. However, later on, the cuts were restored.

DC   **After much resentment?**

GKP   Yes, resentment and pressure from the public servants.

DC   **So how did you yourself regard these new PAP leaders that came into power in 1959 — Lee Kuan Yew, Goh Keng Swee, Rajaratnam and Toh Chin Chye?**

GKP   Generally the civil service was not very happy about them, particularly their pronouncements against the British and the English-educated citizens of Singapore. And the civil service, being mainly English-educated, therefore had a very strong feeling that their standing in the government may be jeopardised. That led to quite a big wave of resignations from the Administrative Service.

DC   **Senior resignations. And how did the PAP respond to these resignations?**

GKP   I think they were not very happy about the situation. Although they were anti-colonial and anti-British, they still respected the British civil service system, provided the civil service was loyal to the country and faithful to the people, and not to any political parties that would come and go. That was the traditional British concept of the civil service as opposed to the American system. So being trained in that system, the civil service viewed the PAP's dealing with the government servants with alarm. However, deep in the minds of these leaders, they did appreciate the loyalty of the civil service to the country and to the people.

DC **So when these resignations took place, what corrective measures did the PAP government take?**

GKP Some of them resigned and, of course, the PAP did not try to exert their influence to retain them. Or some who would resign were persuaded to remain, and I was one of them.

DC **From which ministries and departments were these resignations drawn from?**

GKP Mainly from the Administrative Service, which was spread over several departments.

DC **What about the expatriate officers? How did they feel, how did they respond to the idea of the PAP in government?**

GKP They remained neutral. I think that was partly due to their training in the colonial service, that conditioned them to be loyal to any government that would come to power. Just like in England, they have the Conservative Party in power, and if their personal views are more inclined towards the Labour Party, they still have to serve the Conservative government, and vice versa. So as far as that was concerned, there was no sign of resentment or sabotage from the British civil servants. In any case, their numbers were reduced gradually. And we were told that the Malayanisation scheme would be in full force as soon as possible. And we had to be prepared to take over their posts.

DC **What was the relationship then between the expatriates and locals in 1959?**

GKP Quite cordial. I must say the British behaved in a very gentlemanly manner, knowing full well that the day would come sooner or later when they would have to leave the colony, and leave the government in the hands of the local people.

DC   **In the Labour Department in 1959, what was the ratio of expatriate officers to local officers at the top level?**

GKP   Practically no expatriates there by that time. And at the most, I think there was — towards the end — one secretary, a British secretary in the ministry. He was a very nice man, I could recall.

DC   **In the aftermath of the 1959 election, one writer suggested that conservative business owners, property owners and expatriates held reservations about the PAP in government. For example, Lee Kuan Yew refused to take office until PAP detainees[3] were released, and he gave several of them posts in the government. How did the civil service react to these?**

GKP   They were quite indifferent because they realised that the PAP would definitely do something drastic when they came into power. And they were resigned to fate.

DC   **In 1959, the PAP government had promised a fair deal for workers through better wages and improved working conditions. Lee Kuan Yew had warned of the damage to the economy. There was a tussle between labour and capital, to minimise the impact of strikes. And in order to secure industrial peace with justice, an Industrial Relations Ordinance was enacted in 1960, providing for the conciliation and arbitration of disputes by collective bargaining. And later, an Arbitration Court was set up. What was the effectiveness of the Industrial Relations Ordinance and the Arbitration court?**

GKP   There was one important effect, in that they reduced the number of strikes. And though there was still labour unrest, it stopped in time from deteriorating into unpleasant incidents. And this was done by making reference to the court for arbitration, if the disputes could not be settled by conciliation or any other methods.

---

[3] Lim Yew Hock's government had detained several leftist members of the PAP, such as Lim Chin Siong and Devan Nair.

The Communications portfolio in the Deputy Prime Minister's Office

GKP At that time [in early 1961], there was a Permanent Secretary in the Deputy Prime Minister's Office who was going to retire. So, I was asked to take over from him. Then I became Acting Permanent Secretary to the Deputy Prime Minister.

DC **This was towards the end of 1961?**

GKP That was early 1961.

DC **Could you tell me something about this appointment of Acting Permanent Secretary?**

GKP I was in that ministry until August 1964. And that was a very interesting and exciting period for me. Because the Acting Deputy Prime Minister's Office dealt with several portfolios, mainly communications and other subjects, which were not just under specific ministries to administer. The main subjects were Department of Civil Aviation, Department of Postal Services, Department of Telecommunications, Road Transport Department, Meteorology Department and the Marine Department. About seven or eight of them.

DC **Mostly to do with communication?**

GKP The communication of Singapore. And there were drastic changes during that period of which I took part in. For example, the construction of underground or undersea cables for communications — telephone and telegram lines from Singapore all the way to Borneo, Australia, New Zealand, and up to Canada. And there were also changes in the civil aviation aspect.

DC   **What were the changes?**

GKP   In the nature of the carriage of passengers, the changing of aeroplanes. And at that time, Singapore was one of the five partners in Malayan Airways which consisted of Malaya, Australia, England, and Borneo, and Singapore. And I took an active part in the construction of the airport at Paya Lebar.

DC   **So was there an emphasis in this department on the improvement of communications for Singapore?**

GKP   Oh yes! That period was a very, I should say, drastic period for the changes in this aspect. Before that period, these communication services were pan-Malayan in nature, for example, postal and telecommunications services. They had their headquarters in Kuala Lumpur with the Director-General there. Then that was the period when we separated from the federal control of these departments.

DC   **Mr Goh, how was it like to work under Toh Chin Chye[4] when you were Acting Permanent Secretary in the Deputy Prime Minister's Office?**

GKP   I must say the work was quite challenging.

DC   **Was there any overall plan, or was it done on an ad hoc basis?**

GKP   There was no overall plan because at that time, the PAP had just come into power. And these communication problems were being dealt with as and when they arose. But this was an interactive process, because even if we did not do it, other countries would have compelled us to do it.

---

[4] The then Deputy Prime Minister.

58 • SPEAKING TRUTH TO POWER

DC **What was the organisational structure of the Ministry of Communications?**

GKP Below me as a Permanent Secretary, I had a Deputy Secretary and one Assistant Secretary. Then the departments concerned were Director of Postal Services, Director of Civil Aviation, Director of Meteorology, Director of Marine, Road Transport and ... how many did I mention?

DC **Road Transport, Meteorology, Marine Department, Civil Aviation, Postal Services.**

GKP And Director of Telecommunications, as well as of the Telephone Board.

DC **You dealt with very diversified departments? But as Permanent Secretary, you were directly responsible to the Minister?**

GKP Yes, the Minister, for all the administration of these departments.

DC **How often did you meet the Minister?**

GKP He was a very busy man, being the Chairman of the PAP and a very important cabinet member. I used to see him once or twice a week on important matters. Otherwise it was just through minutes of meetings.

DC **What would you classify as important matters?**

GKP Where policies were concerned.

DC And how often would you liaise with the Directors of the different departments such as civil aviation, postal services?

GKP I had regular meetings with them, practically once a month altogether — exchanging our views on various aspects of communications and any link between the departments to be ironed out. But they were free to come and see me anytime when they had any problems.

DC These departments dealt with very specialised and narrow services, such as civil aviation, postal services. So, when problems of a technical nature arose, how did you cope with these?

GKP I was only concerned with the major policies and administrative problems. The technical problems were resolved by the departments themselves. They had specialists in this field. Like the Telecoms Department, they had people who were well-versed with telecommunications. And civil aviation, they had experts on the subject.

DC So you were only concerned with the administration?

GKP Yes, administration. And if I had difficulties, I could get the help of foreign countries by consulting experts or their counterparts of these departments, which had better experience than ourselves, from the more technologically advanced countries.

DC So how frequent did you enlist the help of outside governments?

GKP Quite often. Sometimes officially, sometimes unofficially. We established very good rapport with them.

DC What were some of these outside agencies that came to ...?

GKP Departments of the similar nature and they were more advanced.

DC In the Commonwealth countries?

GKP Yes, in the Commonwealth countries. And they were quite happy to assist us. Because communications is a field where everybody would benefit if every country improves its services.

DC You said earlier that working in this particular ministry gave you a much broader perspective in work, as you had to deal with many departments whereas previously you only dealt with labour problems. Could you enlighten me on this?

GKP This is very simple. I had so many departments to deal with. In the Labour Department, their only concern was labour relations and industrial relations and to keep industrial peace in Singapore. Whereas all these departments had various types of field of work. And it really broadened your outlook. And most of them were of an international nature. Take telecoms. You can't be running a telecommunication department on your own without having liaison with other similar departments in the world. And postal services too. Similarly, with civil aviation. Your planes must fly to some other countries and you have to liaise with the other civil aviation departments.

DC So how did you find the transition from working in the Labour Department to the Ministry of Communications?

GKP The transition was quite smooth because all the experts of the various departments were there to guide me. What I exercised my discretion on was the administrative aspect of it, and policies, as well as the control of the finances.

DC   **But who would make the policies? Would the policies come from the government in power?**

GKP   Usually it works this way. Now, for example, we were going to expand certain services in the telecommunication field. The Director of Telecommunication would put up his proposal to me, and I would study them and consult other experts in the similar field. Then I made my recommendations to the Minister. If he approved them, then it became a formulated policy for the particular subject. Then I would ensure that this policy was carried out by the departmental heads, both financially, administratively, as well as from the standpoint of the personnel. Because a lot of policies were required, either the expansion of the department, or the employment of more personnel and experts. But we all went on with it very smoothly.

DC   **What about directions from the Minister passing through you and on to the relevant departments? Did they come about in that manner?**

GKP   No. The Minister usually went through me. That's the duty of the Administrative Service. The Minister never went to the departmental heads to give them instructions. Because he would like the problem to be studied carefully and sieved through to a very minute detail before he approves the policy.

If the policy did not go through me, then I wouldn't have known what the departmental heads were doing. How could I then ensure the policies were effectively carried out? Put it in a nutshell, I was fully responsible to the Minister for the administration of these departments.

DC   **So you had to deal with policies of an inter-departmental nature involving several departments. How would you go about co-ordinating them?**

GKP   That was done by constant meetings among the heads of departments with me. Take for example, some road transport problems in Singapore. I would call the Traffic Police, the Registrar of Vehicles, the PWD [Public Works Department] and other departments concerned with road transportation and obtain their views on the matter. Or sometimes I would form a sub-committee to study the problem and make a report.

Becoming Chairman of the PSA

DC So after you had worked in the Deputy Prime Minister's Office, you were transferred to the PSA [Port of Singapore Authority].

GKP Yes.

DC Why were you transferred?

GKP The reason was very simple. At that time, the PSA was run by Europeans. The Chairman was European and the General Manager was European. And quite a number of officers in the senior hierarchy were Europeans. And the Prime Minister's intention was to Malayanise those posts. And I was instructed to take over the chairmanship and to do my very best to introduce more local officers to fill the senior positions. But that was not very easy, because most of these shipping matters required some knowledge of international affairs. And our local officers at that time had not developed that outlook. But anyway, I overcame it gradually by replacing the posts one by one. And finally, when the General Manager, an Englishman, left, I was asked to take over the General Manager's post as well. So, I was concurrently Chairman and General Manager for that period.

DC How did these two posts differ?

GKP The difference was very obvious. The Chairman dealt with the policies of the board, and under him he had a board of something like 12 members, appointed from the members of the public and one or two government servants, to assist me in the formulation of policies. Then as General Manager, I had the various departments under me like the Director of Operations, Director of Administration, Director of Finance, et cetera, to carry out the policies. It was not a very easy situation because you had to wear two hats at the same time. You formulated policies, at the same time you had to carry out policies, which was not a very ideal situation.

DC   So to put theory into practice, try ideas in practice. Then what were your responsibilities as Chairman?

GKP   My responsibilities as Chairman? We had monthly meetings with the board and reviewed the operations, the financial results and discussed our future development, to see which area we should spend some money in, or invest in for the development of the port. Whereas the administrative staff under me were mainly concerned with the day to day routine and operational aspects of the port, which were quite multifarious, because it was a very big organisation with about 12,000 workers at that time.

DC   The PSA was known as the Singapore Harbour Board?

GKP   That was before my time. In fact, I drafted the ordinance to convert it from Singapore Harbour Board into the PSA with certain new concepts of administration.

DC   What were the new concepts of administration?

GKP   More independence from the government in the formulation of policies and administration. It became more or less an autonomous body, dispensing with finances, such as wages without reference to the government. Whereas in the government department, every cent we spent, every man you employed, you had to refer to the Ministry of Finance or to the Public Service Commission. There, in that sense, we could develop the port more effectively and quickly. You see the point? That meant complete control of our own finances and our own administration.

DC   So this decision to make the PSA an autonomous institution, was it a government policy?

GKP   Yes.

DC How did the government arrive at such a policy?

GKP At that time when the PAP came into power, they realised that a lot of these departments or boards became very cumbersome and could not develop very fast. And many other countries had these so-called independent autonomous boards and statutory bodies where they controlled their own finances, where they took charge of their own affairs without much reference to the government. But on the whole, of course, the general policy still had to come from the government. But the control was much less. At that time, I even recommended that the Telecoms Department be also made autonomous. And I did draft an ordinance to make it autonomous. But due to merger with Malaysia, that matter was stopped. And only until a few years ago, this was carried out. And now you could see the result of the expansion of the Telecoms Department. In other words, it's just like a company ...

DC Commercial company?

GKP Commercial company. You have your own directors, you have your own experts and you control your own affairs. And you invest whatever income you have for that particular purpose, that is, operation and development.

DC But who would decide how this money would be spent and invested?

GKP We have a board. For example, when I was in the PSA, we had a lot of money coming in in the millions, so I had a Finance Committee of which I was Chairman. And then we discussed how to invest the money, and get the best interest and income out of the money which was not spent. When we wanted to spend, for example, to build a container port and all that, we had the reserves there. We needn't have to go to the Ministry of Finance, which could have been very tedious. It could have taken three years for them to approve.

DC So who sat on the Finance Committee besides yourself?

GKP I had a few other members from the boards seconded to serve on the committee. We had various committees — the Personnel Committee, Finance Committee, because we could not call board meetings all the time. So, all these small matters were entrusted to sub-committees.

DC   **But the board had overall control?**

GKP   Yes, we had to, of course, report to the board monthly or quarterly, on our investment operations.

DC   **What was the composition of the board?**

GKP   The members of the board were appointed by the government from Chambers of Commerce (the Indian, Chinese, and Malay Chambers of Commerce) and members of the business community who were good in finances or in communication subjects.

DC   **How often would the board meet?**

GKP   About once a month.

DC   **So were members of the board paid an honorarium for their services?**

GKP   No.

DC   **The merger with Malaysia in 1963 did not affect the idea of setting up the PSA in any way?**

GKP   No. And that was the main difference between the efficiency of the Port of Singapore Authority and the other ports in Malaysia, like Penang and Klang, which were in shambles.

DC   **Why were they in shambles?**

GKP   Because of bad administration. And they used to send people down to us for training in various aspects of port operation. At that time, I remember, goods stolen from the wharfs in Malaysia could be brought out of the gate of wharfs because of bad security. And the delays in the ships' turnaround were quite frequent in Malaysia. The legal step I took was the reorganisation of the port activities. I introduced the three-shift system, where we did away with a lot of overtime work, which was very wasteful. So, every worker was guaranteed eight hours work with higher pay, because we had better efficiency and we could charge higher port dues from the shipping companies. And they were very glad anytime the ships came in. They could be discharged and cargoes delivered without delay.

DC   **But were the workers happy about the reorganisation?**

GKP   At first, they were very sceptical. But later on, we assured them that their take-home pay would not be affected. Because with efficiency we increased our port charges and increased our ships' turnaround. In other words, our business improved as an international port. We were able to pay them higher wages.

DC   **What was the response of the shipping companies to the higher charges?**

GKP   They were quite happy because they would rather have had the ships quickly delivered with the cargoes and transshipped to other countries, rather than stay in the port for days, which meant quite a lot of their expenses. The ship is like an aeroplane. If you don't operate, it's a loss.

DC   **When you drafted the ordinance for the PSA, did you draw upon overseas examples?**

GKP   Yes. We did study some of the foreign countries' ordinances. I can't remember which country. We had a lot of examples copied from them.

Changes introduced in the PSA

DC   **So besides re-organising the workers into a three-shift system, what other changes did you introduce?**

GKP   One of the major changes was, I introduced the concept of a container port for Singapore.

DC   **This idea of a container port, how was it to work for Singapore?**

GKP   Well, it was purely by accident, I must say. We heard about container ports or container registration of cargoes, but then we never saw any of these. So, in 1967, I went to the US to finalise the loan of $45 million [from the World Bank] to expand four wharves at the PSA. Then while negotiating for the loan and finalising it, I met a man, to whom I am very grateful, called Austin Tobin, the Executive Director of the Port of New York. He showed me the operation of the container port in New York and Port Elizabeth. He took me up in a helicopter and for the first time, I saw how a container port operated.

So, he told me, "You can save a lot of manpower, save a lot of labour problems and you also prevent thefts from the cargo holds in the ships. And delivery is faster, all transferred by cranes from the land to the ship."

So, I saw the operation. Then I asked him about developments in other countries. He said, "England has just started. Hamburg, Rotterdam are already on the way."

So, I went to England, Holland and Germany to have a look at their container development. Then he told me that it would be a waste of money and time to develop on the old-fashioned method, that is, the usual traditional wharves.

So, having been inspired by him, I went back to Washington to discuss with the World Bank officials, to change my concept of development. But these World Bank people were very fussy. They said, "Look, unless you convince me that there is a need in Singapore, which is very far away from the modern countries in Europe or America, to have its port containerised, we are not prepared to change the method of construction of the wharves." So, they said, "If you could get some experts to conduct a study and make recommendations to us, we would be quite happy to review the whole matter."

So, I managed to get in New York the help of a United Nations expert to come to Singapore, to make a study of the possibility and feasibility of containerisation of the

Singapore Port, with the view to improvement of our cargo handling, especially between the various countries in Southeast Asia. He came and made a study of Japan, Hong Kong, Taiwan, Thailand, Indonesia, Philippines — quite an extensive study on shipping cargoes, statistics, annual turnover. And he strongly recommended that Singapore be the first in Southeast Asia to containerise, so that we could capture this type of business, especially from Japan, which had started already in Tokyo and Yokohama, to Europe and America. So, we would be the link for the transshipment of container cargo. So, he recommended that we should do it fast. And with the money we had already agreed to obtain from the World Bank, and with the land we already had, near the former Yachting Club — we had reclaimed the land — so they said we could start there.

So, I went back to New York again to finalise this concept with the World Bank. And they quite willingly agreed. So then, that was how we started. We got the firm from England to study and implement this concept. It was, I should say, due to luck sometimes. If I had not myself gone to New York, I would have lost this opportunity. Then after we started, all the surrounding countries — Malaysia, Taiwan, Hong Kong — all came to us to have a look.

DC **Did you have to put this idea forward to the board for approval?**

GKP Yes.

DC **How did they respond to this idea?**

GKP They were quite enthusiastic because I had to produce a lot of evidence, literature, and I managed to get the approval of Mr Barker who was the Minister in charge.[5] Mr Barker was a very good man. He didn't make any queries, he didn't order any further investigation, a very straightforward man.

DC **So this ideas was ...**

GKP ... conceived.

---

[5] At that time, E. W. Barker was the Minister for National Development, which oversaw the PSA, in addition to being Minister for Law.

DC It came from your initiative?

GKP Yes.

DC So finance was a problem in putting this idea into being?

GKP Not much of a problem. We borrowed $45 million from the World Bank, and the PSA itself, I think, spent another $50 million. It cost, in total, about $100 million for the four berths. And that was how the container port started in Singapore.

PSA during the political transitions of the 1960s

DC Singapore became a member of the Federation of Malaysia on 16 September 1963. How did that affect the running of the PSA?

GKP That did not affect very much. PSA was an autonomous body and it was not under any jurisdiction of the Malaysian government.

DC But the PSA had liaison with the other ports in Malaysia?

GKP Not only Malaysia, PSA had liaison with many ports of the world, as shipping is international. And the development was also on a worldwide basis.

DC Where was the PSA's annual income derived from?

GKP From many sources, mainly from the ships that were berthed, and from the storage of goods at godowns.

DC   So it was mainly cargo handling?

GKP   Cargo handling. And the provision of pilotage service to ships coming and going out of Singapore.

DC   Before containersation came into being, how was cargo handling carried out?

GKP   Before that period, cargoes were mainly handled by the workers from the ships berthed alongside the wharves. Of course, there were some ships which did not come to the side of the wharves but, you know, in the sea. And the cargoes were handled by lighters which was a bit cumbersome.

DC   So was containerisation a significant development?

GKP   Oh, it was. But still a lot of cargo is handled alongside the wharves. Not all the ships were "eating the rice."

DC   In the mid-sixties, there was a development project at the East Lagoon to provide additional deep water berths, with additional transit shades and open storage space. How significant was this project?

GKP   Well, that was partly a programme to expand the activities of the port, to meet with the increasing amount of cargo handled by PSA. But as I told you before, this project was finally abandoned with the introduction of the cargo port in that area.

DC   And there were plans to extend the port facilities at Jurong too.

GKP   Yes, that was because of the rapid industrial development that took place, and the consideration was that it would be easier for the cargo from the industries to be handled at Jurong, rather than transporting them to Tanjong Pagar, which was a distance away from Jurong. So, there was a little port established at Jurong for that particular purpose.

DC   **Were there any particular plans for expansion during this period?**

GKP   The plan, as I mentioned just now, was at first, the construction of ordinary berths. Then the concept was changed to containerised berths. And we thought that the Jurong wharves were to complement the activities of the PSA wharves.

DC   **These containerisation plans, did PSA have to get loans from overseas associates?**

GKP   Yes. First, a loan was obtained from the World Bank to the value of only $5 million at six per cent interest payable in 20 years' time. It was a very attractive loan. But that was not enough. PSA had, on its own, to pay another amount similar to $50 million to complete the construction of the wharves and the purchase of the equipment.

DC   **What about local sources or on sources of finance?**

GKP   No. We did not go to local sources.

DC   **How did the Confrontation with Indonesia from 1963 to 1965 affect the PSA?**

GKP   The effect was very bad because a lot of transshipment cargo was lost. And that was a very bleak period for Singapore's trade and shipping.

DC   **How was the transshipment service to Indonesia lost?**

GKP   Because a lot of goods exported from Singapore were mainly derived from Indonesia, like the local produce of rubber, pepper and other spices. Because Singapore by itself did not produce any such things. And they were all from Indonesia and re-exported from Singapore to the bigger liners.

DC **So were there any contingency plans to offset this loss of transshipment paid?**

GKP Not to my knowledge, because it's something which happened quite abruptly, and nothing could avert the tide of the shipping depression.

DC **How did the separation of Singapore from Malaysia in 1965 affect the PSA?**

GKP Not very much.

DC **It was not a severe confrontation with Malaysia?**

GKP No.

DC **Singapore, during this period of time, had embarked on industrialisation policies, changes in entrepot trade so as the handling of petroleum. How did the PSA cope with these broad economic changes?**

GKP Well, we did not have any particular plan to avert this crisis. Of course, there were strikes, unemployment and decrease in the demand for labour, but the entrepôt trade still carried on. That was because of the peculiar situation in Singapore, where ships liked to concentrate their transshipment, and also because of our good banking and insurance facilities.

DC **What about the handling of petroleum storage and export?**

GKP Well, this was partly maintained by the shipping or oil companies. They themselves had the tankers to cope with this sort of situation.

DC   **So would you like to review and assess the work of the PSA during the time when you were there? How would you like to sum up that period?**

GKP   Well, during that period, it was a period of intense modernisation in the utilisation of labour, and handling equipment, and introduction of the containerised concept of handling cargoes. And also, we did our best to do away with contract labour, which was not very productive and subject to abuses. So, we had more direct labour during that period.

Abdul Wahab Ghows

Solicitor-General and High Court Judge

Date of interview: March 1993
Interviewer: Elisabeth Eber-Chan

Abdul Wahab Ghows (1921–1997) held nearly all the appointments in the Legal Service at various points in the early years of Singapore's independence, most notably as Solicitor-General, when he drafted several key pieces of legislation for the government, and as a High Court Judge.

Born in Singapore, he graduated from Raffles College, before it merged with King Edward VII College of Medicine to form the University of Malaya. During World War II, he served in the British resistance movement in India, Burma and Malaya, and then worked for the British Military Administration in Kuala Lumpur after the war ended.

In 1949, he left for London to study law and was called to the bar at Middle Temple. Returning to Singapore in 1952, he did his pupillage at the firm of Oehlers & Choa and then joined the Singapore Legal Service at the onset of Malayanisation. For next few decades, he took on a wide range of appointments in the legal service, as District Judge, Official Assignee and Public Trustee, Crown Counsel (later State Counsel), Deputy Public Prosecutor, Registrar of Trade Marks & Patents, and most notably as Solicitor-General (1971–1981) and as a High Court Judge (1981–1986).

In this interview, he shared primarily about his role in the drafting of landmark legislation when he was Solicitor-General, such as the Newspaper and Printing Presses Act, the Hijacking and Protection of Aircraft Act, in revising the Criminal Procedure Code, and the events surrounding these pieces of legislation. He also discussed how he worked with Prime Minister Lee Kuan Yew and the cabinet ministers, and also shared candidly about rivalries in the legal service between its key figures of the day.

Joining the Legal Service

EEC   **What made you decide to read law? This was the beginning of your legal career.**

AWG   Yes. Because I was already about 28 years old, in 1949. Law was the shortest course I could find to get into a profession. I didn't want to do anything else because of my age.

EEC   **Did you save up enough money to all this while, Judge?**

AWG   My father helped me with about $10,000.

EEC   **Your family was still in Singapore?**

AWG   Yes, yes. With my savings also. So I went to England and read law and I did it extra fast. And I came back in 1952.

EEC   **That's right. And this was the real start of your second phase of your career, Judge? You began as a pupil in Oehlers & Choa.**

AWG   And then I was in Oehlers & Choa as a pupil. I attended upon the Registrar doing summonses in Chambers. And only before the Registrar, not before the Court. One day I was waiting outside the Registrar's room. The clerk came up to me and said the Registrar wanted to have a word with me after everybody had gone off. And the Registrar was the most senior local officer at that time ...

EEC   **Mr Tan Toon Lip?**

AWG   Yes, yes, Toon Lip. He called me up and he said, "Wahab, why don't you apply to join the Legal Service?" So I said, "What is there in the Legal Service which you are recommending?" He said, "Well, you know after so many years, you will get so much money. This is your chance of promotion as you go on." It was 1952, in the midst of the Korean War, and Singapore was suffering a sort of slump. So I was in Oehlers & Choa ... Geno Oehlers.[1] He was telling me that, "You see, there's not much work here".

EEC **It was still a conveyancing firm in those days?**

AWG Yes. He said: "You see, there's not much work here and I really don't think I could offer you a job at the end of your pupillage. But see what happens, because as you can see, I have so many briefs on my table but they are not moving." And things like that. Toon Lip was telling me that I had a good chance in the Legal Service. "Why don't you apply?" So I said, "I have to consult my father." So my father was a school teacher for many years, and he liked me to be in Government Service. So I went to see Toon Lip again and said, "Could I bring my father to see you, because he is interested in your offer." He said, "Yes." My father happened to know him a bit. And we went to see him and he spoke. So my father said, "You should apply." So I got the forms and filled them up, and I was interviewed by Gordon Smith who was Chairman of the Public Service Commission. He was a Judge of the High Court and he was the Head of the Public Service Commission. And he interviewed me together with a few others, but most of the talking was between him and me. We were discussing the recent cases. And before I knew anything, I was in the Legal Service. In those days, you need not apply to join the Legal Service. They picked you. The Chief Justice said, "Can you get a couple of chaps?" and told the Registrar to look around. So the Registrar picked me and recommended me to the Legal Service, and true enough I got in. And there was only one other person who was Legal Officer in the Singapore Legal Service, and that was Jeyaretnam.[2]

EEC **Oh, Mr J. B. Jeyaretnam?**

AWG J. B. Jeyaretnam.

---

[1] George Edward Noel Oehlers (popularly known as Geno, after the initials of his full name), lawyer and the first Speaker of the Legislative Assembly of Singapore (1955–1963).

[2] J. B. Jeyaretnam, the Workers' Party Member of Parliament (MP) for Anson in the 1980s, was a District Court Judge and Registrar of the Supreme Court in the 1950s to early 1960s.

EEC So you join at the same time in fact?

AWG He joined a bit earlier than I did. But my seniority was higher because I had spent some months with Oehlers & Choa.

EEC Oh, your pupillage of course. You were admitted after that as well to the Singapore Bar?

AWG Not yet. Before I finished the sixth month, before I finished the pupillage, I joined the Government Service. But my period of pupillage was counted for seniority purposes.

EEC So you joined directly as District Judge and Magistrate?

AWG No. As a District Magistrate, Sepoy Lines.

EEC In those days the Traffic Court was a separate court?

AWG Yes, yes. Sepoy Lines, near the entrance of the General Hospital.

EEC The building has gone now.

AWG Yes, pulled down already. I stayed there and I was in the 2nd Traffic Court.

EEC That was the most junior court at that time.

AWG That was the most junior court at that time. Then I was there from ...

EEC Well, the date of your joining is 22 May 1952?

AWG Yes, I was there till ... I don't know, because after that I was transferred to the Police Court at Hong Lim Green.

EEC Also an old building which has gone?

AWG No, in the shed at the back. There were two sheds at the back, I was in one of the sheds. Anyway, I was there till 1954 as a Magistrate. Then I was appointed OAPT [Official Assignee and Public Trustee]. The person who was in the shed opposite ... there were two sheds at the back ... the person in the shed opposite was Dennis D'Cotta.[3]

EEC At this time the Rendel Commission was sitting and Malayanisation was very much in the air already.[4]

AWG Yes, yes.

EEC There were quite a lot of local officers already in the early 1950s?

AWG Yes. Now, Kulasekaram[5] was in the Official Assignee Chambers as Assistant Official Assignee. Then he became a Magistrate. And there was also Dennis D'Cotta. He was

---

[3] A District Court Judge who became a High Court Judge in 1970.

[4] The Rendel Commission was a constitutional commission chaired by Sir George Rendel, a British diplomat, which paved the way for self-government for Singapore. It convened from 1953 to 1954. The 1955 general election was held under the resultant Rendel Constitution, and saw the Labour Front voted into power, which in turn convened the Malayanisation Commission to speed up the process of localising the civil service.

[5] Thilliampalam (T.) Kulasekaram — later a High Court Judge in the 1960s to the 1980s.

Assistant Official Assignee at that time when I was a Magistrate. Kulasekaram was transferred from the Official Assignee to become a Magistrate, and he occupied one of the sheds behind. I was in one shed, he was in the other. So in 1955, when I was about to be transferred as Assistant Official Assignee, I went to see Kula across the path there and asked him, "You were in the Official Assignee, what do you think of the place?" He said, "You'll like it. The boss is very good." The boss at that time was W. G. Alcock.[6] Anyway, when I went to the Official Assignee, I was Assistant Official Assignee and Public Trustee.

EEC **In the premises of Supreme Court?**

AWG In the Supreme Court, 4th floor. Now, W. G. Alcock was a very good superior, head of department. He would help you if he saw that you were willing to learn. And he taught me how to draft. So that time we were amending the Bankruptcy Ordinance. He was also Estate Duty Commissioner. So he was teaching me how to draft and I worked on the draft of the Estate Duty Amendment Ordinance in 1958. And then his position was Malayanised, and I became Acting Official Assignee and Public Trustee, because I was the most senior legal officer there at that time.

EEC **You had then only six years?**

AWG Yes, that's right, but in the Official Assignee. Because there were two expatriate officers working as accountants. They were not qualified accountants but they were helping with the accounts. So the Governor felt that in the legal department like the Official Assignee and Public Trustee, the head of the department or the acting head had to be a legal officer. So although I was only six years in service, I was appointed Acting Official Assignee and Public Trustee. And that was when I put up my draft Estate Duty Amendment Act which became law in 1958.

---

[6] The Official Assignee at that time.

Becoming Solicitor-General

AWG So I was appointed DJ&FM [District Judge and First Magistrate] in 1970 [...] That was quite good. Anyway, we went on quite well. And then the DJ&FM name was changed to Senior District Judge. But I wasn't there too long because at that time they wanted a Solicitor-General and that post was vacant.

EEC **That was because Winslow had become a Judge?**

AWG Yes.

EEC **And Tan Boon Teik was Attorney-General. And Francis Seow[7] had resigned.**

AWG Yes, that's right.

EEC **How did you get along with Francis Seow?**

AWG We had hardly any contact with each other.

EEC **Never worked together?**

AWG Never worked together. He used to work with me before when I was in Havelock Road; he was in DPP [Deputy Public Prosecutor] under me. I was Senior Crown Counsel,

---

[7] Francis Seow — Solicitor-General (1969–1971), who then practised law privately before notably contesting as a Workers' Party candidate in Eunos Group Representation Constituency (GRC) at the 1988 general election.

he was one of the DPPs under me. But after that I never crossed swords with him. Anyway that time in 1971 they wanted a Solicitor-General, and Boon Teik remembered me from the Whyatt days. That time the Registrar of the Supreme Court was a chap called Tan Wee Kian. And Sam[8] was DJ [District Judge] Civil.

EEC   **T. S. Sinnathuray?**

AWG   T. S. Sinnathuray was DJ Civil under me, he was my No. 2, and Tan Wee Kian was Registrar. So when Boon Teik wanted to fill the job of Solicitor-General, Chong Jin[9] offered him Wee Kian. Chong Jin said, "Wee Kian is a good administrator." So Boon Teik said, "I don't want an administrator, I want someone who can do the work." So luckily, he didn't take on Wee Kian, there would have been a mess. So Boon Teik insisted that I should be the Solicitor-General.

So I went across as Solicitor-General, and Sam stepped into my shoes and became Senior District Judge.

EEC   **So you went back to [the Attorney-General's] Chambers. By this time the Chambers had moved from Havelock Road to High Street?**

AWG   Yes, yes, that's right. So I occupied the room downstairs.

EEC   **Vacated by Francis Seow.**

AWG   Yes, he had done it up very nicely. Now, when I went to AG [Attorney-General's] Chambers, I was shocked at the trouble that was there. There were the upstairs boys against the downstairs boys. Francis Seow's gang was downstairs and Boon Teik's gang was upstairs. So I said, this is no good.

---

[8] Thirugnana Sampanthar (T. S.) Sinnathuray, a District Judge and later High Court Judge, known to friends as Sam.

[9] Wee Chong Jin, the Chief Justice (1963–1990).

EEC **The draftsmen were in the middle?**

AWG I said this was definitely out of hand. I mean, this was the second time I was facing trouble like this. So I got rid of K. S. Rajah, got him transferred out. Isaac Paul Ratnam, I got him transferred out. I told Boon Teik, "Look, I've got to get rid of these fellows, otherwise there is not going to be any peace in this Chambers."

So I got rid of all the ring-leaders and everything was quiet. I said, "Now we all work for the department. There are no upstairs boys, there are no downstairs boys. And I do not ask anybody for his personal loyalty. I don't believe in that. I don't believe in building an empire here. Tomorrow I'll be quite happy to go somewhere else. So I don't ask you for your loyalty. Your loyalty is to the department." So it went on. And I was there for quite a number of years.

EEC **Well, you were acting SG [Solicitor-General] and confirmed in 1974. It was when they still had this acting system which they don't have any longer. Now, during that time in the 1970s, there was a whole number of very very big criminal trials that you did. I can run through them with you Judge. First of all, the Andrew Road murders. You prosecuted that personally?**

AWG Yes, I was prosecuted with Loh Lin Kok as my junior. And when they appealed through a QC [Queen's Counsel], I came down to argue that appeal. And I had two juniors, one was Loh Lin Kok and the other one was Jeffrey Chan. And Jeffrey Chan was sleeping during the trial. Because this case was going on and on for several days, so he fell asleep. So I said, "What sort of a junior are you here? You are supposed to help me ..."

EEC **He might have been doing "getting up" [legal research and preparation] the night before or something. But the Gold Bar murders[10] were followed by the Andrew Road murders.[11] You prosecuted that as well, Judge?**

---

[10] A landmark criminal case in 1972 in which 10 men were charged for murder relating to a gold bar smuggling syndicate.

[11] Another landmark criminal case in 1983 in which a couple and their domestic worker were murdered in their Andrew Road bungalow after a robbery.

84 • SPEAKING TRUTH TO POWER

AWG   No, no, Gold Bar murders was the one I was talking to you about regarding Jeffrey Chan.

EEC   **Not the Andrew Road murders?**

AWG   Andrew Road murders — by that time, Loh Lin Kok had already left. Gerald Fernandez ...

EEC   **It was earlier ... Gerald Fernandez[12] and Wee Toon Boon[13] were the two cases earlier.**

AWG   Yes, yes.

EEC   **You did both of these?**

AWG   Yes, I did both.

EEC   **Gerald Fernandez, because of the corruption case?**

AWG   Yes, yes, yes.

EEC   **And Wee Toon Boon also?**

AWG   No, no, Gerald Fernandez's case I did this as District Judge & First Magistrate, as a senior district judge.

---

[12] Gerald Fernandez was the secretary and legal advisor of the Malaysia-Singapore Airlines (predecessor of Singapore Airlines) who was charged for corruption in 1970.

[13] Wee Toon Boon was a Minister of State for the Environment who was charged for corruption in 1975.

EEC   **Yes, it was heard before you?**

AWG   It was heard before me. And that time, Francis Seow was the Solicitor-General. Do you know he was trying to play dirty on me? Knowing very well that he had already put in his resignation. So he knew very well that I was in the running for his job. So he and Jeyaratnam, who was defending Fernandez, came into my chambers with Fernandez, and asked for a plea bargain. So I said "I am not going to enter a plea bargain, I won't allow it." Jeyaratnam said, "My client will plead guilty and you take into account that he pleaded guilty, so no custodial sentence." And Francis Seow agreed. So I said, "I am not willing to agree to that. I must give a custodial sentence. But if you like, Francis, you can plead in open court. But have you consulted the Attorney-General?" He said, "No need. I am the Solicitor-General, no need to consult." So I said, "Then in open court, I will say that you asked for a non-custodial sentence and I will decide." He said, "No, no, no, I don't want that. I'm not going to say anything, and you will not refer to me." "So in that case," I said, "I am not going to agree to any plea bargain." Because if I had given a non-custodial sentence, the PM will scream ...

EEC   **It was a very serious case.**

AWG   And my chances of becoming SG will be dashed to the ground. But he was trying his best. Because he was going, so he might as well torpedo other people's chances.

EEC   **The Gold Bar murders were very bad.**

AWG   That was 1972.

EEC   **Can you remember anything in particular? It was a long trial?**

AWG   Yes. Actually that was quite an easy one. I was the Prosecutor and I played one against the other. Because Jeyaratnam ...

EEC   There were three other counsels on the other side, wasn't it?

AWG   Yes, yes. Jeyaratnam clashed with the three Indian boys who helped to take the bodies away and dumped them. They also helped to beat these two victims up. But Andrew Chou[14] and his brother tried to put all the blame on these Indian boys. According to the Chou brothers, they asked these boys to take them away and confined them somewhere until they agreed to hand over the gold to them.

EEC   The two brothers?

AWG   The two brothers. But instead they went and killed them and threw their bodies away in the bush. So I played one against the other and got the whole lot of them.

EEC   I must tell you as an aside, that the gold bars are still not disposed of?

AWG   I know. But I think the government can take it away. There were no claimants after so many years.

EEC   During your years as Solicitor-General, you actually did a great deal of other work, Judge?

AWG   Yes, I did a lot of drafting also.

EEC   You did drafting and you represented the government all over the world. The prevention of crimes and treatment of offenders in Tokyo, the Congress of

---

[14] Andrew Chou was the lead murderer who was directly involved in the smuggling of gold bars, and for which he murdered a businessman and his employers. He recruited the help of his brother David for the murder, as well as eight other accomplices, five of whom were teenagers.

the International Academy of Legal Social Medicine in Rome, both in 1973. You were the leader of the delegation to the 5th UN [United Nations] Congress On the Prevention of Crimes and the Treatment of Offenders in 1975. And you delivered a paper on "Crime Control Procedure in Singapore," the conference of magistrates in Australia. And another one, "Human Rights and Legal Drafting in Singapore" at the UN Human Right Course, also at the Institute of Criminology in Australia. And you attended the International Conference on Air Law in Montreal in 1978. And a Trademarks meeting, World Intellectual Committee in Geneva.

Now, you seemed to have had a predominance of criminal topics. Certain non-criminal topics — intellectual property, human rights and legal drafting. What was your preference all this while? Did you prefer to do criminal topics or criminal work?

AWG Not really. Because if you concentrate on one thing, then it becomes boring after sometime. That was why I was doing a lot of legal drafting. Not that I was asked to do it. I did it on my own. When it's necessary, I just produce a Bill. And without any argument, it became law.

EEC This was even when you were Solicitor-General and still carried on doing this?

AWG As Solicitor-General ... for instance.

EEC We had a Parliamentary Counsel by then, did we not, and a Legal Draftsman too?

AWG Yes, but they did not do original drafting like what I did. I originated the drafting. In their case (the Parliamentary Counsel), they were asked to modify certain laws that had been passed in the UK or somewhere, for Singapore. And then they would go and copy it, and make a bit of modification. Whereas in my case, the drafting was original. For instance one day, the PM saw a report from England about the ideas that criminals should not be mollycoddled anymore. That they should tell us what their defence is. I mean, it was not a game anymore. So they [the UK government] published a White Paper and PM had to look at the White Paper. So he called Boon Teik up, and he told Boon Teik, "You show this to Ghows and see what he can do with it." So I took it home and had a look at it. I said it was a good idea.

So I amended the Criminal Procedure Code, taking away the right of silence ... I mean, when a person is arrested, he is asked to say what his defence is. He is warned that if he doesn't say what his defence is, at a later date, he might not be released, and things like that. It was quite a serious amendment.

EEC   **Yes, a real change in the law.**

AWG   A real change in a law. And then I also amended the Arms Offences Act at the same time, so that if a person joins a group to rob or to commit some other crimes, and if one from the group fires a gun, then all the others are liable to be hanged too.

EEC   **Yes, yes, discharging of firearms in public place?**

AWG   Yes, that's right. That was what I did because I discovered that usually in a melee, in the excitement, nobody could identify the person who fired the gun. So everybody would say, "Not me!" And then we cannot prove common intention. So I said, anybody who happened to be in that group is liable to be hanged, unless of course he runs away before that.

EEC   **If it is quite apparent that he is not in the group [when a gun was fired]?**

AWG   If he is not in the group ... I happened to be a member of the Commission where we visited the prison and all that, about caning. We used to say, "These gangsters who are under the age of 18 or so when they commit offences, and you sentence them to Reformative Training, they would escape the cane." That is ridiculous. I mean, these fellows should be caned. So I amended the Act so that if they were sent to Reformative Training, the mandatory punishment of caning would still apply to them. And I also amended the Evidence Act. Because if you amend the right to remain silent, you've got to amend the Evidence Act. So I also amended the Evidence Act at the same time.

EEC **They were consequential?**

AWG Yes, consequential and all that. So when I amend the Act, I would always amend the consequential Acts too.

EEC **Your amendments were challenged, Judge.**

AWG Yes, in the Privy Council. It was reported in the MLJ [Malayan Law Journal].

EEC **I don't have the references here, Judge.**

AWG It was reported in the MLJ where they argued it was unconstitutional, the amendments to the CPC [Criminal Procedure Code]. Appeal dismissed.

EEC **Yes. Must have given you a great satisfaction.**

EEC **So you were Solicitor-General, confirmed from 1974, and you continued right up to 1981 when you were elevated. You did generally everything that came your way presumably?**

AWG Everything.

EEC **So you acted in place of the Attorney-General, you did drafting. I was told by DPPs that when there was nobody around, you simply took the files and went down and did prosecutions?**

AWG That's right.

EEC **You enjoyed your court experiences, didn't you?**

AWG Yes. I did everything.

EEC **At that time, what was the judiciary like, to appear before them?**

AWG That was alright.

EEC **In the mid-1970s, the numbers of judges had dropped to an all time low in terms of numbers, only six. So that must have been pretty busy?**

AWG Yes. But I didn't waste a lot of time. I was very fast with my work.

EEC **Yes. Your reputation was such, Judge, that you just took it and went down and did it without taking assistance or anything of that sort.**

AWG I didn't waste anybody's time.

EEC **So did you get along with the Attorney-General? Your work sort of overlapped in certain respects.**

AWG I know, but he left me to do all the work. Even vetting letters. For instance, every letter that went through the Chambers had to come to me first, and I checked it. If I was not satisfied, I sent it back to the State Counsel. After I was satisfied with it, then I initialled it, I sent it upstairs and Boon Teik, seeing my initial there, would initial it even without looking at it.

The 1977 Vietnam Airlines hijacking[15]

AWG You remember, the Vietnamese hijacked a plane and brought it to Singapore?

EEC **Yes, this was before 1975 actually, Judge? Was it 1974 or 1973?**

AWG No. About 1975.[16]

EEC **I can't quite recall ...**

AWG The Vietnam War ended at 1975, about that time. Boon Teik happened to be out of Singapore at that time.

EEC **You were acting Attorney-General?**

AWG I was acting Attorney-General. Now, of course the PM was mad when he asked me, "Is there any Act we can prosecute them under?" I said, "No." I mean, there was no Act to deal with air piracy or hijacking. So he was very upset about it. Then he didn't say anything more. Then we were wondering what to do with the fellows who hijacked the plane. Then Teow Yeow,[17] without telling me, without asking me about it, postponed the charging of this chap till the evening after all the reporters had gone. And he applied for a custodial order for them to be locked up under the Criminal Law Temporary Provisions for a few days. The idea was for the government to decide what to do.

So when PM heard about it, he phoned me up, "Why didn't you ask me before you did it?" I said, "Did what?" He said, "Why did you lock them up under the Criminal

---

[15] On 29 October 1977, a hijacked Vietnamese plane landed at Seletar Airbase. It was believed that the hijackers were fleeing the Vietnamese communist government and were seeking asylum in Singapore. They killed two passengers on board before the plane landed in Singapore, and ultimately surrendered.
[16] It was in fact 1977.
[17] Tan Teow Yeow, a Senior State Counsel who later became a Judicial Commissioner of the Supreme Court.

Law Temporary Provisions?" That was the first time I heard about it. I said, "Well, I've got to find out about it." He said, "Don't you know?" I said, "No." Then he got very angry. He said, "Didn't you think you should have asked either the Minister or me before you did anything?" So I said, "Yes, Sir!"

There he was, ranting away, then after that he put down the phone. I was very upset. I didn't put the blame on Teow Yeow. I just accepted it, because I didn't know that they did it that way. In fact they never asked me about it. So about half-an-hour or one hour later, I met Eddy Barker[18] and he said, "Don't worry Ghows, don't worry ... I mean, he gets upset about this thing, what you did was right. Because it is the decision of the government that should apply in this case since there is no law." So after some time, we decided to charge them with possession of firearms. We couldn't charge them with murder because the murder took place outside Singapore. And the only thing we could charge them was with illegal possession of firearms in Singapore.

So Boon Teik came back, he heard about it, he was grinning away, happy like hell that he was not in Singapore when this thing happened. So do you know, within two weeks, I produced the Hijacking and Protection of Aircraft Act. Within two weeks.

The Newspaper and Printing Presses Act (NPPA)

AWG Then another time, PM called me to attend a Cabinet meeting. I didn't know why I was called to attend the meeting. Then he was sitting on his high chair at the end of the table, and talking about introducing an Act to curb newspapers being run by millionaires who claimed to represents the public opinion in Singapore. One of them was George Lee.[19] So he said, "The person who represents public opinion is me. I was elected by the public. He was not elected by anybody. He only represents himself. And he has the nerve to claim to voice the public opinion and things like that." Then he said he was going to amend the Act this way, that way. And I was seated down there, I was supposed to be taking notes.

---

[18] E. W. Barker, the Minister for Law.

[19] Businessman Lee Geok Eng, better known as George Lee. The brother of the philanthropist Lee Kong Chian, George Lee managed the *Nanyang Siang Pau* newspaper, which was merged with *Sin Chew Jit Poh* in 1983 to become *Lianhe Zaobao*.

Then he went on leave somewhere, and he told Goh Keng Swee to talk to me about it. Goh Keng Swee didn't know what it was all about. He called me up for a meeting. I didn't take much notice of it because I knew his views were slightly different from the PM. Then I was called up at that time [by the PM to see him] with Boon Teik. Now he wanted it to be done immediately. So I put up a draft, because Boon Teik — of course he doesn't know how to draft anything. So I put up a draft and gave it to PM. He looked at it he said, "No, no, no, I don't like this. It's too fierce. I don't like it." So Boon Teik told me: "Forget it, if he thinks it is too fierce, then we forget it."

But no, he [the PM] called me up. About three weeks later he called me up again with Boon Teik. He said, "This is exactly what I want you to do. But you got to consider all the legal consequences but this is what I want you to do." So he told me what he wanted to do. But I had to put it into a legal language.

EEC **In accepted form?**

AWG In accepted form, and I had to make sure it did not conflict with other laws. Boon Teik didn't know anything. So I went back and thought it over and produced the Newspaper and Printing Presses Act, which has no precedent anywhere else in the world.

EEC **That is true.**

AWG No precedent anywhere else in the world.

EEC **Foreign ownership and matters like that?**

AWG Yes. So when they want somebody to draft something original, they asked for me.

EEC **Not for the legal draftsmen or Parliamentary Counsel?**

AWG No.

EEC There were two in those days in the 1970s.

AWG Yes. But when they wanted something original, they would ask me to do it.

As High Court Judge

EEC Now we come to the interesting part of your legal career. How did the approach come to you for the Bench, Judge?

AWG You see, I was retiring in 1981. The government offered to give me employment for five years after I retired as Solicitor-General.

EEC You had then reached the age of 60?

AWG I was reaching the age of 60 on 30 January 1981. Boon Teik was pressing me to be a Judge. At first, they wanted to employ me as Judicial Commissioner. Boon Teik was arguing with Eddy Barker that appointment as Judicial Commissioner was not appropriate in my case ... I don't know what reason he gave. So they have offered me a yearly contract as a Judge. The opposition was from Chong Jin, I was told.

EEC I see. Well, anyway it was overridden and you duly took your place on the Bench. And that was in February 1981.

AWG No, 3 January 1981.

EEC I beg your pardon, 3 January and the report appeared in February issue. Now, the Attorney-General, in his welcoming address, said indeed you have held nearly all the appointments in the Legal Service and spent some time as DJ&FM before you were appointed a Solicitor-General. This was some six years ago. Now, as far as I can work out, Judge, the only post you have not held were Coroner, Registrar and ...

AWG As Registrar I held for a few days.

EEC Few days? Coroner ...

AWG Coroner, never.

EEC Never. And you were never in the Legal Aid Bureau?

AWG No.

EEC You've done everything else?

AWG Yes. When I was Registrar of Trade Marks & Patents, I drafted the Patent Licensing Act also.

EEC Actually, can you look back with a great deal of pride on your drafting career too?

AWG I did a lot of drafting.

EEC You were known also for the Medico-Legal Society, being prominent in that. Now we come to the years on the Bench. You spent five years?

AWG Five and a half years. Five years and nine months on the Bench.

EEC You gave a very short speech, inaugural speech, Judge. Then after that when you were on the Bench, you have a list of seven ...

AWG No, many more.

EEC Yes, of course. But the ones that we have garnered from the MLJ are these seven.

AWG No, there are more, I see more.

EEC These are on our database, Judge.

AWG Is it?

EEC Yes. We punch them out now in the computer. And this is the one I managed to get hold of yesterday. First of all, did you preferred the human interest sort of case or purely legal case?

AWG Human interest.

EEC Human interest. Purely legal cases could be a bit dry, I think. And you did this one with Tan Poh Kee and Tan Boon Song [a couple], where you gave upon divorce a matrimonial home to the wife?

AWG Yes. She was driven out by her husband's cruelty. He just threw her out with the children and he continued living there. And finally he wanted to force the wife to delete her name from the ...

EEC **Yes, they were joint owners.**

AWG Yes, from the title deed. He wanted the wife to remove her name because after she left the matrimonial home, after she was driven out from the matrimonial home, she ceased paying the instalments. Because she had to rent a room for herself and her children. So this Michael Hwang was appealing for her, he said that she couldn't possibly afford to pay half for the Housing and Development Board flats ...

EEC **In which she was no longer living?**

AWG Yes. And she rented a room for herself and her children. So she was also divorcing on grounds of cruelty. And the divorce was not contested. But then he was ordered to pay her $300 a month and $150 per child maintenance, which he never paid. So arrears of maintenance amounted to $7,130 or something like that. And he wanted her name to be deleted. So I thought this was too much. So I told him to get out of the house for her to get into the house, and for the Registrar to work out the amount that she should pay him back what he paid for the house, but of course deducting the $7,000 maintenance he was owing and all that.

EEC **You remember this very vividly? It struck you very much?**

AWG No, no, I went and read it a few days ago, because everybody was telling me that this is one of the leading cases in Singapore these days. So whenever there is a quarrel between a husband and wife, they refer to my case.

EEC **They refer to this one, Tan Poh Kee and Tan Boon Song, 1982, 2 MLJ.**

AWG Yes. This is a leading case. I mean, he went on appeal, the appeal was dismissed.

EEC Now the interesting one here too is the reciprocal enforcement of Bank of India and Trans Continental Commodity Merchants ...

AWG This was trying the sharp one on us. But I did a lot of research on that.

EEC Yes, allegation of illegality.

AWG Yes.

EEC Now, were you ever asked by the Chief Justice what sort of work you would prefer? Or did you have to do just anything?

AWG Anything he gives me.

EEC You never expressed the preference for anything or the other?

AWG No, no. But I did a lot of criminal work.

EEC You did criminal work. Capital cases as well?

AWG Capital cases as well, but I was of course the second judge. Two judges. I was always the second judge. But I was the one who wrote the judgement every time.

EEC The situation, as you know, is now changed. It is now a single judge. Do you think that's more onerous?

AWG I think so. At least with two judges, we could consult with each other. I mean, it is actually wrong to have a single judge because when the jury was abolished, the government agreed that in future we would have two judges, so that they can consult each other and all that. And suddenly now they reduced it to one judge.

EEC **The jury was abolished in 1969.**

AWG Well, I argued cases before the jury, I thought they were cuckoo.

EEC **It was not a suitable system, you thought?**

AWG No, not in Singapore especially.

EEC **In those days particularly, different level of education perhaps.**

AWG I thought some of the decisions of the jury were quite cuckoo. But the two judges system — because I appeared on so many criminal cases with two judges, I was usually the second judge, and we always discussed.

EEC **So you had somebody else to have bounced ideas?**

AWG Yes.

Hedwig Anuar

Director of the National Library

Date of interviews:
September–November 1998,
January 1999
Interviewer: Chua Chee Huan

Hedwig Anuar (b. 1928) was the first local director of the National Library, at first assuming the post temporarily in 1960, and then from 1965 to 1988.

Born Hedwig Elizabeth Aroozoo in Johor Bahru, the daughter of Eurasian parents, she moved with her family to Singapore at the age of nine. She graduated from the University of Malaya in Singapore in 1951 as a literature major, joining the university's library the following year as a library assistant. In 1955, she was awarded a scholarship to pursue librarianship studies at the Northwestern Polytechnic School of Librarianship in London. After a short stint at the University of Malaya in Kuala Lumpur, she was seconded to the National Library in Singapore in 1960 to serve as director for a year.

After another sojourn in London, she returned to the National Library as assistant director (1962–1964), and then becoming director again in 1965 until her retirement in 1988. She was a founding member of the National Book Development Council of Singapore (today the Singapore Book Council), as well as of the Association of Women for Action and Research (AWARE), whose name she coined.

In these interviews, she discussed the sexism she experienced after her graduation from university, and how she began her career in librarianship. On her long tenure as director of the National Library, she shared about her experiences in building up the collection of the library, the role of the mobile library service which she introduced for the community at large, and her reflections on how the National Library had helped to build national identity.

Joining the University Library

CCH   **Mrs Anuar, you mentioned that in 1952 you joined the Library.**

HA   Yes. Well, of course, I had applied for the Queen's scholarship, and I didn't get it. It went to a man. That was my first realisation that maybe everything was not quite equal.

And the other thing was that I went before the PSC [Public Service Commission] and I didn't get into the Admin Service, unlike the men who were with me in the Honours class who all got in. So that was another indication.

And I've gone before this British Public Service Commission. I remember it was headed by a judge, Justice Brown or someone, and he said, "Oh why do you want to get into the Admin Service? You should become a teacher." And all that, you know, the usual thing.

Anyway, I remember dancing with Sir Henry Gurney[1] at the Convocation Ball [at the University of Malaya in Singapore]. He got killed later right. Ambushed after the Emergency started. Well, maybe it was not the Convocation Ball. Then it was earlier, one of the dances anyway, at the end of the year, I remember. And he also said, "Why don't you become a teacher?" And which of course was the usual thing that most girls did in those days. And after that was social work.

Professor Hough rang me up and told me about this opening at the University Library. "So why don't you apply for it?" So I did. And of course I got in.

So at that time it was a very small library. It was later the Students' Union House, I think. Just a small building by itself in the old Cluny Road grounds next to a few other big houses that were used by different departments. Plus, there were staff houses quite nearby as well. So I knew the library of course, and they were planning to have a bigger library, but that came later.

So I went and became what was called a Probational Library Assistant. It was in April 1952. The Librarian then was someone called Mrs Kennard. Theresa Kennard I think her name was.

So Mrs Kennard was the Acting Head. I don't think she had any library qualifications. The man who had been there all the time was someone called Tan Oh Sai, who had run the library before the war. He may have been a Raffles College graduate, I'm not too sure. But he died a couple of years ago. Anyway, during the Japanese Occupation when the Japanese were occupying the buildings, he had

---

[1] The British High Commissioner to Malaya, who took up his post in 1948 just as the Malayan Emergency had begun.

hidden the books in his house or somewhere. So he had saved a lot of the books, which was marvellous because it was a very small collection anyway at that time. I don't think it was more than maybe 50,000, 100,000 — something like that.

[...]

So, I joined in April 1952, and I was in the Catalogue Department most of the time under Jean Waller who trained us. There was another student, a science graduate, who joined us later — Choy, he was in the Medical Library. The Medical Library was of course separate, which it still is. It was in the Medical Faculty Campus in College Road.

So ours was the Arts and Science one. And at that time of course, there was no computerisation or anything like that. But we had to learn cataloguing. There was no library course in Singapore, but we could do an external course run by the British Library Association.

So we had no formal lectures to go to. We had a correspondence course. So I did this course by correspondence towards the Associateship of the Library Association — the ALA. So I got through two of the papers before I went to England. This was between 1955 and 1957. I think I sat for one paper a year, which was all that you had chance to do anyway. Because you had to do the current year's correspondence course first and then at the end of my two years or towards the end of my two years, let's say about June or something, 1957, I got into University Council Fellowship to study Librarianship in England.

CCH **Before you talk about England, let's come back to the correspondence course.**

HA Yes.

CCH **Did you study at your own free time?**

HA Yes, in my own free time. I wasn't given time during my working days. Exams — they gave you time to sit for the exams.

CCH **Did they give you study leave and such things?**

HA No. I didn't get study leave. Don't think so. No, no.

104 • SPEAKING TRUTH TO POWER

CCH   **So were you selected for the course or courses …?**

HA   You did it on your own or the university encouraged you to do it. Maybe we got an increment for each exam that we passed or something like that. I can't remember the details, but we were assigned a tutor by the Library Association. You registered for the course, the ALA — the Associateship of the Library Association. And there were four papers that you had to take. So I did two before I went to England. So I was already half way through. So that was good.

[…]

There was Cataloguing and Classification, Administration. And then there was one which was Literature of a particular field, a particular subject. You could take it either in the Arts or Social Sciences or Science. Of course I did the Arts one, and that was a breeze. There was no problem with that.

As Director of the National Library

HA   Anyway, I came back to Singapore, and of course I was tremendously busy because I had to organise this move to the new building [of the National Library].[2] And we didn't have much by way of finance, you know. There was no money put aside for the move and I didn't know how to organise this move, and finally thought of having this chain of human labour. Because it was just next door, I mean, the building was just a few hundred yards away from the old building. So, we had done that at the university library when we moved in 1952 or 1953. We'd also had this human chain.

So, I had asked the staff to weed out as much as possible and then to pack up all the books in order, in shelf order and so on. And also to mark which departments, which rooms they would go to and so on. So it was all done in one or two days — the move. Then we had, of course, all the unpacking and re-opening and so on — settling in. So it was a very very busy time, but very enjoyable. And I think there were only about 50 staff at that time, so we were all very close and friendly. And I treated them all to a satay party at No. 2 Nassim Road. From the library attendants upward, and they were so pleased. So that was nice.

---

[2] In 1959, Hedwig Anuar was sent to the Kuala Lumpur campus of the University of Malaya (the university into which Raffles College had merged), to start a university library there. In 1960, she was seconded to the National Library in Singapore to serve as director for a year to supervise the move and setting up of the new National Library at Stamford Road, from its old premises which is now the National Museum.

Hedwig Anuar • **105**

And there were only about three qualified librarians at that time, local librarians. There was George Khoo and Vincent Yap. And they had been the only two who had got scholarships during Harrod's[3] five-year period because, I suppose, librarianship was given low priority compared with scholarships for other fields. So they were qualified and I think there was Rosemary Yip. She was an Australian librarian and she then moved to the Singapore Polytechnic when it opened, and she became the librarian there for many years.

And there were one or two expats, I think, but not for very long. I think they were on contract and they went back, or they were wives of Britishers.[4] Can't remember their names, there were a couple of them during that move, I think.

So it was a very busy time. And then in November the library was officially opened by the Yang di-Pertuan Negara, Yusof Ishak. So he came and opened the library and he noted that we didn't have enough chairs [laughs] or desks, because the furniture was being made by the Prisons Department, you know, to save money. That was the cheapest furniture that we could get [laughs]. So, some of it hadn't arrived yet, and we just had the book shelves but not the tables and chairs for the readers.

And, of course, we had to have a lot of publicity. I gave radio talks and things like that through one of the Radio Singapore broadcasters. We had book reviews. You know, I felt that publicity was very important, so that's what we did. A lot of things had to be done but we couldn't do everything right away. But at least we had the basics.

There were a number of older staff. They all had "A" levels, but they mostly didn't have degrees. But they were all doing the British exams externally. So again I was busy with tutoring them, taking part in lectures, which were organised by the Library Association. Other lecturers like Mr Plumbe and so on also took part. Mr Harrod of course had left before I came, so I never had the chance to talk to him about it, though I knew a little of course of the plans before I had gone up to KL. But I had met him when we formed the Malayan Library Group.[5] He was one of the founder members, of course. And he became the second President, I think, after Mr Plumbe or maybe he was the first President, in fact. And I was the Secretary. And then, later other senior librarians like Mr Clark and Mr Plumbe and all became presidents or chairman of the library group.

So when I came back to the National Library in 1960, it was just a very short period really. It was meant to be a year. So it was like from April 1960 to March 1961 that I was supposed to be there. But it was extended for a couple more months,

---

[3] Leonard Montague (L. M.) Harrod, director of the Raffles Library (1956–1959).

[4] An old term, used in British India and other British colonies at that time, to refer to people from the UK.

[5] A library organisation that united all interested in library work in Malaya and Singapore, which arose from a meeting convened by Hedwig Anuar and Wilfred Plumbe in 1955. It continues today as the Persatuan Pustakawan Malaysia (Librarians Association of Malaysia) in Kuala Lumpur.

106 • SPEAKING TRUTH TO POWER

because then I decided I needed to go back to London to join my husband who had been there for nearly seven years.[6] That was a long time.

So, I asked for leave and instead of going back and then going off from KL to London, I said that I'd just stay on for a couple of months and then go on to London. So that's what I did. So my son and I went off to London in July 1961. And then Mr George Khoo then became the Acting Director for a while. He had been Acting Director before Harrod came, so he was the only local person. And I had known him before as he was a music lover also and used to attend some of the music concerts with Apel and others during the war. Afterwards I knew him and his brother Benjamin, who was also running a choir and things like that. So we all knew one another. I mean, Singapore is small.

So I went off to London and George Khoo was acting [director] and the government thought I was going back to the University of Malaya Library, which I did when we got back from London. I went back to the University Library for a while in Kuala Lumpur. And in the meantime, thinking I was not coming back to the National Library, they got two Colombo Plan[7] experts from New Zealand — Mr Cole and Miss Taylor. Mr Cole was there for only three months and Miss Taylor was to be there for two years. So she was on a contract, from 1962 to 1964.

Then when I went back to Kuala Lumpur, to put it very simply, my marriage really had broken down and I wanted to get back to Singapore. And I was pregnant as well with my second child Shirin. But I still wanted this break, and so I came back to Singapore in 1962, and of course it was very awkward because Miss Taylor was already there and so was Mr Cole. And I needed a job desperately, of course. I didn't want to go back to the University Library particularly. So I applied to the library, and they made me an Assistant Director, a supernumerary in brackets, sort of an extra person there. So I accepted it because it was still a better pay than the Assistant Librarian's pay at the University Library. And I really didn't feel like going back to the University Library.

CCH **Why?**

HA I suppose because I had had this taste of the National Library and I thought it was more interesting. In the University Library, I felt it was not as challenging because the

---

[6] Hedwig Anuar met her husband, Anuar Zainal Abidin, while she was pursuing her librarianship studies in London. They divorced in 1962.

[7] A regional organisation, formed in 1950, representing intergovernmental efforts to strengthen economic and social development of countries in Asia, and known particularly for its scholarship programme.

students and the staff more or less knew what they wanted. You were stuck mainly in the catalogue or order sections, which were very routine things. Although book selection would be interesting, but even with that, a lot of it was decided by the academic staff who knew what they wanted and asked for what they wanted. So it was a matter of serving them, supplying what they needed. There were quite a few expats there too, so I didn't think I would have a chance to move up. Whereas the National Library was new, had a new building, and had a lot of challenges ahead.

It was going to be a much more challenging job compared with the University Library which was expanding steadily. Didn't have any problems because they attracted staff who were better paid [laughs]. They had a lot of expats, which I think Singapore government really didn't want. They wanted to localise, to Singaporeanise the posts as fast as possible. So like these Colombo Plan people, they wanted a local person as far as possible. So I decided to stay even if I couldn't go back to being the director, because these people had come in in the meantime, and that was nobody's fault.

So when their contract was up as Colombo Plan experts, I applied for the post of Director. So I became the Acting Director for a while and then Director [again] in 1965.

CCH **Mrs Anuar, we have to come back to the part when you were asked to come to Singapore on secondment.**

HA That's right.

CCH **As civil servants, did you need to join a political study centre?**

HA Yes, because I was of course very new to the civil service. I had never worked in the civil service before. I had to learn the procedures, the government procedures about getting three quotations for everything. Getting approval from the treasury, attending meetings of the ministry. The library came under the Ministry of Culture, which was a new Ministry of course. Where the Minister was Mr [S.] Rajaratnam, and of course he was a great reader and I had known him before with Dr Goh [Keng Swee] and Mr Lee Kuan Yew and so on. And I think he had contributed to some things that I had contributed to as well. The old Temasek magazine. He used to write a lot, of course, in the *Straits Times*, when he was a journalist. And a great reader, of course, a tremendous reader, and he'd be asking for books all the time. So it was very small, it was such a new Ministry. I think the important thing was the multilingual policy also which was very important for the library to build up the collections in Chinese, Malay and Tamil. And therefore we had to get people who were fluent in those languages. And the collections were very small and there were constant complaints about there not being enough Chinese books and so on. But the thing was, not many Chinese books were available then, because remember that a lot of books from China were banned at that time.

So we had a very restricted amount of literature of Chinese books being imported into Singapore in the first place. And what was published in Singapore again was fairly limited. Some magazines, some textbooks and some literary works, no doubt. And we got these under the Printers and Publishers Ordinance at that time. And then came the Printers and Publishers Act. So at the beginning, one of the first things I did, in fact, which helped all the libraries, was in 1960 when I came, we got the National Library Act amended and the Printers and Publishers Act amended. Rationally, only three copies were to be deposited, and I think we increased the number to five or something like that. So that the university library would also be a depository library.

I got the Printers and Publishers Act revised. That was one of the first things I think we did, so that the University Library would also benefit. We were getting only three copies and one of which was sent to the British Library because of the hangover from colonial times. The British Museum Library at that time, and later it became the British Library.

So I asked for an increase in the number of copies to be deposited although the publishers didn't like it, of course, having to give away so many copies. Anyway, we kept one in the Southeast Asia room, and I think one for the University Library, and two for loan or something like that eventually. And that helped, I think.

And when Miss Taylor came later, she was a very good negotiator. She had worked in the Brooklyn Public Library. She was very pro-American libraries in that sense, and she felt that American training was the best. But as I said, I think, we grew to respect each other and I gave her all the support that I could. And in the end she recommended me to succeed her as director. But anyway, that's later, but what she did was she wrote to the British Library and said, "You have been getting these free materials all these years from Singapore because Singapore was a colony. Shouldn't you give something back to the new National Library?" And she suggested the British Museum catalogue, which was about 300 volumes or so. It was a huge thing, which recorded all the works in the British Library.

So they agreed and they gave us this magnificent collection of so many volumes. So I really had great respect for her in that she was a real go-getter, that she also got the Lee Foundation to give us some more money.

I mean it was difficult days, the government had a very limited budget for books. So we had to go to a lot of donors — chambers of commerce and people like that. I mean my first year had been too limited in 1959, 1960. That was just to move the library. You know 1960, 1961 when I had first come. It was just to move to the library and get things started. And I had started the mobile library and a few other things. But my time was short. But when she came, she had these two years, and she saw that the big thing was to build up the book collection, because the budget was still quite small.

And the National Library Board was started also in my time and the first chairman was Dato Loke Wan Tho, who then died in a plane crash in 1964 when Miss Taylor was here. And he was a very great supporter of the library, of course. And gave us his photography books and things like that. He also had the Gibson Hill collection of books. So various donors including, I think, the Chinese Chamber of Commerce, gave us Chinese books and so on.

Mobile libraries

CCH **You mentioned about having mobile libraries then.**

HA Yes.

CCH **How did you choose the three places — Siglap ...**

HA Yes, and Yio Chu Kang ...

CCH **Joo Chiat?**

HA No, Joo Chiat was a branch library. We used an old community centre. I think it was one of the early community centres during Lim Yew Hock's time, and that was one of the first branch libraries under Harrod actually — Joo Chiat. And Siglap was also an old community centre and that became a small branch library. So we wanted to go further out where it was more rural, so I think one was Yio Chu Kang and another one was ... later on we expanded to about 10 mobile library points. Choa Chu Kang was one, I remember. And then because of congestion in the Chinatown area, we also had the mobile library going to Tanjong Pagar, which was of course the Prime Minister's constituency, so we chose that as well. And Joo Chiat and Siglap eventually were merged when we had the Marine Parade Branch, but there was a good reading population there already because it was a fairly middle class area. So Joo Chiat was one of the oldest I would say. Yio Chu Kang was mainly Chinese, so we would have Chinese.

Then we went round to some of the schools as well. I think the mobile library served some of the outlying schools where it would have been difficult for the children to come right down to the Raffles Library. I think at the beginning, we started with about three points, and one was only a children's library. There were three vans altogether. And the two bigger ones had been given by UNESCO,[8] but Harrod hadn't started on them with so many other things to do.

So, we said we had better start using these mobile libraries. So in 1960 or 1961, we started using them. And so that was for adults as well as children. They went in the evenings at 6 o'clock or night time. So there was always the driver and one library clerk or librarian, and then the two of them would manage. And people would queue up to borrow their books and that was a weekly thing. I don't know when we stopped the mobile service, but gradually it decreased as we had more branch libraries. Ended it finally because the collection was limited to a van, you know. How many books can you put into a van unless you have a huge trailer like they have in the British and American libraries or New Zealand.

Yes, Miss Taylor was keen on mobile libraries too because they had them in New Zealand.

CCH   **So how long do they normally station in one spot?**

HA   I think an hour or two hours something like that — two hours probably.

CCH   **And who would chart the route?**

---

[8] The United Nations Educational, Scientific and Cultural Organization, which donated US$2,000 towards the purchase of the library vans.

HA

The route, well, we would work it out. There was the head of what was called the Library Extension Section. It was Chang Khye Seng, because when he went to New Zealand he saw the rural library services. When he came back, we got him to work on this and so he was in charge of the mobile libraries and the part-time branch libraries which were opened only about three days a week, like one to seven or one to eight o'clock. So you got these morning school children and the afternoon school children together, and then you'd get the adults coming back after work and then we'd open on Saturdays as well. So that was also of course a very popular service. So that was under one person — Chang, and he would work out the route.

CCH **And on what basis, the criteria?**

HA

Take the shortest route, of course.

CCH **Population, size?**

HA

Population as well, yes. Where there was less population, more rural. Because if you have too large a population, you wouldn't be able to service them from such a small van, from this small service. I mean, I forgot how many books the van could carry. I think not more than a thousand books, or probably less. There were fans inside so it wouldn't get too hot.

If you let everybody go into the van, it would be quite hard, it would take a long time because they would have to choose their books. And there was a person, the library clerk, who would be sitting near the door and stamping the books as the borrowers went out. So in the end, what we did was we carried more books in the van, and they'd put the books in the local community centre. And the children would borrow from there instead of going up into the van. And there would be this long queue, as I said, to borrow the books. And the community centre would give us this space for displaying the books. The adults went into the van because there were fewer adults using the van compared with children.

So, in fact, the emphasis had to be on children. I've written about this. Because the children were more literate than the adults. The children were going to school and they were learning to read, and they needed material to encourage them to keep on reading, of course, to develop the reading habit, whereas the adults would take a longer time. If they were not literate, they were going to take a much longer time to be literate.

There was the Adult Education Board in the early years. I know of friends who sent their amahs[9] to learn. Miss Taylor herself, she had a Chinese amah and she, of course, had come from places where there was total literacy and she'd never met illiterate people before. And she sent her own amah. She had a flat in Nassim Hill somewhere. And it was all new to her, it was the first time for her in Asia. She'd worked in New Zealand, she'd worked in New York, which were quite different. So, when she had this amah, she sent her to the classes at the Adult Education Board I think at that time. And she said how this amah was so excited to be able to read the labels on the bottles and understand more things and all that. It was a revelation to her, which was not to us. But that's why I had to explain to her why we had worked the mobile library that way, because there would be fewer adults in these rural areas who could read. And the Chinese materials that they would have would be limited; mostly magazines and very simple stories, legends and those kind of things that were available — same with the Malay or Tamil. It's mostly magazines that they wanted anyway, and things with lots of pictures, which were hard to get.

So, it was the children who crowded around. And then later on, we tried to fit in a programme. I think that they would be told a story first by the librarian there. So that they would get a bit more and in some places, I think, the mobile library went to the school; schools in the rural areas. Probably one or two in Yio Chu Kang itself and a few others.

Because in those days, they all seemed very far away. The roads were not as good. We didn't have the expressways. In my first year as director, I had a lot of invitations to talk to schools about libraries, about reading and so on. And, of course, I accepted because I saw this as part of promotion. And that was important. And I remember one of the first times I went to a school in a rural area, I think it was in Choa Chu Kang, which seemed a long way away in those days. I mean, it's still far. But it's faster to get to now than it used to be.

So I got this invitation, and I drove out there in my car and tried to find the place, and finally I arrived at this school. And I went in and the teacher didn't seem to know that I was to come and give this talk to the school. So I said, "Yes, your principal had written and here I am," and so on. And she was quite puzzled and she herded the children into this assembly hall; the biggest room and it was a primary school, they were all young children. And I hadn't realised that this was going to be young children. And I was not used to talking to young children. So I had to sort of change my talk and make it very simple. Tell them a story, that kind of thing. And then it turned out, like halfway through

---

[9] Cantonese female domestic servants in Singapore.

the programme or towards the end of the programme, they had a call and apparently I had gone to the wrong school! I had gone to the primary school instead of the secondary school, which was next door or a bit further up. And there were two students from that school waiting for me in my office and wondering where I had gone. And they had come to fetch me. If only I had known that they were going to fetch me, I wouldn't have gone. But anyway that was still a mix up, so it was very funny, giving the wrong talk at the wrong school. So after that, I tried to find my way better or to get more details, because I think this invitation came through a phone call or something, and vague directions were given.

Anyway it was fun because we went to all sorts of places. Every time we had a new mobile library point opened, there would be a dragon dance and a big show and all that. And speeches and things like that — the community centre person or the MP (Member of Parliament) of that area would speak. Yeo Ning Hong[10] said he remembered the mobile library, and he said that without it, he would have grown up to be a gangster or something [laughs]. He lived in Chinatown or somewhere.

So a lot of people remember that. The older people do remember the mobile library because it was their first experience of being able to borrow a book, without having to pay for it. There were these rental libraries and there still are. To borrow a book and to see a wider range of books than they would normally experience. I think at the beginning we allowed a loan of at least two or three books at one time, and later it became four books. We only increased it gradually when the book stock grew. Then magazines became available for loan, which we just discarded when they were worn out, because they were popular magazines.

[…]

The mobile library was expanded till we had about 12 points from the initial Tanjong Pagar one, which was the only one in the central area. But we justified that on the grounds that there were a few schools down there. There were a lot of poor children who didn't have access to books. And then we went more to the rural areas. Then as the branch libraries developed, whenever a new branch came and we could block off one of the mobile library points like near Toa Payoh or Cheng San — those kinds of places.

So eventually the mobile library service was phased out in the 1980s. Because when the Queenstown branch was opened as the first branch, then Toa Payoh which was the second branch and a much larger branch, we had to accommodate them rather than the mobile library service and the part-time branch libraries.

---

[10] The MP for Kim Seng who was the Minister for Defence and Minister for Communications and Information in the 1980s.

Vernacular books

CCH **You mentioned that initially there were complaints about the lack, or shortage, of vernacular books in the library. And you mentioned that it couldn't be helped, because basically lots of material was not available. But how did you explain such policies to the public?**

HA Well, you had to write letters and articles and so on. And to make sure that people understood that historically speaking, it was an English library for English language readers, and it was only towards the end of Mr Harrod's term that non-English books started to be purchased and added to the library. So, of course, it would take time to get the same number of non-English books as English books. I mean, the English books had been built up from 1823 or whatever,[11] from the time the library first began. Whereas the non-English books only started to be bought in the 1950s.

So there was a lot of catching up to do, and in fact, we bought a lot of earlier books on microfilm. We looked especially for Singapore imprints. Anything that had been published or printed in Singapore is very important historically of course. And we wanted to have as complete a collection of Singapore imprints as possible, to build up the Southeast Asia Collection. The Singapore part of that Southeast Asia Collection. We said that we should have a hundred percent of everything printed and published in Singapore. And that's why the British Library catalogue was a very important gift which Miss Taylor secured, as I said, through her negotiating skills with the British Library.

Even under the Printers and Publishers Act, in colonial times, they didn't bother very much about the non-English materials. They were concerned to get mainly the English materials, because probably there were not that many British civil servants who learnt the local languages. Of course some of them did. They learnt Cantonese or Hokkien and all, but Mandarin itself didn't even come about till much later. And then, of course the traditional script, instead of the simplified script, meant that sometimes people couldn't read the earlier one or vice versa.

So there were a lot of problems — technical problems with Chinese publications — and we had to explain this. Of course I had the Chinese staff draft

---

[11] The National Library had its origins as the library of Raffles Institution (RI), which was founded in 1823. That library became a public library known as the Raffles Library and Museum in 1874, which then moved into its own building in 1887 (the National Museum building today).

all these first and then translate it. We would send the draft reply to the Ministry, as I said, for approval, and it would be with the translation as well. Because it would go to the Chinese press.

And we also had talks in Chinese by Chinese staff going to schools and so on. We explained that we were trying to build up as fast as possible. I mean, the government didn't help in terms of giving us a bigger budget. We had such a small budget to spread over four languages. And there were equal demands by different sectors for English books; especially for science and technology. There were people wanting books in Chinese, the Malays wanting books in Malay, Tamils wanting books in Tamil.

And of course there were special problems with Malay as well. Because we have to remember that publishing in Malay wasn't very advanced in those days, in Malaysia as well as in Singapore and Indonesia. Up till now, I think, the Indonesian book trade is not well developed, and it's hard to get Indonesian books in the quantity you want. So the problems of book publishing, book distribution in terms of book sales and promotion, in terms of authorship as well, all these problems had to be addressed. And this is why UNESCO was very important to us, and Singapore was a member of UNESCO in those days.[12] As I mentioned, Mr Harrod had attended an UNESCO Seminar on Public Libraries in Asia in 1955. And he tried to follow up the recommendations of that seminar in the development of the National Library; that small countries could combine the functions of a public library and a national library.

Most people don't understand the distinction between the two. But basically, a public library is a lending library, whereas a national library is a reference library. You don't lend the books. The idea is that they have to be preserved forever. And they are mainly for reference, for information.

Your public library material, books and magazines and so on would be loaned to the public and would not be expected to last forever. The books would wear out from time to time and would have to be replaced by newer editions or new copies. And then in terms of a national library, you would have to collect all the materials published or printed in that country. And of course the national collection was part of the Southeast Asian Collection, although we kept the books deposited under the Printers and Publishers Act. They were kept in a separate stack in the Reference Division.

---

[12] Singapore became a full member of UNESCO (United Nations Educational, Scientific and Cultural Organization) in 1965, but left in 1985 because it was asked to pay more dues than it thought was fair. Singapore rejoined UNESCO in 2007.

How the National Library built up national identity

CCH   **And could you elaborate on how the National Library helped to build the national identity in the sixties?**

HA   Well, I would say it was partly through the collection itself. That we had this special collection on Singapore and Southeast Asia, and particularly the books on Singapore. We would buy plenty of copies of those. Any books on Singapore, the publishers would be very pleased because we would buy more than other libraries, which may buy one or two copies. We would buy 10 or more. Books by local writers, books on history, politics, the economy, anything on Singapore would have special preference.

We had this booklist on books about Singapore, which was done every two years. In fact the first one came out during Miss Taylor's time, I think, in 1963. So we kept that up every year or every two years. And I think it's still going on, I'm not quite sure.

Then the Singapore National Bibliography would help to let the libraries and booksellers to know what books were published in Singapore, and who would hopefully buy these books. Exhibitions, national campaigns — we always supported them with our exhibitions, our own booklists. The exhibitions would be opened by a minister or a politician. We had lots of exhibitions in the lecture hall. And we would have talks given by local people as well on different issues, competitions sometimes too. We would help the Ministry, the Publicity Division whenever they ran competitions. We would have the competition forms available in the library. We were a distribution agent for the Ministry's pamphlets.

So I think we publicised the work of the Singapore government with our charts and pictures. The Ministry of Culture would use our mobile libraries also. And they had theirs as well to go round to the rural areas, to the CCs [Community Centres] and all. So all that helped I think to build up national consciousness. And the service being in four languages that was stressed all the time. Using radio, using TV, using the press, using personal contacts, visits to schools — we had a lot of talks at schools. I would give lots of talks to schools. So half the time I would probably be out of the office.

Kwa Soon Bee

Pioneer of Singapore's healthcare system

Date of interviews: September 1995
Interviewer: Lee Liang Chian

Dr Kwa Soon Bee (1930–2016) was Singapore's Permanent Secretary for Health and Director of Medical Services from 1984 to 1996, during which he oversaw the restructuring of public hospitals and the implementation of the "3M" framework — comprising MediSave, MediShield and MediFund — for financing healthcare in Singapore.

After graduating from the University of Malaya in Singapore in 1955, he joined the civil service as a medical officer. He then headed to the United Kingdom to specialise in clinical and laboratory haematology, becoming the first Singaporean to be trained in that subject. He returned in 1963 to lead the Blood Transfusion Service and was appointed Medical Superintendent of Kandang Kerbau Maternity Hospital in 1968, and of Singapore General Hospital in 1972. At the pinnacle of his career in healthcare, he became Permanent Secretary for Health and Director of Medical Services in 1984, and stayed in those roles until his retirement.

In the course of his long career, Kwa set up Singapore's first national specialty centres (such as the National Skin Centre and the Singapore National Eye Centre) and expanded the polyclinic network. He also played a key role in developing the Singapore Armed Forces (SAF) Medical Corps, beginning as a volunteer Medical Officer in the SAF. Later, he was commissioned a Captain, and rose to become a Colonel.

Kwa was a younger brother of Kwa Geok Choo, the wife of former Prime Minister Lee Kuan Yew.

In these interviews, Kwa spoke about the government's family planning policies, in which he was involved at various points of his career. That included the controversial issue of legalising abortion in Singapore in 1970, and how the government addressed opposition from the Catholic Church and the Malay community. When discussing MediSave and MediShield, he also shared about the process of putting up papers, on such complex policies, to the Cabinet for approval.

Role in family planning in Singapore

LLC   **Dr Kwa, you were very much involved with family planning in Singapore. What exactly was the scenario at that time when family planning was being pushed for?**

KSB   I was in KK [Kandang Kerbau Hospital] in 1970, 1971, or thereabouts. I was sent there to take over from Andrew Chew who was being promoted to be DDMS [Deputy Director of Medical Services] (Hospitals). At that time birth rates were still high. All the government incentives for people to adopt family planning were gaining slow acceptance. And so, after all the education of family planning and the use of various devices, the government decided that another approach should be used, and that was to allow abortions as a means of family planning.

So abortion laws were passed which initially allowed abortions to be carried out for socio-economic reasons. Up to then, abortions were only allowed for medical reasons. Beyond that, it was illegal. So laws were changed to allow abortions for socio-economic reasons. At that time anybody can apply for an abortion by filling up a form and stating the socio-economic reason — poor family, income less than a hundred, and all that. They would have had to file in their form and appear before a small committee of three or four persons who would interview them, establish that the socio-economic reasons were there and then approve it, and they would get their abortion within a week.

So I went to KK to tidy up this process of abortion, application and approval, and then to ensure that the means to carry out the abortion within the hospital were there. We organised the clinics such that the patients could come in the morning, get their abortion, rest and then go back. That was all being done as an outpatient. Previously patients were admitted overnight, stayed a day, so they spent two days which was very impractical.

The committee would meet every week on a Saturday. I was one of the members by virtue of being the Medical Director. Another member would be an obstetrician and gynaecologist, and we would approve.

The second approach was to encourage more and more people to accept things like IUDs [intra-uterine devices] in addition to the usual condoms, the usual pills and all that. (People were encouraged to use all those.) But one thing was to go for a permanent ligation. So, our role was to publicise and encourage the acceptance of ligation, especially directed at the low-income families or families which were already big. We were to arrange such that people could get their ligations done with a minimum of inconvenience.

A very important programme then was the post-partum ligation. In other words, as soon as you have delivered your second child or more, we would encourage you to go through an immediate ligation operation within 24 hours, through a simple hole in the abdominal wall, put a tube in and then ligate. Various forms of ligations and sterilisations were being explored. Then they would encourage and introduce these to an outpatient.

My role was just to operationalise the whole concept of abortion and sterilisation to help bring birth rates down. So, it was a multi-pronged approach. From one of incentives, they then began to introduce disincentives such as things like you won't get priority for housing if you have too many children. Whereas previously, the more children you had, would have gained more points for housing. So, it was a perverse incentive.

LLC   **These disincentives were brought in because the incentives didn't work as well?**

KSB   Yes. They made it punitive. For example, people who were poor would pay very minimally for delivery. But then they went on delivering. So, the idea was to introduce accouchement fees, such that for the first and second child you pay the minimum, subsidised fees. Then for the third, fourth and fifth and more, you pay an increasing amount. That was another form of disincentive. Other disincentives: previously you would get priority for schools, now you don't get priority for a school of your choice.

LLC   **Basically, to introduce disincentives was a later measure.**

KSB   Later. That was abortion and KK's reorganisation. My role in abortion came back again in 1984 when I was Permanent Secretary. We had been telling the government: "Look, our family planning is too successful. From having an average of four or five children, people are now having less than two children per family." In fact, it was about 1.8 or thereabouts. And we were not reproducing. The government did not act. So, it went below replacement level for about six to eight years and we still could not reverse it.

We had a total review during my tenure as Permanent Secretary. That resulted in the publication of a new set of policy which was pro-natalist. In other words, we then said in a rather sort of unique way: "We still encourage family planning. We still tell the people to keep to two children, or less if they cannot afford it, so that they could break out of the poverty trap." But we said, "For those who can afford, to have three or more."

This was criticised by a lot of people: "How can you tell certain groups to have two or less and for others, if they can afford it, to have more?"

So, it was discriminatory. If you can't afford it, have two or less. If you can afford it, have two or more. The slogan was: HAVE TWO, OR MORE IF YOU CAN AFFORD IT. It was quite a unique type of slogan, never seen in any country in the world. Whereas previously, ours was: PLAN YOUR FAMILY, STOP AT TWO or HAVE TWO CHILDREN, BOY OR GIRL, IT'S ENOUGH, that type of thing. But now we have changed it entirely: HAVE TWO IF YOU CANNOT AFFORD IT. THREE OR MORE IF YOU CAN AFFORD IT.

So, I was involved at that stage. At that stage we began a whole series of pro-natalist policies to encourage those who can afford it to have more children. So came all the cash incentives. Cash incentives had to be arranged such that only if you were well off could you benefit from this cash incentive. To encourage people to have more children, we can't say, "We give everybody $1,000." Then what will happen is, even the poor will go for it. So, we had to give it such that if you are paying tax, you are in the tax paying bracket, then you will get, say, a tax rebate of $1,000 or more. So over time, the cash incentives were very, very significant.

In fact, that is a separate thing. It started off targeting university graduates. Then it reduced the qualification to 'A' Levels [Singapore-Cambridge General Certificate of Education Advanced Level]. Now anybody who has 'O' Levels [Singapore-Cambridge General Certificate of Education Ordinary Level] and can afford it, will benefit from this cash incentive. They don't give increased maternity leave because that is non-discriminatory, it affects everybody. But they will give it by way of accouchement fees which remain high for your second or more child, but you can claim it as a tax rebate. So, if you don't pay tax, that high accouchement fee is still punitive.

It's controversial. Many people would say: "It's a very discriminatory type of government policy."

LLC   **Actually, this way of doing it is very much tied up with Mr Lee Kuan Yew's worry about graduate women not marrying.**

KSB   It was. It started off more as a procreation measure. Then only did Lee Kuan Yew come out at one National Day rally where he mentioned about women not marrying because they are better educated, or marrying late, or having children late; and men not marrying their equals, men always marrying down. So, he highlighted that problem of the Great Marriage Debate.

LLC The various campaigns for the family planning through the last two decades are very different from the campaigns for the Blood Bank.[1] The crux of the matter is really quite different, although it's for the nation. Looking back at these two areas of work, what would you say you have gained from carrying out these campaigns?

KSB Each is different in its own way. Each requires a different approach and a different technique. In the Blood Bank, it is trying to persuade people to be altruistic, to donate blood which they felt was something so precious that they cannot part away with it and therefore, appealing to them to help and all that. At the same time keeping it voluntary, at the same time encouraging the predominant ethnic group, the Chinese, to come to donate.

Whereas family planning is different. Trying to tell people, the low income group who saw having big families as useful because they were traditionally farmers and they want children to help them, or Malays who believe that it was God's gift to have plenty of children, getting them to change their cultural attitude towards child-bearing required a totally different approach.

How do you persuade women to have their tubes ligated whilst at the same time, convincing her that it is not going to affect her health and all that? How do you persuade a man to undergo sterilisation and still convince him that it is not going to affect his virility and all that?

So, it is dealing with different value systems and different concerns of the different cultural or racial groups.

Personal views on abortion and family planning

LLC Did you agree with those policies like abortion?

KSB As a civil servant, you do not allow your own personal beliefs to come into it. You are employed as an administrator, so you do it. Even personally, I didn't see anything wrong with the liberalisation of abortion because I felt that was the only right thing to do in the face of increasing childbirths, the poverty and the fact that when abortion was not allowed, we saw the ill-effects of illegal abortion.

---

[1] One of Kwa Soon Bee's early key appointments was as Medical Officer in charge of the Blood Transfusion Service in 1963.

So, everything about abortion, I accepted. The indication to be giving abortion for socio-economic reasons was accepted. The only thing I felt was, if anyone wanted to seek an abortion for whatever reasons, they should be responsible enough to seek the advice and treatment early and not wait until it was too late. That was a very strong view I held. It's relative, whether you abort at six weeks' pregnancy or eight or less than 10, to whether you abort when it's 24 weeks when the baby was almost recognisable. I just felt that if you want to have abortion, by all means, be responsible.

The second view on abortion I held was that having had one abortion, please be responsible enough to take the precautions of family planning or other contraceptive measures to prevent pregnancy. And I get very upset when I see people coming for it. So, all you do is to go on counselling, advising and all that.

So, it was natural that with abortions and some feelings about it, I accepted sterilisation even more. People who no longer needed children and have reached their maximum quota of children, I was very keen to get them all to go for sterilisation. I had no problem whatsoever with sterilisation.

To prevent abortion, I always believe that we should advocate and promote family planning through contraceptive devices, through the IUD, through the use of the pill. I think if you take it in its totality as a programme to improve the well-being of the individual family, there's nothing wrong with it. I didn't find it difficult.

LLC **But in carrying out these policies, you had to be sensitive to the public reaction, right? Were there challenges, or rather, difficulties you encountered?**

KSB Not really. Apart from the slight resistance to accepting abortion by religious groups and Catholics in particular, we didn't encounter difficulties. We don't say that the Catholics have to do it. While they may not agree with it, we say, "Okay, we'll leave you alone." But for those who are willing, don't deny them that as a means to family planning. Otherwise they'll resort to backroom methods and illegal abortion which was worse.

Then there were the Malays who did not like abortion and who did not like sterilisation, because they did not believe in limiting their family. In that case, we accept it. We try and persuade them to restrict their family or to accept sterilisation. That's all. Apart from these two groups, there wasn't really a problem anywhere else.

Becoming Permanent Secretary

LLC   **In 1984, you became the Permanent Secretary (Health) and Director of Medical Services. What exactly was the nature of your work as a Permanent Secretary?**

KSB   I think I was appointed Permanent Secretary mainly because Mr Howe Yoon Chong, who was Minister for Health, wanted to bring me up here to begin thinking about restructuring all the hospitals. Already at that time, he saw the need to change the way we delivered health care, to change the system of health financing. He already saw the problems of old age coming up in the year 2030.

His report on the elderly was good in every way and was correct in every way except for one thing, and that was telling the people they could not withdraw their Central Provident Fund savings until they were 60. Whereas before that, it was 55. Because of that one recommendation, the whole report was thrown away and not accepted, and had to be shelved.

I was brought up by Mr Howe mainly to look at restructuring, how we could re-do that. Up to that time, there was only one paragraph in the Government White Paper on the Health Plan. (Very occasionally, the government comes up with a Health Plan.) In 1982, they came up with a Health Plan to say that the government would look into restructuring and would look into the introduction of a savings scheme for health care. That was all in the statement made. And I was supposed to elaborate on that.

Actually, it was by coincidence because I was not banking on coming up here. I had already worked from 1955 to 1982, and I was hoping for an early retirement, to go into private practice. But he did not want me to leave. So, he made all the effort to get me up here. And it fitted the government's plan to allow civil servants to retire and all that. So, it just happened. So, I came up.

When I came up here, my efforts were made towards three things. One was to look into all aspects of how we could introduce MediSave. We started in a very rudimentary way in 1984. Then it slowly evolved to what it is today. MediShield didn't come up until about the year before last. That was 1993. And MediFund did not come up till 1994. So actually, MediSave was the scheme I had to introduce.

Then the ideas of restructuring hospitals were formulated together with the various methods of doing it. Then it resulted in the first experiment in NUH [National University Hospital] which was restructured in 1984 to 1985. The hospital's opening by Goh Chok Tong coincided with the restructuring.

That was the first attempt at restructuring or running a hospital meant to be a government hospital, teaching hospital, district hospital, but run as a "private" hospital. Within one and a half years, the government was satisfied that it had the chances of being successful. So, we were asked to introduce that into SGH [Singapore General Hospital]. Restructuring was the second major task I undertook.

Third, was rebuilding of hospitals. The rebuilding of SGH was in 1981. But since then, nothing was done, although there was a lot of talk. So, I was asked to relook rationalising the building of polyclinics or health centres, and then look into the rebuilding of (if you exclude NUH which was built about that time) Tan Tock Seng, Toa Payoh, KK and all the other centres.

Those were my three briefs really. So, we had MediSave introduced. Then the restructuring started in NUH. Then it went on to the Skin Centre and then it was SGH. SGH was an operational entity and the problems were entirely different. The problems were massive. There was the culture, there was the attitude of the people, there were the operational systems. Whereas in NUH, you could start from scratch and you had no historical baggage to carry with you.

Because of that, we took a different approach. We appointed American consultants on contract for four years to help us convert an on-going hospital in a government mode to a commercial mode. They spent one year studying the system, putting all the plans into action, running in parallel. After one year, we cut over and we no longer existed as a public hospital. We ran as a restructured hospital.

We worked with the Americans for two years. At the end of the third year, we felt confident enough to tell them: "We don't need your services," because the contract allowed us to terminate their services after three years. And we ran, after that, the hospital on our own.

Then in a matter of about two years, the government decided to restructure, almost simultaneously, KK, Toa Payoh and Tan Tock Seng. Toa Payoh and KK went at the same time. Tan Tock Seng was a bit later. At the same time, we established the Eye Centre as another restructured hospital. All these restructuring was done during my period as Permanent Secretary.

The other thing was to bring about drug registration. Up to then, drug registration was not in place. Anybody could import any drugs. So, we had to introduce a simple system whereby no drugs could be brought in unless they were registered.

The last thing was: Over the last two years, how do you license and accredit hospitals, nursing homes, laboratories and medical clinics? Up to then, anybody could just register with the Registrar of Companies and then they could set up their practice. We did not check them for their equipment, standards, et cetera.

So, in 1983, we enacted the Private Hospitals and Medical Clinics Act and Regulations, and began the slow process of restructuring. Today, all hospitals, clinics, labs and nursing homes have been licensed. We are now at the stage of having to review and renew the licence.

Those were the major ones — licensing, accreditation, restructuring, hospital rebuilding. Even now, hospital rebuilding is not quite finished. It will only be in the middle of next year that we finish re-building all our hospitals, including the Dental Centre, and the Institute of Health. The last hospital to finish re-building will be in 1998 when we will take over the building of Tan Tock Seng. That will be the last one. By early 1999, we will transfer the patients. Then we will demolish the whole of old Tan Tock Seng hospital which is the oldest existing hospital today.

LLC **While the first three areas that you mentioned — MediSave, restructuring and rebuilding of hospitals — have really wider political implications, that was why the government wanted to carry these out, things like drug registration and licensing of nursing homes. How did the need for doing this come about?**

KSB Every country in the world would always control what drugs can be brought in for sale. But because we never had our own pharmaceutical industry, we just allowed all and sundry to come in. So, we felt that there was a need to ensure that people were not dumping their sub-standard products or people were not dumping products which had not been approved for sale in their own country of manufacture. We had to protect our public by ensuring that they got drugs that were efficacious. So, the need for that grew up over time. And so we just studied it.

LLC **When you say "we", you are referring to ...**

KSB ... Ministry.

LLC **Ministry of Health. Coming from the Ministry, not from the hospitals' side.**

KSB No. From Ministry.

How the Permanent Secretary works with the Minister

LLC   **Could you give us an insight into the workings of the Permanent Secretary, in relation to the Minister for Health?**

KSB   I think the relationship differs from Minister to Minister. By and large, we find that almost everything that is major or significant, with political implications or considered sensitive, would go to them. All new policies would go to them for approval. They would usually be debated, discussed, modified and then implemented. They usually start with a discussion paper, what we call a Ministerial Paper. It will be studied and discussed.

Minister usually holds a fortnightly meeting with all the senior staff where he will discuss the papers. He will either give his input, or he will readily approve, or he will ask for modification. If it is something that is more or less operational, within the responsibility of Ministry, it will go on. If it is something that has implications beyond the Ministry, affecting other Ministries, or it has political implications, then after acceptance at Ministry level, it will result in a Cabinet Paper being put up. We will write the Cabinet Paper. We will debate it, discuss it, and then it will go to Cabinet for approval before it comes down for implementation.

By and large, any changes to the Acts would require Cabinet approval. Any amendments to the various legislations would require Cabinet approval. Changes to Regulations do not require Cabinet approval. They only require the Minister's approval. That is as far as the authority goes.

When we want to do large things like, say, MediSave, that would be a paper that would go to Cabinet after it has been debated and the system worked out. Then with the Cabinet's input, we will refine it. So also, for MediShield and MediFund.

When it comes to a building programme, the overall building programme for the decade or so will be presented in a very brief summary to Cabinet. Once Cabinet approves in principle, we will then work to refine the projections and the costing. We will then go to the Development Planning Committee [DPC] which is a committee of three Ministers. The DPC is a committee of our own Minister for Health because it is a health project, Minister for Finance because of financial control, and Minister for National Development. If the three Ministers approve, then the project will go through, having got the in-principle approval. So, there is the next step — the DPC Papers on any new developments.

Other than that, there will be day-to-day problems which are of a sensitive nature. The Minister would just call to meet us. But very often, we may go for two or three days on end without having to see him at all. A lot of the work goes in and out by files only. So, you have to learn to write minutes in a brief, concise manner, state what the aim of your paper is, state what your conclusions or recommendations are, and ask his concurrence to confirm that that is the approach that he wants. More than half the paperwork can be done by just files, without you having to see him. But where a subject is controversial and he needs clarification, then he will set a date for a meeting or call you in, and he will discuss it.

By and large, I think Ministers tend to go further down (to the operational level) than is really necessary because they want to be sure that the implementation details are correct. One will expect Ministers to just set the policy and let it be operationalised. So far, I found that most Ministers like to be involved even in the detailed implementation, at least kept informed, and they will then say, "Yes, I agree."

If you are doing a thing like MediSave, how we present it to the public would also be his concern. So, Minister wants to know what is your public communication programme, how would you do it, what media, how is the message to be put across and all that. Whereas theoretically, it could be just left to you. Similarly, when we worked out the details of MediSave, even if it meant keeping to the principle, we would finally give the whole implementation details to him for his information or for his concurrence. They are doing work which need not necessarily be part of their work. I think it's because we are so small as a Ministry. Everything appears in the papers, in the news, and they get asked by their colleagues in Cabinet. They had to account for it.

LLC   **When you have projects like MediShield, MediFund and all that, did you have special project teams?**

KSB   We have usually. If you say hospital building, there will be myself, the Deputy Director in-charge of hospitals, the Head of Development, and the Director of Finance. Four of us would be preparing. He [the Minister] would call us in or set a date for a meeting and we would discuss. Similarly, if it is MediFund, then the person dealing with MediFund or MediSave, the Director of Finance and myself would go in and discuss with him. We are not formal project teams because it's on-going work.

MediSave and MediShield

KSB   The whole point about MediSave is related to restructuring hospitals and subsidy. As long as the government wants to restructure hospitals and decides that it wants to reduce the level of subsidy, the government must provide patients or the public with the means to pay for their health care cost. Therefore, after looking at various systems, it decided that a savings scheme was the best. This savings scheme is different from others in that it is not contributing to a common pool, but it is contributing to your own individual savings which, if you don't use, it earns interest, which you can use for your old age and which will be tax free.

Those, theoretically, were things that we thought would be a reason for you to be prudent in how you use your savings and therefore, not over utilise health care cost. Whereas if you have paid for your insurance policy, and thereafter, everything is free, the human nature wants to take the maximum and use everything, even if it is not necessary. Similarly, if you paid to a common pool like, say, national health care, as a social security, and thereafter, everything you get is for free, the tendency is to over-utilise healthcare.

So, we decided not to go the US way of private insurance and the UK way of national health, but to go for an individual savings scheme with all its incentives for a person to be prudent. So, you save on income tax, you earn interest, you use it for your old age. If you die, it goes to your estate. Again, you are assured of it.

In a way, MediSave is in itself the simplest form of health insurance because it is used within your family. You use it whenever any member of your family needs to go to hospital, and you pay for it. We are really giving an individual savings scheme but you are insuring against your own and your family's future needs. But for a long time, public felt that that money was not theirs. It was squirrelled away somewhere, and they couldn't help wanting to get their hands at it. That was why for many years our emphasis was to tell people: "MediSave is your saving. Use it wisely. If you don't use it, you can always save it."

Today people are beginning to realise that it is their own money to be saved for their future. MediSave is really more for your future needs, when you stop working. When you are working, you are always covered by your company's benefits. So, it was more for that.

We realised that MediSave must work with restructuring. In other words, when you restructure hospitals, you have different classes of wards. From people paying only five to six per cent, you want to gradually increase the amount they have to pay as their co-payment. You must give them the means. That's why we had savings. MediSave will be adequate for the average person. But if you are one of those unfortunate to be inflicted with a major or catastrophic illness, you won't have enough money to cover. You'll soon deplete your savings.

That was why we decided to introduce a modified health insurance scheme. But we didn't want a health insurance like the US system which, having paid, you get everything for free. We somehow wanted to build in a disincentive for you to spend. That was how we developed the idea of only an insurance scheme for catastrophic illness. In other words, you can't fake a catastrophic illness. You must have fallen ill, and you really become very ill. And nobody chooses to be very ill. That is a natural barrier to using MediShield. Because of that and because it is a high risk if you fall ill, we decided to pool the risks. MediSave is not pooled, MediShield is pooled. So, having paid a premium, your risk is shared among everybody, so that those who are well will contribute towards looking after you.

But we also know that, from our experience with the Human Organ Transplant Act, people hate to take out insurance, hate to fill up forms. We knew that if you want to have everybody covered by insurance, it'd be a very difficult feat. So, we moulded it or framed it such that as long as you are a MediSave contributor, you are presumed to be a participant in the MediShield scheme. But if for any reason you don't want to do it, either you are covered for health by your employer, or you had your own money, or you had bought your own health insurance, then you opt out of the system. That way it allowed us to have pooling, maximum sharing of risks by the whole population and a simple way where you are automatically enrolled without having to fill forms.

That was good. All that we did then was to allow you to opt in for your spouse and your children or even for your parents. Why have we allowed parents? That's because MediSave was only introduced in 1984. Many people stopped working in 1984 and they didn't have MediSave. If they didn't have MediSave, they won't have MediShield. That was why we allowed people to use MediSave to pay for their parents' hospitalisation or for insurance. But in time to come, say, 20 years down the line, people who are working today or have been working for the last 10 years from 1984, by the time they reach 55 for retirement, they would have significant savings and MediShield. That's why it's like that.

So, the concept of MediShield is:

(1) To prevent abuse by over-use;
(2) To ensure that is only used to pay for your catastrophic illness; and
(3) Even if you pay for catastrophic illness, you would still have to pay a small percentage or co-payment.

That's the philosophy of MediShield really. The average person stays in hospital for about five days, shall we say. And it's hard to define what is catastrophic. Is cancer catastrophic? Is heart attack catastrophic? Rather than go into the semantics of what is a catastrophic illness, we just say: "Anybody who stays roughly twice the normal length of stay must have got something serious."

So, when you have stayed for twice the normal length of stay, then the catastrophic illness comes into play. In other words, they [the scheme] would start paying for you. So, you would have paid the first portion. Like when you have a motor-car accident, you pay the first $1,000 or the first $500. That's what we call the deductible. That's the concept. Having paid the deductible, MediShield will keep on paying the rest. But you would still have to pay 20 per cent out of pocket so that you don't depend on the insurance for everything. This concept of deductible and co-payment are the unique features which, everybody is now beginning to realise, is the best way to prevent abuse. That's MediShield.

Putting up papers to Cabinet

LLC   **This scheme, with all these intricacies of co-payment and deductible, this fine-tuning of the scheme went through a very intensive brainstorming process.**

KSB   It would go through discussions within the Ministry between myself, Director of Finance and the accountant. Then we would go to Minister with the first cut to say: "This is how we are doing it."

Then he will think about it and he suggests refinements or tell us: "What about this alternative?"

It goes through that process many times before it becomes fairly crystallised. Then it will go to Cabinet for approval. Cabinet might come up with some alternative, usually with a political angle in mind. So, we will do that. We are doing the same when we are talking about how do we cap the earnings of doctors in private practice. So, we are going through the same process. It's very much official. It goes to Minister and then comes down, discuss, goes back.

LLC   **For these discussions, each person would contribute based on one's experience in previous schemes, like as you've mentioned, the opt-out scheme for organ**

transplant. You'll find that these discussions for new policies actually benefit from the long-term experience.

KSB It does. But usually one person has the responsibility of putting on paper everything. Then debating, modifying, recording consensus, recording directives and refining. So, one person has that responsibility, either the Deputy Secretary (Administration) or the Director of Finance or DDMS (Hospitals). He has the responsibility of putting up the final paper.

LLC **Just now you mentioned that you put up a paper, and state very concisely the aims of the proposals, and then your conclusions. Can you give me an idea how long are these proposals?**

KSB You'll be amazed at the shortness of it. Generally, in Health, no paper to Cabinet should be more than four pages, double-spaced, A4 size. Can you imagine trying to put across a concept of a MediSave scheme all in four pages? At most, it might come to six. But I know that the MediSave scheme and all the rest were put across in four pages. MediShield was put up in four pages. Anything more than that, Cabinet has got no time to read. They'll probably turn to our Minister and say, "You tell us what it is all about."

Our Minister ensures that we keep our papers brief. The papers are put up very clearly. The paper would show: "Drafted by so and so by name, designation. Amended by so and so (his superior) by name and designation. Vetted usually by Permanent Secretary." The third person vetting is myself. Then: "Approved by Minister." Then it goes to Cabinet. Everybody's name is there.

Cabinet, over a period of time, will be very familiar with the style and names. "Oh, this paper is by so and so. It's atrocious because he has already been known for putting up very poor papers, very woolly thinking." They soon get to recognise different writing styles. But that is not enough. Earlier on, every paper, after the content, the substance, the principles are all approved by Minister, goes to about four senior Permanent Secretaries to vet for English, style and presentation. This was because Cabinet was very clear that it wanted a precise civil service language. So, it went through vetting.

Slowly the vetting by Permanent Secretaries was phased out because they got more familiar.

Now it is rare for us to send papers for vetting. But the guideline still stands. All papers must be vetted. So, what you do is, telephone the Cabinet Secretary and say, "Who is the Permanent Secretary responsible for vetting this week?" He would say this Permanent Secretary and we'll send it to him. He must vet within the day and return it back because they are only looking at the English and the presentation. They don't know the substance. They are not supposed to change. It is just a matter of saying: "This is too oblique. This is too ambiguous. Change it."

If you compare papers that were written 10 years ago and papers written today, you can see the evolution of the papers. Earlier, they were very woolly, haphazard. Even the format has to be very clear. The headings, everything, the spacing are all very clear.

LLC   **How did this spacing and format come about?**

KSB   All directed by Cabinet Secretary. Cabinet cannot go through different ways of presentation by different Ministries. So, it is very clear.

LLC   **These four senior Permanent Secretaries who vet the papers, do they take turns?**

KSB   They take turns.

LLC   **There are only these four and no other?**

KSB   Four or five. I'm not sure. At that time there were people like Head, Civil Service. They changed. Before, it was Sim Kee Boon, Ngiam Tong Dow and all that. They were changed.

Alan Choe

The Housing and Development Board's first architect-planner, and founder of the Urban Redevelopment Authority

Date of interviews: May 1997
Interviewer: Soh Eng Khim

Alan Choe (b. 1931) was the first architect-planner of the Housing and Development Board (HDB), and the founder and first General Manager of the Urban Redevelopment Authority (URA).

Choe, who studied architecture at the University of Melbourne and obtained a Fellowship Diploma from the Royal Melbourne Institute of Technology, was the first architect and town planner to return to Singapore from overseas. In 1960, he was headhunted to become the first architect and planner for the newly established HDB. His first task was to help the new PAP government achieve its first five-year plan of building 50,000 new homes. He exceeded the target by 4,000 homes.

He formed the URA in 1964 to undertake the urban renewal and redevelopment of Singapore's central areas, becoming its first General Manager. After leaving the URA in 1978, he joined RSP Architects Planners & Engineers, one of the largest architectural practices in Singapore. He later served in various roles such as Chairman of the Sentosa Development Corporation.

In this interview, Choe discussed the reasons for the success of the HDB's housing programme, his experience of working with then Prime Minister Lee Kuan Yew as well as with the United Nations Development Programme (UNDP) team working on urban renewal for Singapore. He also shared about his role in the URA, as well as in the conservation and preservation of Singapore's built heritage.

HDB's housing programme

SEK   **Mr Choe, we were talking about the SIT [Singapore Improvement Trust][1] and the inherent problems from which the HDB faced.**

AC   So, as I said, the key difference between the SIT and the Housing and Development Board (HDB) was that the SIT's agenda was very different from the PAP's agenda. The PAP's agenda had a focus — a very direct focus on what they were after. The eradication of slums was a promise they made on a political platform.

In the case of the SIT, as a colonial government, it was more to demonstrate that they did care for the population at large, but it was done on a very, very small scale. Too luxurious to fit the community. And also the architects that they had at that time would apply just like I did when I first came back [from architectural studies in Australia]. They applied to Singapore what was applicable to Western society. To them, three-storey walk up flats were intolerable.

So you can see that there were a lot of differences in the approach to tackling public housing. And I have said that they missed the point completely, principally because they did not have that political will that the [PAP] government that came into power had. It was the political will that drove the success of the public housing programme. Without the political will, I would say, it would have failed. In all planning matters, it is always a political decision.

SEK   **But the number of flats built was more than originally planned under the first five-year programme.**

AC   Yes, yes.

SEK   **The expected number to be built was 50,000 flats, and then you exceeded it and completed 54,000 flats.**

AC   Yes.

---

[1] The Singapore Improvement Trust (SIT) was set up by the British colonial government in 1927 to address the housing needs of the Singapore population. One of its earliest projects was building the Tiong Bahru housing estate.

SEK **How would you attribute that success?**

AC As I said, the government here has been quite pragmatic. When they went into public housing, firstly they were prepared to accept the fact that they did not want the planners or the architects or the citizens to think that public housing would be elevated overnight to a standard that was too high for them to afford, or too expensive for the government to afford to house everybody. So they were prepared to go into that by building the first generation of HDB flats.

So, in the first generation of Housing Board flats, we had a lot of what is known as one-room apartments. One-room apartments in those days were really basic. Today, they would be our slums. Maybe we won't even let our overseas workers stay in them. But that was how we started the public housing programme to achieve the target numbers. Because in those days, target numbers were a more important priority than the niceties that we can afford today, like the environment, greening of the area, playgrounds, carparks. Those were not there. Just to put a roof over their head.

The most luxurious was the three-room flat. In fact, a three-room flat has only one room. Effectively it only had one bedroom because if you take into account the living room/dining room as a room also, it was a three-room flat. We had what was known as a one-room flat. In a one-room flat they resorted to using communal kitchens, communal toilets. What you had for each family was just a one-room flat — nothing inside.

[…]

And this was the lesson which we had seen from many countries. That their fault was that they followed the SIT. They had architect-planners who were mostly expatriates or people who just practised the theory of architecture they learnt. What was suitable for their temperate countries, they tried and applied it in the East. And of course they have never broken the housing shortage as the Singapore government did successfully.

Imagine if we had a multi-racial community where the Chinese ate pork and the Malays didn't eat pork — and they shared the same kitchen, used the same place to cook and wash up. It would have been a dynamite situation! But you have to give credit that we managed to steer that through. Even toilets — communal toilets, male and female altogether.

SEK What was your contribution in this area [Singapore's public housing programme]?

AC My contribution was that I was one of the many people there. Getting involved very directly with Queenstown and Toa Payoh New Town. Those were, to me, very important in my life. Because as I said, it gave me an opportunity to handle a thing that people would dream about doing, but never had a chance of doing it. But to me at that time, the satisfaction had never occurred to me. To me, it was the fear of what I designed. Firstly, I had no confidence as I had never done anything like that before. Secondly, I knew that it was not going to be a good thing; it was going to be very, very crowded.

You never thought about all those things. All you wanted to do was to tell yourself that you had to live up to what the political leadership wanted and what they promised the people. And I had a good chairman,[2] CEO,[3] and I had to try and do it. Because they were checking all the time, how things were coming along, and to make sure that I could deliver it.

So in those days, the thought of the satisfaction was furthest from my mind. My fear every evening going home was to reflect on the project. My God, how could I do it? The building area was so dense, and I had no experience. I didn't know how it was going to come out when finished, because what you saw was just a piece of plan. You drew it and you tried to satisfy them, they asked you questions — if too low: in number, you had to bump in more units. It was always like that.

Every time I went in there, I knew they were going to throw it back and say: not high enough, increase some more. And up to a late stage when it was all about finished, they would tell me at the last minute: "Sorry, we got word that it is too low, we want to house 600,000 people." 600,000 people! In my training, it would have had to be a big, big, big city for that 600,000. I used to remember that when I go to New Zealand, they tell me that they have 600 acres to one sheep. And I used to tell the guy: you know in Singapore, we have 600 persons per acre. You have 600 acres per sheep. That was how we demonstrated to them how dense our living condition was.

[...]

In America, urban renewal has been used as a political football. They debate a lot amongst the politicians, and it is used a lot to win votes, and it is used a lot for racial segregation. So, urban renewal and public housing overseas is a dirty word. Nobody

---

[2] Lim Kim San. See footnote 5 below.

[3] Howe Yoon Chong, who later joined politics and became a cabinet minister.

wants to live in public housing. There is a stigma to live in public housing overseas, in Western countries, and in Japan.

But in Singapore, you'd never find people feeling low or down, saying, "I live in a Housing Board estate" because there is no segregation. You have the best of people living in public housing, some very successful people. They refuse to move out. You see today over a period of time the car park in public housing you get more and more Mercedes cars, expensive cars, you see more and more of them installing air-conditioners. And there is very little bad association with public housing as overseas. But in Singapore, we are very fortunate. There is never this distinction about people being scared to say that I live in Toa Payoh, or Queenstown, or any of the housing estates.

SEK   **Not even the early days when public housing just came on?**

AC   Not even in the early days. That's why I say we are very, very fortunate. In the UK, I visited some of their public housing, it was really bad. Vandalism was so bad, nobody took pride in the environment because they considered themselves as the rejects of society and accordingly, they behaved as rejects of society. Because they think that the public see them as that, why should they behave well, it is not their property.

That is another thing which the government did very smartly, which was that in the public housing programme, very soon after they achieved the public housing targets, they knew they were on a steady cruise to achieving all their targets. They thought about the other way, which was to make people own the public housing. And I think that was again a very wise move because if you own the property, you take pride. If somebody in your block dirties the wall (and if you have already bought the apartment), you would be very angry, because he is lowering the value of your property. And also, for Singapore where most of the people are migrants coming in to take root in Singapore, there is nothing like making them have a stake by owning real estate.

And they made ownership of housing very affordable. Today you'd find that in Singapore we have a very high ownership of property, one of the highest in the world. Everybody owns a property. Today you find that if anybody who owns a HDB flat in Bishan or Yishun, he can sell his HDB five-room flat for three-quarter of a million dollars, go to Australia and buy two bungalows. So you can see how successful the public housing programme is.

SEK   **Was there any form of public education programme to educate the people at that time about living in satellite towns like Toa Payoh?**

AC   No. In the early days, I must say that there were two major problems in public housing in Singapore that was encountered. Firstly, the case of resettlement — it was a big problem. Because we were moving, as in the case of Toa Payoh, into an area with farms. Can you imagine a family that had been farming for many many years, living off the ground, and suddenly you go in and you tell them, "Look, I want to take over your land, I want to do public housing and in return, I am going to pay you compensation. For a fruit tree, I will pay you so much, for a vegetable plot, so much, and for your house, I will pay you so much. And to re-house you, I will give you a high-rise apartment."

These chaps had never even known the use of water closet or Naco louvres.[4] Naco louvres in those days used to have a lock — when you pushed it up, it locked. We used to have many cases when they rang up the estates department and complained, "This government is stupid, giving us windows that cannot be opened." So not only did you have to educate their mindset to move away from an area — because it was needed for development — to where they would lose their livelihood.

There were two things that affected them. Firstly their lifestyle, they were so used to living off the ground, wearing their pyjamas, shorts and going out to get everything they wanted. You moved them to a high-rise flat, suddenly they could not move about like that, because there were neighbours all over. Secondly, their livelihood. The mindset change was very important. There was strong resistance.

In fact, in the early days the biggest fear was that every time they went and cleared that area, the people would vote against the government. That was their biggest fear.

SEK   **Was that so initially?**

AC   No. This was the funny thing, you see. Before the event took place, you would have expected that if you did that, the people would surely vote you out. Because they had been inconvenienced, and their livelihood was at stake. But as it turned

---

[4]A brand of windows with movable fins to allow flow of air. Naco is a UK manufacturer.

out, it was just the reverse. So I have got to say that I was quite amazed. But it showed over and over again that in new housing areas to which they had moved people, instead of voting against the government, those people voted for the government — solidly. As I said, I still cannot fathom. It must have been that they were more than satisfied.

Meetings with the Prime Minister

SEK **You organised low cost furniture exhibitions and housing exhibitions throughout that period.**

AC Very early on, again, the HDB realised that we had a problem in demonstrating to people what they were going to live in. Because suddenly, they were put into one-room, two-room flats, and they did not know how to organise the furniture, how to make the place more liveable. So the only way would be to demonstrate it to them. And how did you demonstrate to them? The only way was to build prototypes and build up a true-to-scale unit and show them how it could be furnished comfortably and economically, to meet their needs. So, that was the purpose. It was not to "sell" to people.

I was given the task to organise that exhibition. And that of course put me in a very good stead. Because of that, I had to do a lot of things. And of course in the process, I got to meet the SM [Senior Minister], the then Prime Minister [Lee Kuan Yew], quite a lot. Again as I said, those days when you met with the Prime Minister, or every time he wanted a meeting, you would have butterflies in your stomach, because he was such a forceful person. He knew everything and you were fearful what he was going to ask you. And he expected everybody to be like him, but of course we were not even one quarter of him in ability. He was very sharp.

I remember once there was this thing we were going to do in a Malay area, a housing estate. At that time, people expected there was going to be a problem. So, he decided that he was going to tour the area in a jeep. I was summoned by many people. They asked, who is the planner? They said, "Alan, you better go there. Prime Minister said to go to his house." All of us gathered at his Oxley Road house. Waited there. He came out, "Where is the planner?" "Sir, I am the planner." I tell you, it was a frightful experience. If you gave him the right answers, you would straightaway win his confidence and thereafter, his rapport with you was different.

140 • SPEAKING TRUTH TO POWER

So I learned that with Lee Kuan Yew, the first five minutes, if you didn't cut ice with him, you were finished. He was such an intellect that after talking to you for five minutes, he would know whether or not you were worth talking to, or whether he was wasting time on you. So everybody was nervous. Because of that, you find that our standards were so high. He expected nothing to falter. Even the programme parade [in which Lee toured the housing estate in a jeep], I asked one of them: "Does he expect me to follow?" He said, "If he doesn't ask, you had better stay away." I said "thank you very much," and sneaked off straightaway.

Because, if he directed a question to you, he expected you to have all the facts and figures at your fingertips. And that was one of the things I said that, going back and learning it, he was the one that set such a high standard that the civil service became really very influential. Everybody had to be on their toes, nothing faltered because he had such high standards. He expected it of himself, he expected it of the people immediately close to him and all the people working for him. So the net result was all of us were always on our toes, so that generation of civil servants was different.

SEK   **How closely watched was the housing programme by Mr Lee?**

AC   Oh yes, very much so. I think that he followed it extremely closely. He was definitely the architect of the public housing programme, in the sense that he gave the policies, the thrust, and the programme of what he wanted. And he saw it in a much wider picture than all of us. He had also the ability to pick the right people — in picking Lim Kim San[5] who was a businessman, not tried and tested, had never been a contractor, had never had anything to do with building. And true to form, Kim San learned and in the process, won the Magsaysay Award[6] for public housing contribution. And I think he deserved it. He really did. And Howe Yoon Chong too, who later on became Minister. So these are the first generation people who really started with no knowledge, but just the simple conviction that they were going to deliver the goods.

---

[5] Lim Kim San, the Chairman of the HDB (1960–1963) who then entered politics and became the Minister for National Development (1963–1965). Before 1960, Lim was a self-made millionaire businessman who ran a sago factory, and who was also involved in the banking sector.

[6] The Ramon Magsaysay Award, a prize from the Philippines recognising transformative leadership in Asia.

The Urban Renewal Department

SEK — **Mr Choe, let's talk a bit about your days with the Urban Renewal Department. What were the circumstances under which you were appointed as Head of the Urban Renewal Department in 1965?**

AC — When public housing reached a stage where we were able to tackle the main backbone of the housing shortage. As I said, we started off by clearing all the kampungs, the thatched colonies of housing where there was no modern sanitation. The Bukit Ho Swee fire was a case in example — no modern sanitation, and they were all built without any regard for safety. When a fire came, it just wiped the whole estate off.

At that time when public housing was tackled, the government began to look at the sites to clear the next area of housing problems. These were the slums in the Central Business area. By that I mean slums in Chinatown, slums in the Malay areas in Geylang and the North Bridge Road area. When they began to look at those areas, they had to think in terms of urban renewal. That means they had to tear down buildings that were still in a fairly respectable condition. When I say respectable at that point of time, they were liveable, they were certainly better than what the kampung squatters lived in.

That was necessary not only as a means to improve the living conditions of the slum area in the city. But you required that to improve your infrastructure because you had to widen your roads, you had to improve your infrastructure, you had to put in modern sanitation, cabling, wiring. Everything else had to be put in place. You had to set up parks, open spaces, you had to create land for people to build accommodation as required. Offices, hotels, shopping centres, besides housing.

The city centre remained the prime location, except that because it was settled the earliest, you had the old housing and it remains the most prominent area for development today. In that regard, the government decided that they had to go into clearing slums to kick off comprehensive urban renewal. That was how urban renewal came about.

When they started to think in terms of urban renewal, we had no experience in Singapore, as I said. We invited the United Nations to come in to help — the UNDP came in and sent three experts down. At that time, being the only architect planner in Singapore who had worked on public housing for a couple of years, I was assigned to understudy them. And I appointed two architects, so that the three of us would shadow the three UN experts.

SEK   **How long were they here for?**

AC   They were here for a short period of six months. Some of them left after four months, the longest stayed six months. Originally, they sent one person, who did an assessment for about a month. I was very close with that person, touring the whole of Chinatown to see some of the problems, and how to tackle it. After his visit, an application was made to the UNDP, following which they sent a three-men team for a longer period to help us with urban renewal in Singapore.

SEK   **Could you describe the urban landscape in 1965 then?**

AC   Given the landscape at that time, you could see that with public housing coming out on the fringes, the pressure to redevelop the centre became more and more acute. Because we had gone through the crisis and development was taking place, the urbanisation of Singapore was a natural event. And with that you found a lot of people wanting land for development. They wanted to build offices, hotels, shopping centres and so on.

The landscape at that time had very little of this. All we had were the city centre slums, the old Smith Street, Pagoda Street, Temple Street. There were still slums all over the place there. Very congested, but people happily going about their normal course of work.

On the fringes of the city, you had housing estates coming up all over Toa Payoh, Queenstown and so on. So unless something was done to the city centre, we were going to have lopsided development.

SEK   **As Head of URD [Urban Renewal Department], what were your vision and responsibilities then?**

AC   My responsibility was to try and work out strategies, plans and possible solutions for the government to study, and to implement a comprehensive urban renewal programme. From day one, I realised that in urban renewal, you cannot take things in isolation. I had to work very closely with the Housing Board, because one of the lessons in urban renewal is that you cannot begin to clear people unless you have alternative accommodation to offer them.

So the first thing I had to map out for the government was to make sure that there was sufficient housing built, not only to meet the normal requirements in the original plans. The original plan was to take care of the increase in population, plus the kampungs that they cleared on the fringes. Now I had to tell them that I was going to clear X number of areas in the city centre, and how many families they had to re-house for me. So I had to add my programme of public housing to their needs.

So that was my first target objective — to ensure that they had enough public housing to meet my needs for resettlement. Then, I had to map out a programme to see what was needed to help stimulate Singapore's economic development. Because I saw urban renewal as being very much tied up with economic improvement, not just social development, as in the case of many societies. In the Western societies, urban renewal is only used for social improvement, but in the Singapore context, I have always viewed urban renewal as a means to stimulate economic development. That is, to make available sites to build many of the kind of infrastructure we needed. Not only improving roads, transportation and so on, but clear the land required to build hotels to improve tourism, land required to build offices to generate investments from outside of Singapore. Also, you had to have better accommodation to meet the needs of people coming to Singapore to work. So there were a lot of opportunities.

SEK **What was the decision of the government then to relocate the people to the outskirts of the island, maintaining the city area for commercial use?**

AC Not quite. In the early stage of experimentation, once I was charged to do urban renewal, I prepared a comprehensive plan, not just covering one small precinct. I actually did a master plan covering the whole of the city centre, stretching from Precinct North I at that time as I called it, Crawford Street near the gas tanks right down to the south, which is the old Outram Road jail. That covered a very large area of Singapore, which included Shenton Way, Robinson Road, Chinatown, Little India. The whole lot was within that precinct.

So it was a very large area — I have forgotten the exact number of hectares or acreage. Unless you did it that way with a comprehensive plan, you could not begin to tackle urban renewal properly. In many Western countries, they take one plot at a time in isolation, and there is a lot of political wrangling between one [town] councillor with the next. So it is a dirty word — urban renewal. But we wanted to do it differently.

So this means getting everybody involved. Offices were in the plan because we had already mapped out Shenton Way to be the extension of the Central Business

District. Then there was Orchard Road. Orchard Road was outside of the plan, but we had all the time to bear in mind that Orchard Road would continue to be a tourist belt, and how we could balance off other areas to supplement Orchard Road. So we created the Havelock Road area where today you see King's Hotel, Miramar Hotel and the Apollo Hotel.

Those were all under urban renewal. Those were sub-areas we thought necessary to create the secondary tourist market, rather than just building first class hotels. And then we sited areas to build major commercial complexes like People's Park. People's Park was one of the first sale sites we launched to build a comprehensive shopping centre with housing. So when we did urban renewal, it was not just all offices. We wanted to introduce housing into the city centre, so that we could bring nightlife into the city centre.

We learned that New York after office hours is a dead city. So learning from that, we introduced some housing. So you'd find that in the early urban renewal scheme, we had quite a bit of housing in both north and south. The Ellenborough Market HDB estate, which is now slated for demolition, was one of those — we had apartments, we had shopping below.

SEK **Why was Orchard Road not included in your overall plan?**

AC Orchard Road at that time was not a slum. That was why we did not include it. Urban renewal, essentially means that the first objective is to clear slums; your second objective was to improve your infrastructure so that the city could grow. The third objective I had in mind was to make opportunities for investment and to develop things that would help our economy grow. That is, to build hotels, offices, shopping centres, better housing. In Orchard Road at that time, you had Ngee Ann Kongsi's cemetery. You had the Singapura Hotel, and you had a few other hotels.

The establishment of URA

SEK **You were appointed as GM [General Manager] of URA in April 1974. What were the circumstances that led to your appointment?**

AC I think very simply at that time when we started urban renewal, I was one of the first persons nominated by the government — because of my background and training — to try and look into the possibility of doing urban renewal in Singapore. And being one of the first persons involved when it became necessary to enlarge the Urban Renewal Department (URD) from a unit to a department, and a department to an authority. I suppose it was more or less logical that I started the ball rolling by becoming its first Chief Executive, with all the training experiences and the benefit of guidance from various people given to me.

SEK **What about your responsibilities as GM at URA?**

AC The responsibilities in the initial stages were less on planning. Because part of the process of urban renewal at that time was to try and think out policies and programmes that could help the government implement urban renewal. Urban renewal at that time was a relatively new thing — I would say none in the region dared to venture into urban renewal. Only the highly developed countries like America and the UK went into urban renewal. But even so, when they went in, it had not been an extremely successful or happy kind of experience for the governments or the people affected.

So when we embarked on it, as the first General Manager, I had to spend a lot of time in thinking out programmes, policies that would enable us to avoid going into the same pitfalls as the highly developed countries. I suppose one of the benefits of starting late is that you can learn from the mistakes of others.

In Singapore, our need to do urban renewal was more pressing than in America and the UK. When you looked at the central area, it was mostly lacking in modern sanitation. Our road network was reaching a stage where unless you did something, traffic in the central area would come to a standstill. There was no modern sanitation, there was no way to grow. And land was needed very much for a new metropolis to be built in Singapore, and we didn't have land.

So our need was a desperate one and we could not afford to wait like other countries. In the case of Thailand, Malaysia, elsewhere, they have a lot of land. All they need to do if they are not happy is just to extend the perimeter of the development. They have a lot of hinterland, which we do not. So our needs are quite different, very urgent notwithstanding the fact that we are very fearful of going into a new venture. But we had no choice.

One of the most important things that I had to convince the government on was that we should not — in learning from other countries — go into a urban renewal programme when we did not have a strong public housing programme. Because in America and the UK, what they do is that when they resettle people, they give them a sum of money and say, "This is your cash compensation, out you go." And in many cases they just move into another area and you create a new slum, because they have just moved in and are crammed into another area, because there were no suitable alternative provided.

The second condition that I found very necessary is that unlike America and the UK, where they depended heavily on the private sector to come in and work with government, we had to do it slightly different. Because over there, one of the accusations they faced was that resettlement is used as a means to clear people in order to reward the good friends of the government. To come in, take advantage and exploit the land and the people, to make a lot of money.

So in the Singapore context, we devised something that nobody had done in the world. Not the Americans, not in England, and not in any other place. We decided that we would devise our programme such that after clearing the land, we would make the land available in a very transparent system for people to come in and bid for the land. So that there would not be the same kind of stigma or accusations levelled at urban renewal, that it is to favour a few rich friends of the government. And our difference is that instead of allowing the private sector to decide what they want to build, we tie the Urban Renewal Programme to a Master Plan.

So my preoccupation as the first General Manager was to look at strategies, policies to help make the programme workable. At the same time, to make sure that there were investors who would come in to participate in urban renewal. Otherwise, it would become a totally government programme, which was wrong. You cannot expect the government to come in to build hotels, shopping centres, office buildings, luxury housing and so on.

So we had to devise a new programme to entice the private sector, which meant tying it up with incentives and so on, to invite private sector participation, but in a very transparent system. Of course, starting urban renewal also warranted building up a team. At that time, we did not have specialists. So I had to slowly think of the specialised areas that we had to do and how to recruit the people, to build up.

And of course to draft the first set of urban renewal rules and regulations and the Urban Redevelopment Authority Act, which had to go to Parliament for approval, because urban renewal involves, very importantly, designating areas for renewal. In those days, I must say that people were very fearful. They used to joke that whenever I walked around a place two, three times at night, that was a signal that that area was going to be acquired by the government — that it would be redeveloped. Because once that area was designated for renewal, it warranted compulsory acquisition of the land.

So it is quite important that the Urban Redevelopment Authority Act took into account the powers to compulsorily acquire land, the powers to relocate people, and the powers to offer the land for redevelopment, and also the powers to get other agencies to come in to build the roads, modern sanitation and the whole works. In the early years it was very exciting and challenging, in the sense that in everything you did, you had to try and improvise and think of new things that suited our local circumstances.

Conservation and preservation

SEK   **Could you elaborate on the URA's work with regard to Central Area planning?**

AC   Well, in the early days, one of the key things involved in the central areas before we could even talk about clearing slums was to very quickly work with the other government agencies, in particular, PWD [Public Workers Department]. In those days, the Road Department, Sewerage Department all came under PWD. The infrastructure in the whole central area was inadequate, so we had to put in new infrastructure in whatever we do. We also created a Master Plan for the central area to define areas where we thought the business centre and the financial core should be, and the areas which we thought suitable for tourism, and so on. Those were some of the targets we looked at.

SEK   **So it was done in conjunction with PWD?**

AC   Yes, many other agencies, with PWD in particular and also HDB.

SEK   **You mentioned conservation projects. What about preservation of buildings — did that come later?**

AC   I would say that very much as a result of urban renewal, which highlighted the importance of the preservation of areas, the government formed a Preservation of

Monuments Board.[7] Because there was no point for you to designate buildings or areas for conservation unless you had the powers to rent it out. Under the URA Act, we could only designate areas for conservation, but we did not have the funds nor the need to go in to do the actual conservation. We would conserve it in the hope that the private sector would come and play their part. In certain instances where buildings were involved, it was important that you had an authority with the powers to designate a building for conservation, that nobody should carry out indiscriminate renovation or tear down the building. So that called for special powers.

So, as a result of the conservation programme, the government decided to set up the Preservation of Monuments Board, which had special powers for designating buildings for conservation. They could also acquire buildings for conservation, if need be. So that was an offshoot of urban renewal.

SEK **Could you list some of the areas that the URA identified as conservation areas in the early days?**

AC As I have said earlier, we thought that urban renewal would be a useful means to help with tourism development. In this regard we have identified areas that we want to highlight the very colourful, different racial groups that we have in Singapore.

SEK **Was this done in conjunction with the then STPB [Singapore Tourism Promotion Board]?[8]**

AC Correct. We did it first. We did it first because we identified areas more from the urban planning point of view. At that time we had identified that a very distinctive area around the Sultan Mosque [Kampong Glam], which was itself a highlight. We designated that area to be conserved as a Malay area, where we have some nice buildings and streets like Arab Street and so on. Then we identified the Serangoon area for conservation as an Indian area. Then we identified Chinatown — Temple Street, Smith Street and the like — for conservation.

---

[7] Now a division of the National Heritage Board known as the Preservation of Sites and Monuments division.
[8] Now the Singapore Tourism Board.

So when we talked about conservation in those early days, we immediately thought in terms of our rich cultural heritage. It led to us saying: why don't we use that effectively as a means to also add to the tourist attractions that Singapore had to offer? And if we could conserve that, it would give visitors and young Singaporeans a chance to have a taste of what Singapore was like in the early days.

SEK   **When you said that areas were earmarked for conservation, what exactly do you mean? Did the URA go in actively to solicit for public support to renovate or restore the building?**

AC   Yes. Now this is a very interesting point you raised. In those days, we could only designate areas, which meant we would not allow people to tear it down and put up a new high-rise building that would spoil the character of the whole area. So those were our powers. But with regard to getting people to come in and build, that is a different story because it requires a lot more incentives, to make sure that the people would want to do it. Because in most cases, people object to conservation.

Let's say you own a whole row of old shophouses in Chinatown. You know very well that near you, people are tearing them down and in its place, they build high-rise office towers which are worth a lot of money. So if we conserve your area, you stand to lose out. So that was quite a big problem for us that every time we conserve areas. We faced opposition from land owners who would agitate and say, "Why do we do that? Is there grounds for us to do conservation? Singapore has such a short history, why should we conserve when we have so little?"

But the counter-argument I offer is that it is due to the very reason that we have so few heritage buildings, that we have to be even more concerned and conscious about preserving the little we have. Because if we just let go, we would have nothing to conserve. While we were not able to put in force at that time, I had at that time floated an idea with the government that maybe we should allow people who owned these properties to bequeath it to the state, and have it offset against taxes. There are various ways to put a sweetener to encourage them to do conservation. It's all related to dollars and cents. If they do get some kind of a trade-off, they would not mind.

The other thing that is now being implemented was that if you want conservation, you must give a sweetener to people. What is being implemented is that if you do a conservation area, you don't have to pay development charge, you don't have to provide car park charges if you don't have enough car parks. These are incentives, but not big enough. But I am glad that the Act [Preservation of Monuments Act] and the whole lot is so great that people will do it.

A good example is Boat Quay, by the Singapore River. On the side, you have the United Overseas Bank (UOB) Head office, you have the OCBC [Oversea-Chinese Banking Corporation] head office, worth a lot of money. Yet those row of old houses in Boat Quay, they are conserved. Fortunately, the people who own those properties have accepted that they do have a role to play — some of them out of pride, because it was their forefather's building, and they would like to preserve it. The good sign is that today with the conservation of Boat Quay, people — although they are not getting a windfall on real estate — they are able to rent out their shops into nice restaurants and so on that is giving them a fairly good rental return. It is working, that people over the years have seen the benefits of urban renewal.

On the guidelines on conservation, I must say that the people who are doing it now are doing an excellent job. But my own view is that they are doing it a bit too stringently and rigidly. To me, conservation means you try and preserve the original character of the building, especially the façade and so on. The other important thing I feel is that conservation is only meaningful if you are able to inject life into it. What you don't want is to conserve a thing like an empty museum, which people can walk through but which is devoid of life.

What we are now doing in conservation is that if the floor is a timber floor, the authorities will insist that it be retained as a timber floor. That, I think is quite tough on the owners, because the building code authorities, fire authorities and health authorities have a different idea, and these things do not meet their standards today. Because they [timber floors] are combustible, or are unhygienic. But yet the URA insists that you must conserve it exactly as it was. What they have done in other countries is quite successful. They will retain the whole façade, tear the interior down and then fit in with quite nice new things inside, so that you would still have the character but also the modern amenities that meet with the building code and safety requirements.

Achievements of the URA

SEK   **What would you say are your overall achievements as General Manager of URA?**

AC   I think, to me, the most satisfying thing was to be able to introduce the Sale of Sites programme in Singapore under the Urban Renewal Programme. Which I am very proud to say that today, we are still the country at the forefront to do this. No country in the world has come up with it. You can only do this with a strong government. And in our programme, what we have done is that we have been able to see very quick redevelopment of the Central Area through this need to invite the private sector to come in.

You take the case of when we started urban renewal. We didn't start it that long. We launched our first sale, second sale, one sale after another. And with each sale, you could see that the skyline was changing. The skyline in Singapore changed dramatically as a result of our Urban Renewal Programme, because in the past, the private sector had great difficulty in selecting good sites to build their office, the hotels, the shopping centres. Secondly, if they found a good site, they had no means to clear the squatters or get the infrastructure. So, when you do not have the sites or the opportunity, you cannot bring about investments.

I would say that the thing that I am extremely satisfied with is that urban renewal has not only helped clear slums and put in modern infrastructure, but we achieved the very important dimension of economic development for Singapore, as well as tourism.

In our first sale, we found out that Singapore was extremely short of hotels. There was a lot of demand for people who wanted to build hotels, but there were no good sites. And because of the lack of hotels, tourism suffered because your room rates are very high, and there are not enough rooms. So, in the first sale, I deliberately singled out hotels as the most important one to go out.

It also brought about opportunities for architects who previously never had the opportunity to do nice, big skyscrapers. So if you look at it, Shenton Way is a good example. We designated Shenton Way because we knew in the third sale that we needed a lot of first-class offices to shape Singapore as an important centre for finance and business. So we created the whole belt of Shenton Way for office towers starting with UIC building, Robina House, DBS building. All these were part of the urban renewal.

So Shenton Way came about because of the Urban Renewal Programme. In the planning of Shenton Way, we allowed for vistas of the sea. So that we learned from other countries that you do not build a solid wall such that only the ones facing the sea would enjoy the sea view, and the ones across the road would not. Also, the programme gave architects unprecedented opportunities to do big buildings. So, together with that you see all these, even in Marina Square.

URA took the responsibility to get tax concessions for developers. I was able to put forward to Cabinet that in order to get the private sector to come in to build, you had to give them incentives. And surprisingly, the government agreed when I asked that property tax be reduced by half. At that time it was 36 per cent. It turned out government was fully with me. They gave us 12 per cent instead of 18 per cent. And they gave them 20 years of concession.

So that enabled us to really set off urban renewal like fire. It went off like hot cakes and we have never looked back. And I am very happy to say that even up till today the Urban Renewal Programme is very much structured on the same formula that we formulated right at the beginning. They made basic refinements, but the main Sale of Sites programme remains the same. And with that we were able to achieve a lot for Singapore.

Chan Chin Bock
Chairman of the Economic Development Board

Date of interview: December 2002
Interviewer: Jason Lim

Chan Chin Bock (b. 1933) was the third Chairman of the Economic Development Board (EDB), and the first to have risen through its ranks.

Chan began his career as a teacher at the Anglo-Chinese School, which he also attended as a student. After subsequent stints as an editor with *The Straits Times* and as Public Affairs Manager at the Ford Motor Company, he applied to join the nascent EDB to promote Singapore as an attractive destination for foreign investments. As Chief of the Investment Promotion Division, he was deployed to the EDB's first overseas office in New York, and became known as one of EDB's early "road warriors." He quickly rose to become Chairman of the EDB from 1972 to 1974, remaining in EDB until his retirement.

In this interview, Chan discussed the economic thinking within the EDB in the early years, and how Singapore's failed push for a common market with Malaysia in the 1960s turned out to be impetus for the newly independent country's journey to globalisation. He also shared about the rationale behind the appointments of all the Chairmen of the EDB — of which there were seven up to the point of this interview with Chan — as part of the government's strategy for the economic development of Singapore.

Joining the EDB

JL **Why was it that after two years in the Ford Motor Company, you moved to the EDB?**

CCB Well, EDB wanted Promotion Officers because at that time, EDB wanted to do exactly what Ford was doing. Ford was trying to create a good image of the company, its workers and its products after the strike. EDB wanted to create a good image of Singapore as an attractive investment location. So, they were looking for people who had this type of experience of changing public perception and public image, you see.

JL **They approached you or ...**

CCB No, they put out an advertisement for the kind of people that they wanted to hire in order to kick off our industrialisation programme — people who had experience in creating images for the public for certain desired goals, you see. In the case of Ford, it was to create a good corporate image and a good product image. In the case of Singapore, it was to do the same thing but not for any particular company, but for the whole of Singapore as a country.

So, they spelled it out in their advertisement and I applied for it, because I thought that I had the right experience to go one step further. Instead of just doing it for Ford, why not do it for the country?

So, I applied for the job and went for the interview. The interview panel consisted of some of my present friends in EDB. Joe Pillay was there, Dhanabalan was there, I. F. Tang was there on the interviewing panel.[1] The advertisement didn't say specifically what type of background they were looking for in candidates, but only mentioned certain types of skills in handling publicity and media, all of which I had. But when I came here [to the EDB office] for the interview, I discovered that one of the key target industries for EDB was the automobile industry. Because I had a background in the automobile industry, I became more suitable for it, so they offered me the job.

---

[1] In reference to J. Y. Pillay (then deputy secretary of the Economic Planning Unit at the Ministry of Finance), S. Dhanabalan (then an economist with the EDB) and Tang I-Fang (then a consultant for the United Nations Development Programme (UNDP), who later became the second Chairman of the EDB).

Early years at the EDB

JL **We know that EDB's vision for Singapore is to be a vibrant and robust knowledge-based economy today, and in view of that, Singapore aims to be a compelling global hub for business and investments. But I would like to go back to the 1960s when EDB was set up. You joined in 1964. What was the role of the EDB at that time, and what kind of people was the EDB looking for?**

CCB Well, I must say that as Singapore developed more and more economically from one decade to another, the bar has been raised and we have become more and more ambitious about what we would like to be. But way back in the 1960s, we were less ambitious.

If you read SM [Senior Minister] Lee Kuan Yew's book[2] from the very beginning, he said that all he was interested in was to find good jobs for Singapore's two million people then. That didn't sound very ambitious, but after you have found jobs for two million people, you would want better jobs. Then you would want higher technology, you would want higher economic value added, and so on.

So, in the very beginning it was rather simple. The Singapore government has been very, very pragmatic in its economic policies. So, the first thing the government thought it needed to do to succeed in industrialisation, to give itself a better chance of success in industrialisation, was to have a common market with Malaysia.

I joined EDB about seven months after Singapore had become part of Malaysia, and at that time the job was very simple. If I thought at that time about some of the things that I would have to do in 1998 or 1999, maybe I would have been frightened off, because it would have seemed like that was such a tough job to do without the fundamentals.

But world trade was booming in the 1960s, and of course every country started off with industrialisation. The economic wisdom at that time was that you started on the first steps of industrialisation by making the things that you used to import from other countries, thereby saving on foreign exchange and providing jobs for the local population. And that approach, that theory for industrialisation in the 1960s was quite widespread throughout third world countries. The economic term for that was import substitution.

So, we started on an import substitution drive and when I was hired, my first interviewing team consisted of some very bright people already in EDB at that

---

[2] Lee Kuan Yew, *From Third World to First: The Singapore Story: 1965–2000.*

time. I went to the EDB boardroom and I was interviewed by the senior managers of EDB at that time like Joe Pillay, S. Dhanabalan, I. F. Tang and they had external board members like Mr Bill Lim who was in charge of the Singapore Institute of Management at that time. And one of the things they were trying to assess was what exactly my connections and contacts in Malaysia were, because one of the basis for industrialisation was to get businessmen to invest to make things that would supply not only the Singapore market, but also the Malaysian market, in order to make full use of the common market arrangement.

So, that didn't seem like a very tough job, because I had gone to Malaysia many, many times when I was working in Ford. Because at that time Ford was considering to invest in a plant that would produce cars for both Singapore and Malaysia, and I was very familiar with that.

And also when I was in Ford, I was headhunted to reverse a negative mindset about the company and its workers, because when I was hired, it was at the end of a very long strike — a 110-day industrial action which was highly publicised at that time. They had a Barisan union,[3] which called on the workers to strike for 110 days.

So, after that, the Ford management thought that people would have lost confidence in Ford, in buying Ford cars, Ford products and Ford services. So they thought: they should get somebody to change the mindset. So, I was hired to do that and somehow, EDB got wind of that part of my job in Ford. EDB wanted me to launch a PR [public relations] programme that would encapsulate or corroborate the government's decision to join Malaysia in a common market.

Because in my recently published book called, *Heart Work*, two of my colleagues at that time, Joe Pillay and Ngiam Tong Dow, mentioned that they had to go from school to school to explain to "O" level students what the common market meant for Singapore, and to get them to go back and persuade their parents to vote for the common market, because we had a referendum.[4]

So, EDB thought that, well, maybe two years down the road, if the common market had actually proven to be a big plus for Singapore's industrialisation, we could publicise this. And by publicising this, we could corroborate the government's decision to join Malaysia.

So if you read my CV, there is a part of it that says Public Relations, because EDB had no public relations, no mass communication department, because we don't

---

[3] As in a trade union that was controlled by Barisan Sosialis, the left-wing opposition party at that time.
[4] The 1962 national referendum on merger with Malaysia.

deal with the public. The wisdom of that time was that the government was quite authoritarian, so we didn't really have to explain every economic policy and every economic strategy to the man in the street.

The publicity that was meant to be part of my job was to organise publicity campaigns throughout Singapore and Malaysia, to showcase how successful a common market arrangement would be for Singapore as well as for Malaysia. It was a win-win situation and we could both benefit from it, and I was hired to promote that idea.

But of course, that was seven months after we joined Malaysia. After another four months, I was told, "Forget about Malaysia, we are now going to bet on the world," as we said at that time. So the decision that was made by the government was: "Forget about the common market, if we don't have it, never mind, we'd have to try and survive some other way. Instead of betting on our neighbour for a common market to help us industrialise, or betting on the region, we should actually bet on the world."

By the time we took that decision in 1968, we had already begun to globalise. Whereas people started using the word "globalisation" in earnest only around 1990. But Singapore had begun to globalise as early as 1968, when we made that decision to bet on the world.

Lee Kuan Yew had two meetings; one in Africa and another in Cambridge, Massachusetts, in the US. And these two key meetings heavily influenced him to adopt for the government a kind of globalisation strategy for us in 1968. Of course, you know, if you had actually organised your country and your policies and your conditions to participate in a global economy as far back as 1968 before globalisation became in vogue, that means you have a first-mover advantage. We were over 20 years ahead of the rest of the world.

By the time they talked about globalisation, all of Singapore's economy was already oriented towards a global marketplace.

JL **But in 1964, 1965, the period when Singapore was part of Malaysia, you mentioned that everyone was looking at this win-win situation for Singapore and Malaysia through the common market.**

CCB Right.

158 • SPEAKING TRUTH TO POWER

JL   **But did the common market eventually takeoff?**

CCB   No, it did not, and that's why sometimes in my crazier moments, I have had a thought that maybe it was a blessing in disguise that the common market didn't take place. Sometimes in my quiet moments reminiscing at home, I'd say, "Well, what would have happened? What would my job have been, and what would have happened if the common market had come about?" I do not know whether it is too far-fetched or not, but at best today, we would be in a situation like Thailand where Bangkok is the commercial centre, the financial centre where all the manufacturing is, and the rest of the country is agriculture and tourism. I think that that would have happened to Singapore too. Singapore would have been that commercial, financial and manufacturing hub of Malaysia, where all the commercial activities would take place, and the rest of Malaysia would be focused on agriculture and tourism just like Thailand, if we had continued to be one country. And, well, if you look at Thailand today, what has it achieved? Today Thailand's GDP per capita is about $3,000, and ours is about $30,000; we have done 10 times better than that situation that I described, you see.

So I tell myself that not only did we win big in going global from that time, because of the loss of the common market, but we gave ourselves a couple of decades of headstart to build up to the state of globalisation that we know today.

JL   **At that time when Singapore was a part of Malaysia, what were the EDB's corporate targets?**

CCB   Well you see, both countries had their fair number of entrepreneurs. Singapore had its own bankers and entrepreneurs, and Malaysia had its own traders, tin miners and other kinds of entrepreneurs. And one of EDB's targets would have been to strive for joint ventures between entrepreneurs in Malaysia and entrepreneurs in Singapore, and we would have tried to get cross-investments. In other words, we would have tried to get Singapore entrepreneurs and investors to invest in projects in Malaysia, and then get Malaysian entrepreneurs to come and join Singapore business people and bankers to invest in projects in Singapore.

So, it would have been very, very local. It would not have been global whatsoever. Even if somewhere down the line, we found that the scale was too small and the pace was too slow, and if we had tried to persuade our partners in Malaysia to go global,

I doubt that they would have agreed. Because at that time the political environment was such where anything suggested by Singapore would be answered negatively, and vice versa.

So, maybe it's just for the best that we didn't have that, because, as I said, what you would have is a situation like Thailand today. With an even smaller population. At that time, if we had the common market, we would have had a total population about 18 million. At that time Thailand was about 25 million and then out of the whole country, one particular pivot would shine like Bangkok. It would have had a higher per capita than the rest of the country because of its urban nature, but not very high.

The origins of DBS Bank

JL **You mentioned that the two Indonesian Chinese came down and set up the National Iron and Steel Mill. And you mentioned DBS Bank. But DBS Bank came up in 1968 right?**

CCB That's right.

JL **But the National Iron and Steel Mill was founded earlier?**

CCB Yes. But before there was a DBS Bank, EDB itself would invest or give loans. When EDB was organised, it was a one-stop shop for everything; somewhat like what it is now. Now we have come about a full cycle of 40 years, but at that time, if they said to Singapore, "We need some loans for this project" or "we need an equity partner," then EDB, in order to secure the project, would have had to go in on its own.

So in those early years, we had very active equity participation and a very active loan portfolio in those early industries. And then, a year later when DBS was formed, we transferred the portfolio of our investments and loans to DBS. EDB was actually the precursor, it was almost the early venture capitalist offering equity participation as well as loans to those projects, before DBS was established. Some of the people who were in EDB, who were familiar with the projects, also went over to DBS. And that is the reason why Mr Hon [Sui Sen][5] went over as Chairman and President, and Mr Dhanabalan went over as Executive Vice President.

I don't mean that at that particular stage of our history, there were no financial institutions. UOB [United Overseas Bank] was there, OUB [Overseas Union Bank] was there, OCBC [Oversea-Chinese Banking Corporation] was there. So why was there a need for a DBS Bank, or for EDB to play that role, and then later for DBS to take over? That's quite an interesting question.

The reason was that those early banks like UOB, OCBC and OUB were all set up to finance trade, not industry. And the difference is that when you are a bank that finances trade, you have a very fast turnover. You can finance the commodity trader and you would know within a matter of days whether you have made money, and whether you are going to have your loan repaid or not.

But in an industry like National Iron and Steel Mills [NatSteel] was by virtue of being in manufacturing, it would have had a long gestation period, and most of our banks at that time would not give long-term loans. And if it was just like overnight loans for trading, for instance. You couldn't go to Goh Tjoei Kok[6] and say, "I will lend you 50 million dollars, but on an overnight basis." They couldn't have run NatSteel like that, because they needed long-term loans.

So, they came to EDB for those long-term loans which we subsequently passed to DBS and, of course, this was many, many years before they went to the public markets for capital.

Tenure as EDB Chairman

CCB   When I came back [to the EDB] in 1971,[7] that was when EDB initiated the EDB Training Centres, which we set up as joint ventures between us and potential investors. And that occupied my time as EDB Managing Director for a couple of years.

---

[5] Hon Sui Sen — the first chairman of the EDB, and the first chairman and president of the Development Bank of Singapore (DBS). He joined politics in 1970 and was the Minister for Finance until his death in office in 1983.
[6] Goh Tjoei Kok — the Indonesian-born Vice-President of National Iron and Steel Mills Limited, who later founded Tat Lee Bank.
[7] From 1968 to 1971, Chan Chin Bock was based in New York as Centre Director for EDB's operations in the US. It was one of EDB's first two overseas offices (the other being in Hong Kong), which proved to be so successful in attracting investments into Singapore that they have grown to 19 today (as of 2019).

JL   **How did you all setup the EDB Training Centres? Were you all looking for particular skills at that time?**

CCB   Yes. Most of the skills that we wanted at that time were the so-called artisan skills — skills that are foundational for any industrial society. That is, tool- and dye-making and all that. We looked around the world, making use of our overseas centres that were set up in earlier years for getting investments. We identified companies that were highly regarded in their own countries, as well as internationally, as the best trainers of those skills. And many of these were found, strangely enough, not in America but in Germany, Switzerland and Japan.

So, we encouraged these companies to come to Singapore and jointly set up training centres. Philips, the Dutch company, was one of them, and Rollei from Germany was another one, and then there are others.

And the scheme was roughly like this: we would provide the land and pay for the building of a school for training; the training centre. And the company would supply trainers and the software for training and all that. So, the training school became a joint venture between EDB and companies which had been identified as leaders of that type of industrial training at that time.

So, under that scheme we set up one with the Germans called the Rollei Government Training Centre. The one with Philips was called Philips Government Training Centre, and so on.

JL   **Then where were they located?**

CCB   Well, the Rollei Government Training Centre was in Punggol.

JL   **Oh, is it?**

CCB   Because for this type of training, for these skill-intensive activities, we had to go to the heartlands, because the workers were coming from the heartlands.

JL   **And the Philips Government Training Centre?**

CCB   That was in Jurong; there were some in Jurong, some in Punggol, some in other places, but they are all heartland locations. One was in Bukit Merah and so for the four years I came back to Singapore [1971 to 1975], I had a dual role for much of the time. We continued to try and get the investments in. By that time, my overseas network was already completed. So, having worked in the first overseas centre of the EDB, I knew exactly what the conditions were and so on. So, once I was back here, I was able to direct those activities much better, and at the same time spend half of the time formulating our policies and negotiating with these companies to set up the training centres. Because persuading one of these companies to come into a joint venture training centre with us was even more difficult than getting them to make an investment.

JL **Why was that so?**

CCB Because there was no bottom line for them. Whereas if they made an investment, if it worked out, they would have made a lot of money. The company itself did not directly benefit, only indirectly. We fine-tuned the scheme where the company that helped us in setting up this training centre could have access to half of the trained people for their project.

So, we combined both the investment promotion as well as the training functions. Say for instance we set up in Punggol a training centre for 200 people. When those people graduated, the company would have had the right to take in 100 of them, if they had plans to invest in Singapore and had operations here. And then the other 100 were placed by EDB with other companies. That was how we ran our training scheme.

JL **Other than these EDB Training Centres, were there any landmark projects in the time when you were Director of the EDB?**

CCB For instance, one of those landmark projects that came about during that time, which was officially inaugurated by SM, was by Seiko, the watch maker. They had a plant in Woodlands. So, they participated with us in the training programme, and then they took the workers and started up their own investment.

And then for our part, the other 50 per cent that came to us, we used them to promote skill-intensive industries from America. American companies do not have a tradition of training. In any case, much less of a tradition of training than the Germans or the Swiss. But there were still, of course, skill-intensive companies that were desirable for Singapore. So, in order to get them, we promised we would give them the nucleus of the trained workforce from one of our training centres. And that made it attractive for them. One of those companies which is actually hi-tech and highly admired even to this day which Pock Too[8] may have told you about is a company called Sundstrand.

JL **He's now the ...**

CCB He's now the President of the holding company, Hamilton Sundstrand Asia Pacific. But Sundstrand was our first aircraft equipment project that needed highly skilled workers. So, we got our training centres to promise them that some of the most highly skilled workers would be earmarked for the Sundstrand project even before they started. Their engineers would come to our training centres, evaluate the kids, choose them and say, "Okay, when I start up, can you give me these people?" So, we provided the nucleus of their trained workforce and then the company itself, of course, supplemented them by sending another batch to the US to train in the plant over there. And this formed the core of the highly skilled workforce.

The chairmen of the EDB

JL **Would you like to talk about the seven chairmen [in the history of the EDB] and what are your impressions and differences among these seven chairmen?**

CCB Well, in a way, each one of them had a personality and the training that fit each phase of our development. When Mr Hon was the first chairman, for instance, EDB was a new organisation. So as the first chairman, he had to have a sound reputation and be respected and admired by investors, both locally as well as overseas.

---

[8] Ng Pock Too started his career at the EDB in 1968, serving as Deputy Director from 1980 to 1982. He was later Political Secretary to Prime Minister Lee Kuan Yew and was Member of Parliament for Nee Soon Central.

So you needed an older person, and he was then the Head of the Civil Service. He was eminently suited for that role because he had the stature, he had the reputation, he was respected and admired by local and overseas businessmen and bankers, and so he kicked it off.

After he stepped down, I. F. Tang, who was a member of [Albert] Winsemius's industrial mission, took over from him. And I. F. brought a lot of experience because just like our EDB consulting group now, but he did it under the UN [United Nations], and he had visited many countries and witnessed industrialisation in many contexts. So he was the right person to follow through with Mr Hon's activities.

And then he passed it on to me. Because by that time, communication and promotion with the Americans was very important. Because we had decided to switch from an import substitution strategy to an export oriented strategy. And the American investors and MNCs [multi-national corporations] were our primary targets. So they looked at the whole organisation and they wanted somebody who understood the way American companies thought and made decisions.

JL   **So, after you the next Chairman was ...**

CCB   After me the next Chairman was Ngiam Tong Dow.

JL   **What were changes then under him?**

CCB   When it came to Mr Ngiam, it was more or less a repeat of the rationale from Mr Hon, because he was also the Head of the Civil Service when he was appointed chairman of EDB. He was not as old as Mr Hon, but he was one of the more senior people in the Admin Service.

Therefore the government considered him a suitable person. Then he rallied for a few years. Then EDB had to make a decision again, because each one of them didn't want to do it for too long, you see. They wanted creative thinking all throughout the line. So he had to make a decision whether to ask the government to get somebody else from outside, in which case they would have looked at the Perm Secs available, or they would have looked internally.

So, they asked me at that point of time whether I wanted to come back from my overseas stint. For the years that he was the chairman, he asked me whether I wanted to come back. So, I said, "No, I think, I am doing a great job overseas because I am getting the investments. It's easier for them to find somebody from the pool of Admin Service people to take over from him."

So, he looked around and he decided to appoint somebody from inside, and that was P. Y. Hwang [Hwang Peng Yuan]. And so P. Y. Hwang was there for some years. Technology became very important and none of us right up to that point had a background in technology.

So when technology became important, Singapore's biggest reservoir of technology was with MINDEF [Ministry of Defence] and MINDEF organisations. So Philip Yeo, who was then Perm Sec of MINDEF, was asked to come over so that he could start us on the technology strategy. And that applies even today — Teo Ming Kian [the next EDB Chairman] was also Perm Sec for MINDEF. In fact, they wanted to retain both of them. So that's why they are co-chairmen.

JL **Mr Philip Yeo and Teo Ming Kian?**

CCB Both were from MINDEF, and both are now providing the leadership for Singapore's push to build up technology. Because it's been known all over the world that there is a nexus between technology as used in the military establishment and technology as used in a non-defence area.

Both of them, in addition to being MINDEF people are also part of the ST Group [Singapore Technologies Engineering], which employs the most engineers.

So, in pursuit of that technology nexus, the leadership of EDB shifted to Philip Yeo, and then to Teo Ming Kian. And if you follow that logically, you can ask me, "How about now?" Now it is the biomedical sciences; should you not get somebody like Lim Pin or somebody like that? Maybe you should or a doctor or somebody like that. But they think that technology for MINDEF also covers the biomedical sciences through their defence technology organisation, DSO [Defence Science Organisation National Laboratories]. So, that's why they remain until this phase is completed, and when we feel that we have built up all the technological sectors.

J. Y. Pillay

The man behind Singapore Airlines

Date of interviews:
January–February 1995

Interviewer: Irene Quah

Joseph Yuvaraj Pillay (b. 1934), better known as J. Y. Pillay, was a veteran civil servant who served in many roles. He was especially known for growing Singapore Airlines into a world-leading airline as its first Chairman, when the government was the major shareholder in the airline.

Born in Klang, Malaya, Pillay studied engineering at the Imperial College of Science and Technology in London. After stints in the UK and Malaya, he joined the Public Works Department in Singapore in 1958 as an engineer, before joining the Ministry of Finance's Economic Development Division in 1961. He was seconded to the Economic Development Board (EDB) when it was set up in 1961, before returning to the Ministry of Finance where he became Permanent Secretary in 1968. He was appointed Co-Chairman of the Malaysia-Singapore Airlines (MSA), becoming Chairman of Singapore Airlines when MSA split into two entities in 1972. He continued in this role until 1996.

Over the course of his long career, Pillay has held various positions including Chairman of the Development Bank of Singapore (DBS) and of Singapore Technologies Holdings, and Managing Director of the Monetary Authority of Singapore (MAS) and of the Government of Singapore Investment Corporation (GIC). From 2005 to 2019, he was Chairman of the Council of Presidential Advisers.

In these interviews, Pillay shared his experiences in running and growing Singapore Airlines in the early years, and on how civil servants have run business enterprises for the government. In reflecting on his role as Permanent Secretary at the Ministry of National Development, he discussed how civil servants work with ministers and the political appointees in Singapore.

Joining the civil service

IQ   **After you returned to Malaya [in 1958], you found a job with the PWD [Public Works Department] as a mechanical engineer. So you worked there for two years.**

JYP   Yes.

IQ   **Did you have many expatriate colleagues in the PWD?**

JYP   Yes, at that time there were quite a few still in the PWD. I found the job there very interesting because for the first time, I suppose, I really held responsibility for something. It was pleasant. Kuala Lumpur at that time was a much smaller place than it is now, easy to move around, almost a village-like atmosphere. There were lots of my contemporaries from London, maybe some from my old school in Kuala Lumpur. So I wasn't short of friends. It was quite a happy time over there. No regrets.

IQ   **What were the conditions of service then?**

JYP   Actually at that time, there was not too much difference between the conditions in Singapore and the conditions in Malaya. Both countries had only recently emerged from the colonial period. So they retained many of the administrative procedures and systems that the British administration had introduced.

IQ   **Were there any differences, say, in terms of salary between a local engineer and an expatriate engineer then?**

JYP   Not really, other than the expatriate allowances. The basic salaries were the same. They must have had some allowances. I can't recall what they were. I don't think it mattered too much to us. But the process of Malayanisation was quite rapid during that period. Though I was there for two years, it was coming along quite rapidly.

IQ   **Did you feel that there was any discrimination?**

JYP   Not by the time I came back. Merdeka was achieved in 1957. So it was three years before I started working there. No, there was no problem.

IQ   **You mentioned that in 1961, you came over to Singapore to work.**

JYP   Yes, in 1961.

IQ   **You started in the Economic Development Division.**

JYP   That's right. I joined the Economic Development Division. They had, I think, a unit called the Industrial Development Unit, which didn't last very long. Once the EDB got going, I was seconded to the EDB fairly soon after I joined. I can't quite recall when. It couldn't have been more than six months after I joined the EDB.

IQ   **When you joined the Economic Development Division in 1961, you joined as the Assistant Director in Engineering.**

JYP   Yes.

IQ   **That was what I saw in the government directory. Can I clarify with you? When you joined the Singapore Civil Service, you were actually in the Engineering Service, which was the Professional Service?**

JYP   Yes, that's right.

170 • SPEAKING TRUTH TO POWER

IQ   **When did you make the switch to the Administrative Service?**

JYP   It must have been around 1968 I think. I had to pass some exams. I think it was 1967 or 1968.

IQ   **When you moved back to the Ministry of Finance?**

JYP   I moved back to Finance in 1965 to the Economic Planning Unit. I don't think I was an Admin officer then. I think I joined the Admin Service only in 1967 or 1968 after I had got through the exams. In those days we never thought too much about one service or another service, because we were moved around quite freely. But somebody must have suggested in that period that I should enter the Admin Service. I said okay. It required me to pass examinations in Law and in Malay. I think it was called Part II or Standard II Malay. Maybe also the Instruction Manuals as we knew then. So I had to go through those wretched exams which meant that I had to take some time off, about a week or so, to mug up. It wasn't really difficult.

IQ   **This exam, was it similar to, say, during the days of the Malayan Civil Service when they had this course called the Devonshire Course, where candidates who joined the Admin Service had to undergo a few months of training at Oxford?**

JYP   No, we didn't get those privileges. These were just some standard examinations that were set here on Criminal Procedures and the Instruction Manuals, if I remember rightly, and the Second Language. In my case, it was merely Part I and Part II.

IQ   **How long did you have to attend for the courses?**

JYP   There were no courses. We just studied on our own.

IQ   **You studied on your own.**

JYP   Yes. But for Malay, of course, I had a guru.[1] It wasn't too difficult. Maybe it took me a year or two to get through Part I and then Part II.

Becoming Chairman of Singapore Airlines

IQ   **One of the first government companies which you headed was the Singapore Airlines in 1972 when it started functioning as an independent national carrier. Could you relate to us the circumstances leading to your appointment as its Chairman in 1972?**

JYP   Let's go back a little earlier to mid-1969. I was appointed to the Board of MSA [Malaysia-Singapore Airlines], the joint airline owned by Malaysia and Singapore largely, together with some other minor shareholders. I was then in the Ministry of Finance, Permanent Secretary in Economic Development Division. A vacancy arose, so I was appointed as a kind of representative of the Ministry of Finance which, after all, owned the shares.

At that time, the Chairman of MSA was Yong Pung How. But shortly after I joined the Board, within three months, he retired and Robert Kuok became the Chairman. Then in 1971, it was decided that there would be a Chairman each. Let me just go slightly before that. In late 1970, the two governments decided to split the carrier in the sense that Singapore would develop its own airline, and so would Malaysia. That decision was taken at the end of 1970. And in 1971 March, there was a Chairman appointed from each country. I was the co-Chairman for Singapore. The co-Chairman for Malaysia was Tun Ismail Ali, who was the Governor of Bank Negara. That was the situation. Then we carried on. The target date for the two carriers to go their own way was 1st October 1972.

So I suppose because I was the co-Chairman of MSA, I just continued as Chairman of Singapore Airlines. And Singapore Airlines duly took off on 1st October 1972.

---

[1] Guru — literally "teacher" in Malay.

IQ What were the reasons for the split of the MSA?

JYP The reasons were fairly simple. The two governments, who were the major shareholders, had different ideas of what the airline should be doing. Malaysia was very interested in knitting together the country — West Malaysia (as they used to call Peninsular Malaysia) and East Malaysia (Sabah and Sarawak). So they wanted to focus on domestic services. Well, we were not terribly interested in that. We were interested in going international and developing the international routes. So there was a conflict of objective and it was entirely appropriate that each country should go its own way.

IQ Were you involved in the negotiation process?

JYP Between the two governments?

IQ Yes.

JYP Yes, between Singapore and Malaysia. That started, I think, at the end of 1970 and continued through 1971. I don't know when we finally signed the agreement. It must have been some time in 1971 or 1972, I can't quite remember.

IQ Mr Pillay, do you recall any of the problems or challenges faced during the negotiation process?

JYP A bone of contention was the division of the assets and the valuation of the assets. On the valuation, we finally settled on book value. On the division of the assets, everything that was in Singapore came to Singapore. Of course, we paid for it at book value. The assets in Singapore, of course, formed the bulk of the fixed assets because the operating base and the HQ was in Singapore.

Then the aircraft. For the aircraft, we took the long-haul aircraft, essentially the 707.[2] There was an argument over the 737.[3] Finally, I think we took only five of them. They probably took all of them and the Malaysians bought new aircraft. Then the F27s[4] and the other aircraft. I can't remember what other aircraft were flying around in Sabah and Sarawak. We left it to the Malaysians. In the end it ended amicably.

Growing Singapore Airlines

IQ   **Mr Pillay, when SIA [Singapore Airlines] became an independent national carrier on 1st October 1972, what was your vision for SIA then?**

JYP   It was very simple. We had already, even before 1st October 1972, placed orders for two [Boeing] 747 aircraft which arrived one year later. That was in September of 1973. The intention was to really develop our international services and make our way in the world. That was a very simple objective, or mission.

IQ   **Looking back, in 1972, the decision to buy the 747 Jumbo Jet was a correct move. But then with the benefit of hindsight, do you think that was a bold decision to take?**

JYP   Yes, it was, because we were the first Southeast Asian carrier to buy the 747. Maybe we were probably the first carrier outside Japan and Australia in the Asia Pacific region to buy the 747. I can't recall whether Air India had the 747. But the Japanese and

---

[2] The Boeing 707, Boeing's first jet airliner, used mostly for long-range flights from 1958 to 1979.
[3] The Boeing 737, used mostly for short- and medium-range flights, which has been continuously manufactured since 1967.
[4] The Fokker F27 Friendship, a turboprop airliner developed by the Dutch aircraft manufacturer Fokker from the 1950s to 1987.

Qantas did. That was it. It took some time before the other Southeast Asian carriers decided to emulate us. But we were the pace-setters. No doubt about it.

IQ   **How was SIA going to compete with other national carriers, other airlines, from maybe some of the more developed countries?**

JYP   You mean at that time or now?

IQ   **At that time.**

JYP   At that time it wasn't too much of a problem, because there were very strict IATA [International Air Transport Association] rules pertaining to fares, level of service and standards. And they were designed really to help protect carriers. They were not consumer-friendly, they were producer-friendly. So we had no problem running around these people, doing a bit of discounting here and there, improving the level of service and the quality of service. Eventually we had improved our service to a point where we were quite outstanding in terms of our service not only in the air, but on the ground as well. So we had made bold moves in the international arena to expand our services on a systematic calculated basis, while at the same time, improving our service quality and working hard to reduce our costs. In those days we had certain advantages. Labour costs in Singapore were generally lower. But now that advantage has been largely eroded.

IQ   **I was going through some news clippings from the early seventies. It seems like after the break from the MSA, SIA went through a process of restructuring in terms of management and organisation. Why was there a need to restructure the SIA after the split?**

JYP   I can't remember any specific restructuring. But restructuring is a continuous process. Sometimes it's a minor restructuring, sometimes something more significant. But that goes on all the time. I don't think we are particularly addicted to restructuring. Indeed, the structure and the basic bare bones of the organisation are essentially the same. You may split departments, add some, occasionally dissolve some as the airline expands. We didn't engage in, what is now called, re-engineering. There was no major move to change the structure just for the sake of change. We don't go in for that sort of activity. We had enough to do without stirring things up.

IQ **Were there a number of staff from the former MSA who joined the SIA after the split?**

JYP Yes.

IQ **Those who worked in Singapore?**

JYP Yes. All the ground base staff in the Head Office and in the Engineering Base and, of course, the ground services. They all continued to work here. The flight crew (both flight deck), the technical crew as well as the cabin crew, were given the option. Well, in fact, all of them were given the option of joining either MSA or SIA.

Some of the Malaysians among the flight deck crew decided to go back to KL, those who were based in Singapore and who were Malaysians. But many Malaysians remained with SIA. Then, of course, we just had to add to the numbers. In those days the numbers were quite tiny compared to what we have now. We now have just over 10,000 in the parent airline and 25,000 in the group as a whole; about nearly 7,500 if I am right, or closer to 8,000, in SATS [Singapore Airport Terminal Services]; about 3,500 in SIA Engineering. And we've got SilkAir and several other smaller companies.

Well, I think some restructuring takes place whenever we hive off an activity into a separately incorporated company like SATS. SATS was born in …

IQ **… 1973.**

JYP 1973, you're right. April 1973, just six months after SIA took off. That made a lot of sense. SIA Engineering Company was formed only three years ago. SilkAir, five or six years ago, it's a new activity.[5]

---

[5] Previously known as Tradewinds Airlines, it was renamed and rebranded as SilkAir by 1992.

IQ   **On the question of competing with other airlines, what was the strategy of selling SIA abroad?**

JYP   Essentially the superior service that we offered, plus our excellent network in Singapore as a hub. That continues to be our leitmotiv, our hallmark to this day.

In Singapore Airlines, when we started way back in the early seventies, we built a small entity in an industry that was still in its infancy in our part of the world. The industry has now reached, I would say, maturity in our part of the world, at least in Singapore. Which does not mean that there isn't scope for expansion. There is scope for tremendous expansion in the region and in Asia. But nonetheless, we'd reached a certain stage of development where we are virtually on par with the rest of the world, anywhere else in the world.

But in the early seventies, our industry was young. And we (you may call the players) were also young. And young people tend to be a bit callous. We were prepared to stick our necks out, to take more risks. There was less to lose. I can't remember what the net worth of SIA was in those days. But it couldn't have been more than a couple of hundred million dollars if at all, compared to about $8 billion today.

We were confident in our ability because we thought we had a good management team, a reasonably good product which was gaining acceptance in the world for its quality, and its reliability. We had been growing quite rapidly and we thought we could continue to grow rapidly. By rapidly, I mean 20 to 30 per cent a year compared with eight to 10 per cent now. But, of course, the quantum bite at 20 to 30 per cent a year was smaller than a quantum bite at eight to 10 per cent now.

Still, in this business, relativity is the name of the game. And we were growing extremely rapidly. We were able to afford a much higher, what we called, debt to equity ratio of about four to one, since we were growing extremely fast, we were making money and we could service our debts. Right now, we have no debt at all. So we'd become a very conservative organisation.

Well, one thing led to another. We made increasingly larger investments in aircraft. We were bold. We were the first to introduce the [Boeing] 747 into Southeast Asia. We branched out. We considered the world to be, shall we say, our oyster. And the world meaning really Asia and the developed world — Australia, Japan, Europe and eventually the United States and North America. Certain parts of the world where we are still not prominent, or even active in some cases, are Africa and Latin America. We don't fly at all to Latin America. To Africa, we fly to Egypt (if that can be considered part of Africa), to South Africa and to Mauritius.

But we don't really fly to what is known as sub-Saharan Africa. Not really.

Anyway, to go back to those days. It was a time of very heavy expansion. We were supremely confident of our abilities. We took risks but we believed that they were calculated risks. And in the event, we demonstrated the validity of our risk-taking because we didn't have to go to the government for subsidies or for handouts of any sort whatsoever. The only injection of capital we had when we started off in 1972 was the share of the assets that accrued to the Singapore government by virtue of its stake in the former Malaysia-Singapore Airlines. And for 10 years thereafter, we didn't go to the shareholders for any money. It was only in the early eighties that we sought a further injection of capital from the government. And that kept us going till our listing in 1985, almost 10 years ago. At the time of listing and as part of the listing process, the company issued fresh capital which brought in $250 million. And that's it. The last 10 years we haven't gone to the shareholders for any funds. Rather, we have been distributing dividends very generously to the shareholders. And we are now in a position — I just said a few moments ago — of not having any debt.

I don't know whether this gives some flavour to the answer as to how we became risk-takers. Maybe we were fortunate. I don't like to call it a gamble. Our calculated risk-taking succeeded. And with each success, we were prepared to take bigger stakes as it were. So our orders became larger in terms of dollars and cents. But they did not necessarily become more risks. In fact, it could have been less risky because our base was larger, our experience was greater, more widespread, and we were confident of our ability to make those investments.

Right now, we have made an investment when we placed an order for aircraft of $10 billion or more. It didn't particularly worry us because these are measured investments over a period of time. And we know that we can generate the cash through profits and through our depreciation to meet the investment outlay.

IQ **Would you say that your business sense has been acquired over the years while on the job?**

JYP As in anything one does, one learns from one's experiences on the job and one should improve with time. It does not always happen because occasionally, mistakes are made. Some people get demoralised with their mistakes. We have made mistakes but we've never become demoralised as a result of these mistakes.

178 • SPEAKING TRUTH TO POWER

IQ **You mentioned that even before the official split in 1972 from MSA, SIA had already placed an order to buy the 747. Was that part of a calculated risk?**

JYP You may say so because there were other aircraft that were available. The 747 was the largest. There was also the DC-10[6] which was about two-thirds to three-quarters the size of the 747. There was the Lockheed Tristar,[7] about the same size as the DC-10. And neighbouring airlines bought those aircraft at the time when we placed the order for our 747.

So the concern expressed in some circles was: Why are we going for the jackpot? Why not the smaller aircraft? But we had done our calculations. We showed that the unit cost of the 747 was much lower than for the other two aircraft. And we felt that there was enough demand from the traffic perspective to justify the larger aircraft. So we bought the larger aircraft. It proved a success. We bought more 747s.

Later in the decade, towards the end of the seventies, we decided we also needed a smaller wide-bodied aircraft, and we bought the DC-10 for certain routes that did not quite justify the Jumbo. Well, the DC-10 eventually had a chequered history and we got rid of them.

That's an interesting episode. Why did we get rid of the DC-10s so fast? That was towards the end of the seventies and the early eighties. There was some disturbing crash of the DC-10 and other incidents concerning the DC-10 in the fleets of other carriers. We were consolidating our reputation and our image. We didn't want a company like SIA flirting with danger. So we took the decision to get rid of the DC-l0s.

In retrospect, it may not have appeared to be a necessary decision because the DC-10s continued to fly, although the plane itself is becoming somewhat obsolescent and has been replaced by the MD-11. But at that time, we wanted to preserve our reputation for solidity, safety, shall we say. Risk aversion, when it comes to essential matters like safety and security — I think that decision could be justified on those grounds. Who knows, had we retained the DC-10, there would have been a flurry of excitement from time to time whenever an incident occurred to a DC-10 somewhere else in the world in some other airline's fleet.

So while we were prepared to take risk, shall we say, we were not prepared to sacrifice certain principles of safety and security. And we were not prepared to bet the company, we were not prepared to risk the entire company financially. No.

---

[6] The jetliner produced by the US manufacturer McDonnell Douglas from 1968 to 1988, for medium- to long-range flights.

[7] The Lockheed L-1011 TriStar, produced by the US manufacturer Lockheed Corporation from 1968 to 1984, for medium- to long-range flights.

I think that philosophy prevails to this day. We may appear to be very bold players in the market, but our decisions, our actions are always well thought out. We've got certain safeguards should things not go according to plan, should events not unfold according to plan, as it never will be, since we can never see the future. We are human beings. We do not know what's going to happen. Nobody anticipated the Kobe earthquake[8] which is affecting some of our services now from Osaka. Or the Mexican crisis[9] even; it descended upon us suddenly. These are events which cannot be foreseen, but which we know will happen from time to time. Therefore, we should have some reserves to help us through times like those.

The world economy is improving now, but it's not going to improve forever. So while we expand, we expand at a steady pace. We don't go too excited when times are good. And we are not terribly depressed in times of sluggish growth.

IQ **You mentioned that six months after SIA took off, SIA had already set up the Singapore Airport Terminal Services (SATS). What was the reason for diversification?**

JYP It wasn't diversification. Those services were being offered as part of, I think, the Marketing Division. But Marketing Division had so many other things to do. So it made sense to hive these people off, to give them their head. It helped SATS and it helped marketing.

IQ **You said that SIA's intention was to expand on international routes when it became an independent national carrier. How was this expansion carried out?**

JYP First, you have to get the traffic rights. Then you've got to get the aircraft, the equipment, the people. Then you move in. Once you moved in, you assess the route dynamics and the market. If you think you can expand, you expand. So you offer more services.

---

[8] A major earthquake struck the Japanese city of Kobe on 17 January 1995, which claimed more than 6,000 lives.
[9] Mexico experienced a currency crisis in December 1994 when its government suddenly devalued the peso against the US dollar, which had a spillover effect on other South American economies.

That's what they do everywhere. They're still expanding into some of the destinations that they started operating two decades ago. The business expands, the economy grows. There's a greater demand for goods and services. Even Cold Storage and all these retail outlets, they expand. People consume more. More people, more mouths.

IQ   **As Chairman of SIA, did you have to liaise and negotiate with the relevant authorities and countries for the traffic rights?**

JYP   No, that's done by the management, the appropriate department.

IQ   **By the management of SIA?**

JYP   The International Relations Department would do that.

IQ   **It doesn't have to go through, say, one of our ministries, for example, Ministry of Communications.**

JYP   Yes, of course, because all these are bilaterals. Sometimes, the airline to airline negotiations have to be given the stamp of approval by the governments.

IQ   **I was going through some old newspaper cuttings. It seems like in the late seventies and early eighties, SIA faced some problems regarding traffic rights in the Australian and the American sectors. For example, in 1981, SIA was attacked by several US airlines of dumping "unofficial below cost" tickets and the unfair advantage enjoyed by SIA, that it was actually enjoying government subsidies. For a state national carrier like SIA, outwardly it seems to enjoy the backing of the government and thus has a competitive edge over other airlines. Would you like to comment on this?**

JYP   Yes. Traffic rights, we were having a lot of problems at one time. Now, not so bad. They felt that our costs were low, we had competitive edges, that we were not following IATA. Well, all the IATA rules pertaining to restraint and competition have disappeared. So we were really in the vanguard. What we were doing then is now done by everybody else. So we had those problems but those are the usual problems you face as a business or as a government anywhere. They are not earth-shattering. They're just one of those things. Right now, the problems are how to keep and to retain staff, the wage escalation, the strength of the Singapore dollar. Those are the problems of the nineties. In the next decade, it may be something else. The role of management is to tackle these problems, if possible, to try and anticipate them.

IQ   **Do you see yourself as a trouble-shooter?**

JYP   Trouble-shooter suggests that the trouble has already occurred. Everyone likes to say: "Oh, we anticipate problems." But you don't anticipate all the problems. Then you have situations, like the strong Singapore dollar is a situation. You live with it. It has brought low inflation, which is good. But it also means that productivity has to keep going up every year. When the economy is growing at 10 per cent, wages and salaries also grow very rapidly.

IQ   **What forms of assistance does the government give, say, to a state enterprise like SIA?**

JYP   Government doesn't give very much assistance. There's not much the government can do. And in any event, our government has a policy of keeping people on their toes. So when the PWD calls for tenders for a project, whether it's road making or bridge building or putting up a government building, there's no margin of preference given to a government company. You know, we've got several government companies doing construction work — Sembawang Engineering, Keppel Engineering. But they don't get any special privileges over a private company. There's no intention of giving privileges.

Of course, the government has a general policy of helping Singapore companies to compete, to become stronger, to export goods and services. But that applies to all companies, not just to government companies. All Singapore companies. Maybe even MNCs. We've had to take up the cudgels when MNCs had problems of high tariffs or quota restraints in foreign countries. We didn't say: "Is it a government company?" Or even: "Is it a Singapore company?" It is a company. Maybe an MNC that is producing goods in Singapore and so the government helps it.

IQ **Does the government sometimes act as a guarantor, for example, if SIA were to buy some aircraft?**

JYP Not anymore. Now SIA doesn't borrow money. At first, of course, yes, we borrowed from the Asian Development Bank, which required a government guarantee. Later, it dispensed with the government guarantee, so SIA was able to go to the commercial banks to get a guarantee. But now SIA doesn't need to borrow. If a government limited company wants to borrow money, it's very unlikely that the government will offer a guarantee these days. Companies are quite conservative. They can finance their expansion through their cash flow, supplemented if necessary by raising capital.

The SIA sarong kebaya, and reasons for SIA's success

IQ **From what I read from the old newspaper clippings, the Singapore Girl with her sarong kebaya was the uniform which SIA retained after the airline split from MSA. In 1974, the French designer Pierre Balmain was again commissioned to design a new international image for the Singapore Girl. Again, the kebaya was retained. I'm curious to know why was the sarong kebaya retained by the new SIA management in 1972 when we became independent?**

JYP This essentially is like the conservatism of the company. Conservatism has both pejorative and favourable undertones. In this case, I think I'm using it in the better sense. They don't change unless there's a good reason to change. If they think they've alighted on a winning theme, they see no need to make any changes. So they felt that this uniform was a winner and they just stuck to it, they clung to it.

IQ It seems like there has been a continuous promotion since the start till today to consistently use the Singapore Girl on SIA's advertisements. Well, this is unlike other airlines which sometimes tend to shift their emphasis. Could you describe how SIA have chosen the Singapore Girl advertising concept to sell the airline?

JYP I think this came from the interaction between our Marketing Department and the advertising agency. So they tried it out. It worked. Now it has become, what you called, a leitmotiv for the airline. It's a success, so why change? It's not to say that it hasn't been occasionally modified from time to time. But the leitmotiv still prevails to this day. So if you've got a winning formula, don't change it unnecessarily.

IQ How long would this Singapore Girl image last?

JYP How much longer?

IQ How long do you see it last?

JYP I don't believe they have any deadline, like saying: "Well, it has been going for 20 years. Therefore, another five years and then we'll change." I don't think so. It's like the Shell logo which represents the Shell Company and also represents the prominence of their goodies. If you ask the Shell company: "When are you going to change your symbol from a shell to something else?" they'll say, "Why should we?"

IQ You were earlier talking on SIA's stress on quality, superior in-flight service. How do you see SIA going to maintain this trend?

JYP Through unremitting effort. There's no mumbo-jumbo and no black magic. It's just the right policies, constancy of policies. Not shifting about, jumping around from one day to the next, not losing one's head. And then responsible management with careful recruitment of people and, above all, keeping them happy, which means your reward system must be appropriate. No favouritism. People know that if they are treated fairly, objectively, and they'll respond. So you got to maintain morale. Morale is the most important factor in any organisation.

Again, this is not something unique to a particular organisation. It applies to every institution. You want to succeed. Whether it's a government department, or a non-profit-making institution like SINDA [Singapore Indian Development Association], or a company, whether privately-owned or government-owned, you got to ensure that your policies or the way you are managing people are appropriate. That makes a difference. Of course, you must have a business strategy. You can get your personnel policies right, your business strategy should follow.

IQ **You stressed on the superior quality for the in-flight service. Does it mean that SIA actually looks for, in its recruitment process, certain qualities in our air hostesses?**

JYP Yes. Not only in air hostesses but in everybody they recruit. Whatever it is that the carrier wants in a specific area. If you're recruiting office boys, then you look for the right caliber to make a good office boy at least for a few years. You don't expect him to remain an office boy till he is 65, even if you want to retain him. But if you recruit a young Admin Officer, then you expect that he will work until he is in his 60s. You hope he will remain with you if he is good. Qualities have to be tailor-made to the job specifications.

IQ **Mr Pillay, I'm sure you must have been asked this question many times before. In your view, what would you attribute to be SIA's success formula?**

JYP Again, it is hard work with honest, competent people. Again, this applies, as I said, to every institution that I know of. There should not be any sudden shifts in policies which will only serve to confuse and demoralise people — confuse them at best and demoralise them at worst. There's no magic formula. The aim is to be able to survive from day to day, from year to year, from decade to decade. For that, you got to make sure that the people you work with are satisfied, happy, motivated, and that you've set appropriate mission, goals and objectives and targets for them, both strategic and tactical. Then they will perform. Otherwise, if something is missing somewhere, they won't perform. That's the difference between a good government and a weak government, a good bureaucracy and an inefficient bureaucracy, or a dynamic institution and a laid back institution.

The same goes for your Ministry. Are you in MITA [Ministry of Information and the Arts]?[10]

IQ   **Yes.**

JYP   Same goes for MITA as for MND [Ministry of National Development] or any Ministry.

IQ   **So SIA would place a lot of emphasis on training and development. This would help to raise the morale and retain the staff.**

JYP   It would help to improve performance and it will also show staff that they can improve themselves. That will help to improve their morale.

IQ   **Mr Pillay, what would it take to keep SIA going successfully?**

JYP   No doubt about it, the same formula with the same basics. It doesn't mean that in 10 years' time, SIA will have the same configuration of aircraft or network or whatever as it has today. It might even, who knows, shed some of the activities it has now. It might have taken on some new activities. But those are incidental. The main consideration is to retain the essential elements, principles, philosophy of good government or good management. There's no other way. If you can make sure that your people are there to continue to lead and man the company, the group, the institution or whatever, then it'll be all right. If not, things will go downhill. Countries go up and they go down. Companies go up and down. It's not something preordained. It's because somewhere along the line, there has been a break. It may not be perceptible, but there has been a discontinuity. In the past, it was forgotten. The future then is at stake.

---

[10] MITA and its functions have since been restructured into the Ministry of Culture, Community and Youth (MCCY) and the Ministry of Communications and Information (MCI) at this time of writing.

Foreign ownership and the partial privatisation of SIA

JYP Retaining these companies [such as Singapore Airlines] in the government's stable just in order to enable the government to exercise influence over those companies is not a good justification for retaining government control. The reason why the government still has such a large stake in SIA is very simple. There isn't enough in the market for government to divest more of its stake. The government still retains about 55 per cent of SIA. No particular reason why it shouldn't. But how much can you release? If it talks of releasing another 10 per cent — the stake is down to 45 per cent — the market price of SIA shares will be badly hit because there'll be so much more supply in the market.

The capacity of our market is not that great. The proof of that is in the spread between the domestic price and the foreign price. If you look at any counter where there is a foreign limitation, you'll find that the foreign price is almost invariably higher and sometimes much higher. In the case of SIA, it's almost 65 per cent higher in the foreign counter compared to the domestic counter. For some of the banks, that's quite a spread. And I think for SPH [Singapore Press Holdings], the spread could be even larger. It's because there is a worldwide demand for the foreign counter. But the demand for the domestic counter is limited by the number of Singaporeans, their wealth and their inclinations. Singaporeans are not confined to investing in Singapore. They can invest anywhere in the world.

IQ **I think SIA at one time was in favour of raising the foreign ownership in the airline, right?**

JYP It's essentially 25 per cent. But when we had the share exchange with Delta and with Swiss Air, the ceiling was raised to whatever it was, by an amount we provided to those two carriers. So it's about 27 to 28 per cent now for the foreign share. There is no particular reason why it should be at 27 per cent rather than at 37 per cent. No particular reason. But there're no plans to release more shares or to expand the foreign content partly because of the technical problem of doing so. Of course, there is a premium and some people will benefit.

If we expand the foreign component in the SIA capital, we'll have to move some domestic shares to the foreign tranche. That means some of those domestic investors will get a windfall. How to determine who should those investors be? Likewise, a sudden expansion of the foreign component will result in the price of the foreign share falling. That won't be too well received by the foreign shareholders. So there are these technical problems which will make it quite a tricky business to raise the ceiling for foreign shares.

IQ   **In particular, what is the impact on privatising, say, SIA?**

JYP   What is the impact? This was in 1985. Well, I suppose you can say that the SIA people now have to be very conscious of the return on equity. In the old days, you could argue that as long as they declare the dividend to the government, did not go running to the government for too much money from time to time, it didn't matter too much what the return on shareholders' funds or equity was. There was no such thing as watching the share price every day. I suppose the company could just expand at will. Never mind the marginal increase in profits or the marginal return on additional shareholders' funds was lower than the average. It didn't matter too much. But now you got to watch this very carefully. You don't want your return on equity to fall below maybe a certain threshold. Otherwise the market will just mark your shares down.

That is the sort of discipline on the company. You have to be very prudent in its expansion. It doesn't mean SIA cannot expand. But it cannot expand recklessly. An additional discipline. And it acts not only on management but also on the unions and the workers. They realise that they can't just demand more and more. They've got to improve productivity and try to get the return up, or at least keep the return stable.

IQ   **Mr Pillay, just now as you mentioned, partial divestment and privatisation. With that, the control of the government-linked companies still rests with the government.**

JYP   Yes.

188 • SPEAKING TRUTH TO POWER

IQ   **Do you see that as not actually enhancing local entrepreneur development?**

JYP   The answer to that in "yes" or "no" terms must be "yes". It does act as an impediment. But I suppose the next question should be: does it matter? This is where there are differences of view. Some will argue: "Why should it matter so much?" Because the private sector has freedom to invest in any industry here. There's nothing to stop it investing in the financial sector.

Of course, you may not be able to start a new bank that easily. Even the government is not able to start a new bank easily. In any other field of activity, the private sector can march in. No problem. Sometimes, of course, you got to get a government permit.

Besides Singapore, there is the region, there is the world. Our entrepreneurs are to be found all over the world. You go to Australia, you find him there busily buying up properties or developing properties. You go to Malaysia, London or where have you, and you'll find them.

I don't believe that just because the government has a stake in these few enterprises in Singapore that the private sector is, in any significant way, handicapped or impeded in flexing its muscles. No, not at all. But theoretically, yes, there may be a slight impediment. Does it matter? I don't think so. But I would rather look at this from the perspective of government, not from the perspective of the private sector. That's because I am a government wallah.

I think the government has to ask itself from time to time: "Are we being distracted from our essential task by occasionally having to cast a look over our shoulder at these government companies which are expanding?" So far so good, no major scandals. But you've got to be careful. If a scandal does arise, it's going to be very costly, and it will raise the question again: Well, should the government have such a large stake in so many enterprises?

Civil servants in business, and the Directorship and Consultancy Appointments Council (DCAC)

IQ   **We know that a small core group of permanent secretaries like yourself are being also appointed as directors of a large number of state enterprises. So far your training and experience as an administrator have been acquired through**

the civil service. But when you were entrusted the directorships to oversee the running of such state enterprises at the initial stage, how did you personally prepare yourself? Or were there any government efforts to prepare you in the running of such business enterprises?

JYP Generally, a civil servant starts when he is very young. He's appointed to a board as a director. So he attends board meetings, listens and contributes whatever he can. By and large it's a learning process. He does not manage the concerns. Even the chairman, if he is a civil servant, does not strictly manage the company. Management is left in the hands of the professional managers. But it's true that a civil servant who is the chairman can influence the course, the direction and the pace of change of the company. That's possible.

So the ones who have a flair or a knack or the insight for the running of a company will eventually make it as chairman. Of course, leadership is an essential ingredient. There's not much mumbo-jumbo in managing a company.

The elements or principles of good management apply across the board to the government bureaucracy, to the private sector, to non-profit organisations and voluntary groups. The principles do not change. They don't change either from one period to another period or from one country to another country.

But, of course, the mission is different for each organisation. The government has its own mission which is not necessarily to make the greatest amount of money. It's really to provide maximum satisfaction to the largest number of the electorate. The purpose of a company is different. It likes to satisfy the customer, whoever the customer is, whether local or foreign. But it does not aim to satisfy everybody in the country, that is, all the electorate. In the process, of course, the company must show a reasonable profit in order to sustain its growth or to ensure its survival in the future. For a voluntary group, non-profit-making, the intention again is something else.

There you are, I think there's no problem for a good level-headed person with leadership qualities and some administrative managerial skills to function in any of these environments. Of course, he has to remember, when he is in one type of institution, what the central mission of that institution is. That differs from a government ministry to a company in the private sector, whether it's a government company or a Singapore private limited company or a multi-national or a small and medium-sized enterprise. The principles are the same. It's just the mission that is different. And you adjust also to the scale of the operation.

Of course, there is that quality some people draw attention to, which is business sense. It doesn't always follow that a good civil servant necessarily has good business sense. Whether he can acquire it, I don't know. Perhaps he can, after a long exposure, get a better understanding of business dynamics. But business sense also implies being able to take risks. And that's where excellent judgement is called for. That sort of risk taking is not normally necessary in a government institution. Civil servants don't take that sort of risk.

IQ   **The selection for directors for the state enterprises from the small group of top civil servants is undertaken by the Directorship and Consultancy Appointments Council (DCAC) of the Finance Ministry. Mr Pillay, can you tell us who sits on the DCAC?**

JYP   The DCAC actually meets very infrequently. I think now it's just once a year. But papers come round, principally recommending changes in appointments of directors on companies. Most of that work is done in the PSD [Public Service Division]. The Secretariat of the DCAC resides in the Public Service Division. That's where all the ideas, I suppose, germinated.

The people who sit on boards are not only the very, very senior civil servants, because we try to induct promising youngsters also, so that eventually they will acquire experience and then take over the leadership of some of these companies. Of course, these companies have been accumulated over a period of time. The interesting question is whether they are required to remain in the public domain, meaning within the government's stable. Many people have argued that many of these companies are not "strategic". They're just commercial companies, so there's no particular reason for them to continue to be in the public domain.

On the other hand, there is such a thing as the legacy of history or the burden of history, or maybe sheer inertia. Many of these companies continued to remain in the public sector for historical reasons, even if there are no strong economic or social reasons for them to be government companies. It's not difficult to identify those companies. If you were to identify those companies that must remain within the public domain and cannot be in the private sector, you would end up with very few such companies.

The others don't really have to be in the public sector. But they are there because some time in the past, they were formed. Of course, once you formed a company, you can't tell it, "Don't grow." It grows and it expands and it moves into different areas. It diversifies and sometimes becomes a conglomerate. Occasionally that leads to trouble because when you try to handle too many diverse unrelated activities in one group, focus can be lost. And the group may not have the capability or the competence to engage in so many vastly different activities.

Take Singapore Airlines. They know how to run an airline and the ancillary business of supplying the carrier with airport services, flight catering, engineering services. But SIA people are not experts in hotel management, or in car rental, or even as a travel agency business or tour operation. So they don't participate in those activities. But they were so inclined in the past, as some carriers have done. Just as well they did not, because the history of the other airlines that moved into these unrelated activities like hotels makes depressing pleading. They didn't come out well at all.

So it's best, as far as possible, to remain within an area where you have the competence. They called it the core competence. Try not to depart too far from your core competence.

IQ **For example, in terms of the Government Linked Companies (GLCs), I mean, you mentioned that they have gone into areas that could be commercially done as a private company. Do you think that could be a reason to encourage local entrepreneurship in Singapore? I mean, it could have been run by some other local companies and not by civil servants and so forth.**

JYP Not by a company in the public domain. Yes, they could have been done that way. In fact, even now the government does have or did have a policy of, what they called, diversification. Indeed, there was a report that was published, I believe, in 1986 on this matter of privatisation of the government's stable of companies. So some effort was made. But then of late, there's nothing much. Instead, GLCs had expanded probably as fast as the economy, if not faster. So their share of the economy could even be higher now than it was 10 years ago. I don't know. I haven't seen any figures. But I should be surprised if it is.

IQ **Coming back to the DCAC. How does the DCAC decide and select the directors for deployment to the companies owned or controlled by the government holding companies? Is it set down by the PSD?**

JYP The role of PSD is essentially to appraise the potential of government servants. As I said earlier, the more promising ones are then earmarked for this pool. When a suitable vacancy arises, they look to see whether there is a proper fit between the individual and the company, and they nominate him. That's how civil servants get to serve on these boards.

IQ **Are there any guidelines or criteria for the selection?**

JYP They must have some guidelines pertaining to the potential, or what we called, currently estimated potential (CEP) of the individual, his age and presumably, his prevailing substantive rank or grade. Those are the general criteria.

Ministry of National Development: The relationship between civil servants and the politicians

JYP It's been a real pleasure and satisfaction for somebody like me to witness the evolution, the growth of the civil service, you may say, to its present pinnacle, if I'm not too dramatic. I believe we have one of the best civil services in the world in terms of its professionalism, discipline, dedication, its ability to deliver the goods and to satisfy the people. I like to think I played one small minute part in it. I'm quite proud to be a civil servant. That's why I'm glad I did not accept the blandishments of the private sector in the past.

IQ **Maybe you could tell us about your years of experience as a Permanent Secretary. What would you consider as factors for a successful working relationship between a Permanent Secretary and the Minister?**

JYP I think there must be trust and mutual respect, and the readiness on the one hand, of the Minister to prepare to accept what the Perm Sec says or advises or comments on, at its face value. That the Minister will not agree entirely with the Perm Sec is understandable.

On the side of the Perm Sec, he is to recognise that whatever the differences there might be, in the end it is the Minister who takes the decision and he carries the responsibility and who should be prepared to defend his position (the Minister's position) and to defend his civil servants.

I think what a civil servant does not like is a Minister who will not accept the consequences of ministerial responsibility. If the civil servant sees that the Minister is a bit wobbly in that respect, then the civil servant is going to climb up. He's not going to take any risks at all.

IQ   **Were there any occasions when there were major differences in opinions over policy issues with the Minister?**

JYP   It's not a question of major policy differences. I think in Singapore, the differentiation is such that the Cabinet decides quite firmly on major issues of policy. There's no doubt about that. Of course, the Minister cannot participate in every single issue in the implementation of the policy. Sometimes certain issues of minor policies emerged during the implementation itself. So there can be a difference of opinion on the lesser issues of policy. Well, those issues may be referred to the Minister. I don't think civil servants will get terribly agitated if the Minister takes a different view. After some time, you'll get to sense what the inclinations of the Minister are and you adjust to adapt. They are not wicked people so they are not going to recommend or to decide policies that conflict with the conscience of the civil servants. That's why I don't think I've had any problems here in respect to the voice of my conscience.

IQ   **Could you cite us some of the major policies which you had a hand in formulating and what were the challenges which you faced?**

JYP   Strange that after all these decades, it is difficult for me to identify a major issue of policy that I had a major input. I suppose civil servants are modest. They think that whatever policies they may have had a hand in shaping could not be major by definition. They must be minor. Anything major is decided by the politicians and often initiated by the politicians.

I made history in this Ministry. Mind you, I'm not an expert in any of the areas of this Ministry. But matters like the upgrading of old HDB precincts, as far as I can see — the idea was formulated and worked upon by a Ministerial team in 1987. Its report wasn't published. Upgrading was one of the proposals in that report. It was chaired incidentally by Goh Chok Tong when he was Deputy Prime Minister.

There are so many little things I've dealt with. But if there were any specific issues I could put my finger on, I didn't mind to contribute. A lot of people participate in policy formulation. Ultimately it is the CEO who decides on major initiatives. Here in Singapore, in the government context, the Prime Minister or the Minister deals with some aspect of the Ministry's policy.

It's a bit tricky for me to answer that. We should not be under the illusion that civil servants are movers and shakers of events.

IQ **Mr Pillay, in our last session we were discussing the role of the civil servants in policy formulation. You mentioned that very often the shape of the policy would have been decided upon by the Cabinet, and you mentioned specifically like the setting up of a ministerial committee to look into policy matters like the upgrading of old HDB estates. Is such an example of setting up a ministerial committee an exception rather than the rule? Do you often have ministerial committees being set up?**

JYP You're quite right. That was a very special one. My point really was that the political leadership initiates change in public policy, whether in Health or Housing or Transport. Then the civil servants chip in with their expertise, you may say, of the technicalities. Civil servants do, however, play quite an important role in initiating change with respect to the management of the civil service like personnel, budgetary matters and the like.

IQ **How often would there be instances where civil servants were pro-active in policy formulation based on the directives and objectives of the Cabinet or the Minister?**

JYP When you say pro-active, as in significantly in initiating policy — no. Any significant change in direction, in my experience, is initiated by the political leadership.

IQ **Would it be correct to say that the role of the civil servants would be to crystallise those concepts into concrete proposals for implementation then?**

JYP Yes, I think you could put it that way. That the civil servant's job then is to shape these ideas on change, and translate them into specific programmes and plans for action. But they also have the responsibility of pointing out the pitfalls. In other words, to examine the proposal from the perspective of the expert, if you may like, which means the technical expertise residing largely in the statutory boards and departments, and the coordinating link between the statutory boards and departments and the political leadership. And that coordinating link is provided by, what we called, the Administrative Service.

So the Admin Officer is the conduit between the politicians and the specialist services or the professional services, which means they have to modulate the proposals from the specialists who are the professionals. And they modulate them through their understanding of the political imperatives and necessities to strains. So in a sense, you may say the Admin Officer is a kind of handmaiden of the politician.

IQ **One of the policies that comes to my mind is the HDB policy to reverse the re-emergence of communal enclaves in some housing estates. I think that was in 1989 when Mr Dhanabalan was the Minister for National Development. Was this again a ministerial policy initiative?**

JYP I don't know the history of that. That was before my time. I don't know whether it was introduced in 1989 or earlier. But the intention was to disperse the population so that there was no overwhelming presence of any one community in a particular locality. Of course, it's difficult for that to apply to the majority community, because they account for 78 per cent of the population. So wherever you go, they will be in the majority.

Yes, indeed, that's a political initiative. That will not come from the civil servants because that is intrinsically not a matter for the civil service to decide, although the civil servants or some branches of the civil service could, in this case, have drawn attention to possible implications of non-dispersal, you may say. Very possible. But the decision whether to proceed or not is a political decision, not a civil service decision.

It cannot be so. When the political decision is made, the civil servants just get to work. It's not a difficult matter to implement from the ground. But, of course, presumably it has to be sold to the public, and that selling has to be done by the politicians. And the explanation and even the tackling of the place.

IQ   **Mr Pillay, could I check with you, when did the meetings for the Permanent Secretaries start?**

JYP   You mean the gatherings of the Permanent Secretaries?

IQ   **Yes.**

JYP   Oh, as far back as I can remember. Let me see. I know they were held in the seventies.

IQ   **Even further back than that.**

JYP   Further back than that, quite candidly I can't recall. Perhaps not in the sixties. To the best of my memory, it must have been some time in the seventies, perhaps early seventies.

IQ   **How often were the meetings held?**

JYP   In those days, once a quarter I believe. That was the pattern for a long period of time. In the eighties, I think we started interspersing these formal quarterly meetings with the informal meetings halfway through the interval. So we used to meet every six weeks. But every alternate meeting was a formal meeting, and in between we had an informal meeting which was sometimes just a lunch and nothing else. But quite frequently in the recent past, in those so-called informal meetings, we used to discuss some matters of substance as well. Now the practice is to meet once a month. The intention is to meet once a month.

IQ **Do you have a fixed meeting venue?**

JYP Well, we usually meet, for some reason, at the Ministry of Environment Building. They have a penthouse on top. But I don't know whether that is the crucial feature because we have a penthouse here as well and several other government buildings have penthouses. We don't need a very large area to dine, I mean, two tables, at the most three tables. Then we go down to their conference room which is, I think, on the fourth level for the meeting proper. But conference rooms can be found in every government building. Anyway, it has become now the norm to meet at the Environment Building.

IQ **What was the objective of holding such regular meetings among the Permanent Secretaries?**

JYP When it started, I don't know what it was. Maybe I can say what it is not. It is not a kind of pre-Cabinet meeting where Permanent Secretaries get around the table to discuss what should go to Cabinet. It's not at all. Nor is it a meeting where policy matters on specific issues are discussed like housing or whatever. We essentially discussed internal management matters for the civil service, the changes in practices and procedures which are constantly evolving. Occasionally we may discuss a subject of general application throughout the civil service, like information technology or some security issue. We usually get a briefing from the ISD [Internal Security Department] or the SID [Security and Intelligence Division]. Sometimes the Ministry of Finance outlines some changes in budget procedure. Of course, there are frequent briefings or explanations by PSD on the changes of management of the civil service. Those are the sort of topics that we discussed.

IQ **It would be very useful because all the Permanent Secretaries are actually kept informed of what is actually happening in other ministries and so on.**

JYP Well, not in other ministries in the sense that we discussed policy matters pertaining to a specific ministry like Health, Communications, National Development or Education. No, not so. We didn't discuss education policy or whatever, but certain common issues concerning the management of the civil service, or developments that affect the entire civil service. Information technology is one.

Ngiam Tong Dow

The maverick Perm Sec

Date of interviews: July 1995
Interviewer: Irene Quah

Ngiam Tong Dow (b. 1937) has held a wide range of key roles in the course of his long career in the Administrative Service, most notably in promoting the economic development and industrialisation of Singapore, in the early years after independence.

After graduating from the University of Malaya in Singapore in 1959, Ngiam worked for a short stint as a reporter for *The Straits Times* before joining the Administrative Service. He began as Assistant Secretary at the Ministry of Commerce and Industry, and then moved to the Economic Development Division at the Ministry of Finance. Through the 1960s, he held positions such as Chief of the Investment Promotion Division at the Economic Development Board (EDB) and Executive Director of Intraco, the trading company formed from operations within the EDB.

He was appointed Permanent Secretary at the Ministry of Finance in 1972, becoming Singapore's youngest ever permanent secretary at the age of 35, although he was already an acting Permanent Secretary at the Ministry of Communications in 1970–2. He was subsequently Permanent Secretary at the Ministry of Trade and Industry (1979–86), Prime Minister's Office (1979–94), and the Ministry of National Development (1987–89). He was also Chairman of the EDB (1975–81). The last position he held, before he retired in 1999, was as Permanent Secretary at the Ministry of Finance, which he had gone back to.

In these interviews, Ngiam discussed a wide range of topics in his signature outspoken style, such as the difficulties he faced in negotiating on issues of the common market with Malaysia during merger. He respected Goh Keng Swee highly, particularly during the time they worked together on economic development and industrialisation for Singapore, and in which he self-deprecatingly described himself as Goh's "chief arranger of factory openings." Ngiam also candidly shared about his disagreements with Goh, who opposed building the Mass Rapid Transit (MRT) system.

Joining the Administrative Service

NTD After my Honours year [at the University of Malaya in Singapore], I went to join *The Straits Times*. Once I got my degree, he[1] made me a journalist. He paid me, I think, $750. Then I applied to join the Administrative Service. Today it's much better. In those early days, the civil service only offered you appointment way after everybody else was offered. So, I joined *The Straits Times* first. Only six months later, then the appointment letter came.

Yes, I applied to join the Administrative Service. Then one day I was sent to interview James Puthucheary,[2] who was then the Chairman of the predecessor of the EDB [Economic Development Board], the Industrial Promotion Board. I was sent to interview him. So, I went to see him in his office at Fullerton Building. He asked me what was I doing in *The Straits Times*. So, I said, "Well, I am waiting for your Administrative Service job." I don't know whether he made a phone call, whatever it was. But soon after, I received my letter of appointment. Then I joined, I think, in August 1959. I think our exams finished in March. So nearly six months later.

Mr Hoffman was very disappointed I didn't want to make journalism a career. I decided that it was better to join the Administrative Service.

IQ **In your university days, did you envisage being a civil servant?**

NTD No. I was on an open bursary. That meant I was not tied down to teach. In fact, I thought I would become a journalist because I was already a cub reporter.

IQ **Between the years 1955 and 1959, there were a lot of developments that took place in our political arena.**

NTD Actually we were quite detached. The English-speaking undergraduates of the University of Malaya were quite divorced from political events. Our job was to study. The only people who were politically-minded were members of the Socialists'

---

[1] Leslie Hoffman, the first local editor-in-chief of *The Straits Times*, who was Eurasian Singaporean.

[2] James Puthucheary was a pro-PAP trade unionist and lawyer. Together with his brother Dominic, who was a founding member of the PAP, they defected to join Barisan Sosialis when the party split. They were both detained in Operation Coldstore in 1963.

Club. Maybe in my innocence, I joined the Socialists' Club also. But even then, I didn't feel it. All that we knew was that suddenly one day, I think, we saw the riot cars near Chinese High School. I think the students were very political.

IQ   **Mr Ngiam, you joined the Administrative Service on 1st August 1959. I believe your first job in the civil service was at the EDB.**

NTD   No. I spent the first few months at the Ministry of Commerce and Industry at that time. I think the Permanent Secretary then was Mr Abu Bakar Pawanchee. I just spent two or three months there. I think Mr Hon Sui Sen then became Permanent Secretary of the Economic Development Division of the Ministry of Finance. I don't know how. But anyway, when his Principal Assistant Secretary, the late Mr Henry Oh, left the service to join IBM, Mr Hon, somehow, asked me to be his assistant. So, I thought it was quite interesting.

The Division only had the Minister (Dr Goh Keng Swee), the Permanent Secretary (Mr Hon Sui Sen), myself, as the Administrative Assistant, and the office boy. There were only four of us starting the Division.

I think it was very interesting because both Dr Goh and Mr Hon were great teachers. Since you had nobody below you, whatever assignment they gave you, you got to attend to it yourself. That was really a very rapid learning process. Actually both of them were great mentors, teaching you how to get things done. When you write a submission, Dr Goh and Mr Hon would correct it like in school. Then they would send back your essay to you. You will find that their corrections (Dr Goh's in green ink and Mr Hon's I think in blue ink) were just changing a word here, changing a word there. They made your written piece of work much better than your original. That was how they taught in the early days. They used to send the corrected work back to you. From there, you can see how the argument was sharpened, how your facts become refined. This was more or less a one-on-one kind of a teaching. So, I was very fortunate in a way. I grew up very rapidly under Dr Goh and Mr Hon.

IQ   **In those few months that you were at the Ministry of Commerce and Industry, what were you doing?**

NTD   I can't quite remember. All that I remember was that the Deputy Secretary was an Englishman. He was more interested in making sure that your commas were in the right places, your full stops were in the right places. He never really taught. But when I went to join Mr Hon, it was a world of difference. Dr Goh used to have confidence in you. Although I was very new to the service, one day he called me up and said, "I want to see you." So, you'll be face to face with him. Then he'll tell you what he wants done. Then you would go and get it done or write him a paper. Whereas the old British Civil Service was very hierarchical.

In a way, it was good to go into a pioneering organisation where there was no structure, no hierarchy, where you were the only guy at the bottom of the heap.

The Political Study Centre: Changing the minds of civil servants

IQ **Mr Ngiam, can I ask you whether you attended any of the lectures conducted by the Political Study Centre?**

NTD As a young officer. That was why I made friends with the much older officers. Some of my life-long friends were actually made at the Political Study Centre. That was held in Goodwood Hill in those days.

IQ **Number 4, Goodwood Hill.**

NTD I can't remember. Anyway, the lecturer then was Mr G. G. Thomson[3] at that time. Later on, he was assisted by Mr Gerald De Cruz.[4] Mr Thomson really could start talking and never end. I think at that time, it was really, I would say, changing the mind-set of the colonial civil servants. That was the whole idea of the Political Study Centre.

IQ **Not so much of the young administrative officers like yourself who have just joined.**

---

[3] George Gray (G. G.) Thomson, the Director of Training at the Political Study Centre (1960–1969).
[4] Gerald De Cruz, a journalist and writer, one-time Organising Secretary of David Marshall's Labour Front, and lecturer at the Political Study Centre and later other institutions such as the National Youth Leadership Institute and the University of Singapore.

NTD Really, the older officers who were so used to it. As civil servants, although we signed off as "Your obedient servant," we were really the masters of the people. But with the PAP [People's Action Party], no. It's the other way around. Which is right. We are truly the servants of the people. Unless the civil service changed its attitude, the Barisan Sosialis side would have had a heyday. That was actually essence at peak, I think. That the civil service had really to prove that it could serve and it could deliver results. Otherwise the leftists would have said: "Well, these English-educated chaps are colonial-minded," and so on.

It was part of a political battle. But fortunately, I think I would say most Singapore civil servants changed. Those who couldn't change, particularly the very senior chaps, it was a pity in a way because they were able men. They left the service. Of course, they thought that the PAP was Communist. So, they all migrated or left the service. But I think the fact was that they couldn't change.

In the early days it was really a colonial service. Because I remember when I was in the Ministry of Commerce and Industry, there was such a thing as a cablegram from the Secretary of State.[5] You know, the instructions would come all the way from London. Foreign exchange policy, this policy, that policy, sterling bloc — all would come from cablegram.

I think it should be in the Archives. You should see some of them. That means some young administrative assistant in the Colonial Office in London giving instructions to the Governor of Singapore. They called it cablegram or some gram or other. It was a telegram. You can see that all instructions are given here. Instead of the directions coming here from the Minister, in those days it had to come from London. So, the Governor in a way was, I would say, like the Mayor of a city probably. No major policies were set by him.

IQ **Do you remember what were the course contents of the lectures conducted at the Political Study Centre?**

NTD That I can't quite remember. I think the message was more or less about the fight against the Communists. I think SM [Senior Minister, Lee Kuan Yew] wanted to wake the English-educated up. I remember his famous thrashing was that we were like goldfish in a bowl, and then we were thrown into a tank with piranhas. What was going to happen to you? Yes, that was a kind of thrashing.

---

[5] The UK had a Secretary of State for the Colonies until 1966, when the role evolved to become the Secretary of State for Commonwealth Affairs, and later was merged with his counterpart in the Foreign Office to become the Secretary of State for Foreign and Commonwealth Affairs today (effectively the UK's foreign minister).

204 • SPEAKING TRUTH TO POWER

1959–1965: Goh Keng Swee and the political context

IQ   **Mr Ngiam, in 1959 when you joined the service, the PAP government had just assumed power sometime in early June 1959. It was said that at that time, the new government inherited an empty Treasury with deficits. Added to that was a whole host of problems like shortage of housing, unemployment and so on. Later on, there was a withdrawal of the variable allowances from the civil servants' salaries.[6] I wonder whether you recall this incident?**

NTD   I never missed the withdrawal of the allowances because when I joined, there was no allowance already. But I would say that in the early days, there was so much to do. Unemployment was a real crying problem. Dr Goh used to tell me. He said, "Every time I pass by a school, I get very depressed."

So, I asked him, "Why Minister? Why are you getting depressed when you pass by a school?".

He said, "I see so many kids coming out of school. Where are they going to get their jobs?"

That was really a pressing problem. The first task was to create employment. So, after 1959, I joined Mr Hon. We started the Economic Development Board [EDB]. And then we were seconded to the EDB in 1961 when the Board was started. That was when I think Mr J. Y. Pillay, Mr S. Dhanabalan, all of us, were seconded to join the EDB.

The whole idea was to get any kind of industry. We didn't talk about high-tech, low-tech or whatever. Anybody who was prepared to put some money in and create jobs for Singaporeans was very welcomed. I used to be, what they called, the Promotion Officer for Dr Goh. That means I was the chief gong-banger. I banged the gong for him. So, he used to tell me, "I want to open more factories." Every week I had to open two or three factories. So, I used to go and scout around all the new companies begging them to open their so-called factories.

As I said, we welcomed any type of employment. There was a factory making joss paper. We called it a factory. There were factories making hair cream, making kaya, jam. He used to go and open them. All he asked was: "You write me a one-page speech." He just goes there, makes a short speech and then gets the TV to cover.

---

[6] Upon taking office in 1959, the PAP government removed the cost of living allowance for civil servants in the middle and upper salary brackets, because it said that it had an anticipated budgetary deficit of S$14 million. The cuts were restored in 1961.

Dr Goh was really a strategist. His whole idea was to create confidence. So, the more people see the Minister opening factories, the more confidence there would be in Singapore. It's just like the classic tactic, the Chinese war tactic. When you are really down to your last troop, you circulate a troop around the city to give the impression that you are very well defended. So similarly, the same tactic was used.

I used to be his chief arranger of factory opening. And I still remember quite a number of them, especially the Indonesian Chinese. They were the ones that really believed in some industries in Singapore, like National Iron and Steel Mill. Mr Goh Tjoei Kok was actually from Indonesia. He was a rubber merchant. His group, together with one or two Singapore groups. Then other factories like Ocean Garments.[7] Mr T. P. Tay — he was from Indonesia. They all came under the immigration scheme. If they put down half a million dollars or a hundred thousand dollars (I can't remember the figure) they were given permanent residence. So, they started all these small factories. Ming Tai Garments. Today, Ming Tai is a big property developer. They were from Hong Kong.

The main thing was to create employment. Once you create employment, and when a person has a job, he becomes more responsible. Employment was the best antidote to Communism. It's only when a chap is unemployed that he listens to the leftists. But once you gave him a job, he would not.

Then we, of course, started the HDB [Housing and Development Board] programme for housing. A roof over his head. A job and a house. These were the two main programmes. No amount of speech making and writing essays will convince the man in the street. You give him a job, you give him a house, he becomes more responsible.

Even family planning. The moment the wife can go out to work and add to the family income, quite naturally she will want a smaller family. Of course, we also pushed for family planning. One way was through economic development. You'll find in most countries that the more the income goes up, the lower the birth rate. The more the income goes down, the higher the birth rate. This is a just a natural phenomenon. I think we succeeded quite well.

Then of course in 1963, we entered Malaysia. We wanted a common market. But the Malaysian side never lived up to their words. I think Dr Goh sent myself and Dhanabalan. I am not sure whether Mr Pillay was also sent. We went around the schools preaching the merits of a Malaysian common market. A propaganda campaign. But

---

[7] In the course of the 1960s and 70s, the company also opened a number of OG Department Stores, the abbreviation of Ocean Garments.

we knew even on the day, that if we entered Malaysia, that the Malaysian government would never allow Singapore to have its own industries.

I remember Guinness Stout. I can't remember his name. [Lord Guinness, who chaired the Guinness company] came here. He even put down a deposit for the site in Jurong somewhere to put up his stout factory. Then he took a trip to Kuala Lumpur. He came back, he told us: "I went to see Tan Siew Sin.[8] He says, 'Over my dead body that you have a stout factory in Singapore. If you want a Malayan market, you must come up to Kuala Lumpur.'"

There was no sincerity at all. So, we went into Malaysia, I would say, mostly on economic grounds. I don't know about the political grounds for that. You must ask SM [Lee Kuan Yew]. The whole basis was totally misconceived because the Malaysian government never wanted us to thrive. In fact, speaking on economic terms, I think we were relieved when we were kicked out of Malaysia. Then straightaway we had our freedom. Otherwise, they'd impose a whole host of tariffs in Singapore too. So, there was no sincerity.

I spent quite a bit of time on the common currency negotiations. Again, no sincerity because they wanted us to hand over whatever little reserves we had to Kuala Lumpur, to manage against the issue of currency. So, Dr Goh said, "No. We can have a common logo. But your currency, you issue against your own reserves. Our currency, we issue against our own reserves. And the reserves will remain in our hands."

Again, Tan Siew Sin said, "No. How can it be? It's a sovereign country."

So, I think we broke apart. Might as well. Singapore Airlines was another classic case. We split Malaysia-Singapore Airlines. I think maybe from their point of view, they were right — the airline had to serve all the towns in Malaysia. But we are Singapore. We wanted an international airline. That was how we can make a living. So, we parted company. I just read recently that MAS [Malaysia Airlines] is lamenting the fact that they are required by the government to serve all these little towns which are loss-making.

I won't say that we made a virtue out of necessity. But sometimes adversity turns out to be a blessing — being kicked out of Malaysia. When we came out of Malaysia, our industrial development, instead of being based on imports substitution, was export-oriented. We were one of the first countries in the world that went for export-oriented industrialisation. And we succeeded because the world is a much larger market. We welcomed foreign investments. Today, I think every country is practising that virtue now. So, I think the advantage of the so-called Singapore common sense is being reduced now because the other countries are also practising the same thing.

---

[8] Malaysia's Minister for Finance (1959–1974).

IQ When we were separated from Malaysia, the question to ask was: Could we survive economically and could we defend ourselves? What was your reaction when the separation came in August 1965?

NTD As I said, maybe when you are younger, you don't fear anything. The sentiment then was, okay, we were now separated from Malaysia. On the defence side, I didn't take part. On the economic side, well, you had to go and get more investors to invest in Singapore. That was why EDB set out to get the electronic factories like Hewlett Packard, Texas Instruments. All came in the early seventies actually.

Maybe because we didn't know the ramifications, but we had no doubts. I don't think Mr Pillay — you can ask him — had any doubts at all. Although our problems at that time were horrendous, in a way our appetite was very small, it was finite. We were only about two to three million people. It was not too difficult to provide employment for a city of two or three million people, if you adopted the right policies, and you opened yourselves to the world, and use other people's strength to solve your problems.

The main advantage of export-oriented MNCs [multinational corporations] is that they bring the markets with them. We didn't have to develop our own market. Of course, you can say that it is a long-term weakness. But I don't think so. So, they brought the markets, we had cheap labour at that time. That was how we found our niche in the world.

That is the fact of life in Singapore. We mustn't become complacent. We must keep on changing and be flexible. So, Singapore was a finite problem. I would say. If I were an economic planner in India or China, I wouldn't have the same confidence because the magnitude of the problem is tremendous.

When Mr Lee Kuan Yew said in those days, "I promise you a hope," I think the people of Singapore believed him because it could start quite easily. In no time at all, a few housing estates were coming up. People could see with their own eyes. But if suppose you are the Prime Minister of India or China and you make the same promise, the chaps in the farm will say you are mad. Where is the house?

Our promises were credible because we could deliver them in a very short period of time. Whereas if you are a much bigger country, even if you put in superhuman effort, the impact will be very marginal at the beginning at least. That's why the Chinese in a way are quite smart. They started off with Shenzhen today, in southern China. Then the other provinces could see what can happen if you opened up a province to the world.

So, Singapore too. Similarly, we can also follow that. In the HDB programme, they used to knock off one part of the slums and then shift the people temporarily elsewhere. Then they were back to the first block of flats. And it went on leap-frogging. Promises can be made but they must be delivered in a reasonable time frame.

The common currency problem after separation from Malaysia

IQ   **Can you tell us more like what role did you play in the common currency problem which you mentioned earlier?**

NTD   On the separation of Singapore and Malaysia, the two countries initially thought that we should continue to at least share a common currency. So, negotiations were entered into. They were quite arduous negotiations. But in the end the agreement could not be reached because of a very basic difference in approach. I think Singapore's view was that the reserves, which were to back Singapore's 'S' series of the currency, would have to be in our control and management. Similarly, we also agreed that for the 'M' series of currency, the Malaysians could manage their own reserves. But I think the Malaysian Finance Minister could not agree to that. Therefore, that was the breaking point. In the end we decided to go our separate ways — Singapore to issue its own currency and Malaysia to issue its own currency.

IQ   **Do you recall, on the Malaysian side and on the Singapore side, who represented the two countries?**

NTD   On the Singapore side, Mr Sim Kee Boon, myself, and I think Mrs Elizabeth Sam. The Minister then was Mr Lim Kim San. I think Dr Goh was then the Defence Minister. Anyway, he was the adviser. I think it was Dr Goh who insisted that if we could not control our reserves, then we could not have a common currency. Actually, looking back, I think a common currency between two sovereign countries in fact is an impossibility, because it means you have got to coordinate your fiscal and monetary policies very closely. I think the needs of the Malaysian economy and ours are quite different. We are a trading nation and therefore, we need a strong currency to trade. A stable currency is important. Malaysia may want to stimulate the growth of their own economy. Even if we had agreed on the management of the reserves backing the currency, I think in the end there would have to be a split because the economic policies diverged.

IQ **On the Malaysian side, who represented?**

NTD I remember the Governor of their Central Bank, Tun Ismail.[9] I think Thong Yaw Hong, the Permanent Secretary of their Treasury and some younger officers. I can't remember their names.

IQ **I recall in our first meeting you spoke about the Green Paper.**

NTD In all those negotiations between government and government, I think the Prime Minister (now SM Lee Kuan Yew) said: "Whatever correspondences we write, our position should be so reasonable. One day it has to be published. So when it's published, people can see that we were very reasonable." So, we were very careful in drafting any written correspondences between Singapore and Malaysia. Indeed, within weeks after the break, we published our Green Paper to give our side of the story, including all the exchanges of correspondences, the respective positions taken and so on.

IQ **The Singapore Currency Board was also set up in 1967. Were you responsible for setting up the Board?**

NTD I was in the Economic Development Division then, in the Finance Ministry. But the Currency Board, I remember, the day-to-day operation was under the Accountant-General, then Mr Chua Kim Yeow, I think, if my memory serves me right. But I remember Mr Sim and I knew next to nothing about how to design currency notes. I think Mr Sim made a special trip to England — Bradbury Wilkinson.[10] Even our coins. In fact, within a matter of six months, we had to introduce a new series of currency notes. The first series, I can't remember. I think maybe orchids were the motif, if I'm not mistaken. Orchid and then Ship series which is the present series. But anyway, the

---

[9] Tun Ismail bin Mohamad Ali, Governor of Bank Negara Malaysia, the Malaysian central bank (1962–1980).
[10] Bradbury Wilkinson & Co. was a British engraver and printer of banknotes and postage stamps. It has since been acquired by De La Rue, the company that currently prints banknotes for the Bank of England. It continues to be common practice for countries to print their banknotes abroad.

first series I think revolved around the Orchid, HDB Flats, our National Day Parade, on the Nation-Building Theme.

The UN Industrial Mission survey

IQ **When the UN Industrial Mission was here, what kind of assistance did it extend?**[11]

NTD I would say our role was a supporting role. I would say making sure that we had enough office space and secretaries. They used to be housed where the hotel training school is now. I can't remember the name. Off Tanglin. Not Goodwood Hill.

IQ **Nassim.**

NTD Nassim Hill, that's right. They were housed there. Then I think Mr [I.-F.] Tang used to discuss closely with Mr Hon. When I read that draft, it made some sense to me, like on ship repair. We had some basis. Our people had some mechanical knowledge. And then re-rolling steel bars, old ships break down, cheap labour. We can re-roll into construction material. I would say all the low-tech industries. Any industry the people were prepared to provide employment, we welcomed them. I don't think Dr Winsemius went on the basis of import substitution.

Wherever we had created a local demand for some industrial products, then of course he'd recommend. For instance, our HDB programme required construction materials — cement mills, timber, furniture. Of course, he pointed out: "Well, this is your own internally-generated demand." It was a practical report. Whatever is practical to do, we should try and do.

Then industrial estates. As I said, the whole idea was to build the standard factories because we wanted companies to just invest in equipment, not in the

---

[11] In 1960, the Singapore government invited a United Nations Survey Mission team to conduct a feasibility study of Singapore's potential for industrial expansion. The team was led by the Dutch economist Dr Albert Winsemius, who then became Singapore's long-time economic advisor.

building. Then land policies. In fact, we didn't sell the land to them. We leased it to them. Initially, since we were not sure, rentals were very low. But every five years, we revised the rental. As you succeed, we also want to get a better return on our land. But if you don't succeed, then it's too bad. Both of us lose something.

His was basically a practical report. He also emphasised training quite a bit. I think our training was a practical way because we told the MNCs: "Look, we don't have the ready-made labourer for you. But if you take our boys and girls, you send them to your companies in your own country, give them six months training and then send them back to work in your factory."

Like Seiko, for instance. Even the Japanese recruited, I think, one or two hundred people. Then brought them to Japan and let them work in the Japanese factories for six months to a year. Then they came back and started their own factory here.

It was a practical way. In fact, it was really the right way because the curriculum, whatever it was, was set by the future employer. And he was training them in his own premises. They provided, I think, the living expenses. We provided the airfare, that's all. So, I think it was a practical way.

IQ **The report, however, stated that a common market would be the only solution to a development programme, which did not materialise at all.**

NTD It didn't materialise. That's why we entered Malaysia for a common market. But as I said, my personal recollection is that it was never to be. The Malaysians were not sincere.

IQ **Do you think that during that period, in such an arrangement, we had actually more to gain?**

NTD On paper, maybe. They have a bigger population. Maybe we think that being a city and being a port, we could be faster than they on a level playing field. But as I said, they never intended it to be a level playing field. All they wanted was to take over control of the levers and then make sure that Singapore stays in the dumps.

Formation of the Petrochemical Corporation of Singapore

NTD I would say in the early days, there was less reflection and more action. Today, I do not know. Today, maybe we think a little bit more. It may be good, it may be bad. In the early days, I think we just thought 10 per cent of the time and did 90 per cent of the time. Today, I think we seem to be doing more studies and more thinking and not enough action. We must invest in industries. Today, I think it has come to a time where we cannot expect other people to bring in their capital to set up factories in Singapore.

Today, it is time the EDB takes a risk with the entrepreneurs. I think EDB is beginning to do that. But we have got to put more of our money where our mouth is now. That was what we did for PCS [Petrochemical Corporation of Singapore]. Who in the world would have thought that Singapore, without any oil resources or any gas resources, could become a petrochemical centre? The Chairman of Sumitomo convinced us that it was feasible. And we went through it with him, through thick and thin. It was a project that really taught me things. The Japanese are very thorough, very tenacious and they obey their leader absolutely.

Mr Hasegawa was the Chairman. He met Mr Hon. In his memoirs, surprisingly, he titled the chapter on Singapore "By divine help" or "By divine plan." Why? Because he, being a Japanese, was a Catholic. Very unusual for a Japanese. And Mr Hon was a Catholic. So, when the two men met, they had complete trust in each other.

When I became Chairman of EDB in 1974, the first job thrust on me was the signing of intention. We had a ceremony in the MND [Ministry of National Development] Building's penthouse for the signing of intention to build up a petrochemical industry. But I tell you, it was a real uphill battle. Of course, our strategy was right. And because of luck too.

The Iran-Iraq war broke out. The Mitsui plant,[12] which was supposed to go to Iran, was aborted. We were in the queue. Straightaway when one fellow fell out, we took our place in the queue. And petrochemical investments were very high because it's capital intensive. So, I think we are right.

---

[12] A major petrochemical plant that was being built in southern Iran by the Mitsui Group of Japan, and which had been badly damaged by Iraqi air raids in 1984.

IQ   **The project initiative to start this joint venture came from us, or was it from the Japanese side?**

NTD   I would say from the Japanese side. I would say that I really enjoyed this project, although it was very tough. The Vice-Minister of MITI [Ministry of International Trade and Industry] summoned me to Japan. He said, "I have no time. But since you want this project, I give you five minutes to explain to me why you think this project can succeed in Singapore?"

IQ   **Five minutes?**

NTD   He said, "Five minutes — you explain to me."

So, I really had to put on my thinking cap. I said, "(a) You are going to Singapore because you want a Southeast Asian market; (b) We are becoming one of the world's refining centres. And we have the supply of naphtha. So, it's very stupid for you to bring the naphtha back all the way to Japan, make the final product and shift it all the way back to Southeast Asia."

His name was Mr Yano. I remember him distinctly. He said back: "Yes, you are right."

The project was determined in five minutes. After I left, he supported us. He said, "The Singapore thinking is correct." The second part was right. We had the refining centre. After that, he said, "You said that you have the Southeast Asia market. Your ASEAN, how long is it going to take?"

But I think I would say it's the courage to invest a large sum of money at the right time. And once we are in this sort of project, you are ahead of the others in the queue, although it's a cyclical project.

IQ   **We were one of the first, right?**

NTD   In the region, yes. At the beginning, it was very difficult because there was a slump in the industry. But later on, we had got back all our capital.

214 • SPEAKING TRUTH TO POWER

IQ   **You mentioned just now that it was an uphill task.**

NTD   Yes, all sorts of problems. In Singapore, there were so many doubters. I think the only person who believed in it was Mr Hon and EDB. I think even SM [Senior Minister, Lee Kuan Yew] didn't believe in it. Dr Goh also didn't believe in it. Howe Yoon Chong also didn't believe in it. They said, "You are wrong."

I remember SM once telling both Mr Hon and myself. He said, "You know, if this project fails, all the good that you have done in EDB will be wiped off in one stroke."

What can you say to Mr Lee when he put it in such harsh terms? Really harsh terms.

IQ   **But how did yourself and Mr Hon foresee it?**

NTD   We thought that our basic thinking was correct. The growing market was here. Secondly, we had the supply. Thirdly, I think we were quite efficient in our infrastructure. Of course, most important, we had in Sumitomo a partner who was very loyal. Actually, to my great regret, after the whole thing was going so well, we went and sold off our share to Shell. So Shell was laughing all the way.

IQ   **That was in the eighties, right?**

NTD   Yes, in the eighties. Shell didn't take the risk. We took the risk. When the money was rolling in, we went and sold it away. I was very disappointed with that decision. The Japanese have not forgotten. When I went to see MITI, he [Mr Yano] said, "It's a national project. You understand, national project? That means through thick and thin, you, as a government, must support this project. We, as the Japanese side, through thick and thin, will support this project."

So, when we sold it to Shell, he said, "You have broken your word. Your people, we cannot trust."

But unfortunately, Mr Hon passed away. So, this background wasn't properly fed in. By that time, I had already left MTI [Ministry of Trade and Industry]. I had come to Finance. Nobody asked me whether it was the right thing to do or not. So, we sold it away. Shell's profits since then are far more than what they paid us for it. But the main thing is not so much the money. It's keeping faith with people.

Dr Goh used to tell me that whatever we agreed to, we must honour. Because however painful it is for us, we must, as EDB, honour our word to the investor. If we don't, that's the end for us.

So, I was very disappointed when we just tore up. I think until today, the Japanese have not forgotten that Singapore did not honour its word. That's because there was no institutional memory. So, it's a real pity. Yes, we learnt all this.

As Chief of the Investment Promotion Division: Singapore's business philosophy and economic policies

IQ   **Mr Ngiam, in 1961 when you became the Chief of the Investment Promotion Division ...**

NTD   That's why I told you I was the chief gong-banger. I used to see people, try to get industries, any type of industries, to come into Singapore.

IQ   **What kind of publicity programme was planned?**

NTD   Actually no publicity. We told the investors that we were hungry for work, we were very diligent, although unskilled people. Low cost. I would say cheap labour. Although I did not participate in this, Mr Tang told me.

At that time the Americans wanted to impose textile quotas on us. You remember, in the very early days, they wanted to impose textile quotas. So the American delegation came. We had to sell them the idea as to why they should give us more quotas. Mr Tang was a very wise man, very cunning and very wise. All that he did was just to take the American delegation for a drive through the city and passed by some of the places that were on strike. He said, "These people are on strike. The Communists are about to take over Singapore. If you don't give us any quota, Singapore will be gone."

So, the American delegation came back and gave us a quota much much more than what we ever expected. You must be cunning, you know. So, in the end, we had such a high quota that the government made some money out of the quota. We tendered the quota out to our exporters.

Being the Chief Promotion Officer really meant trying to get industries in. I remember the Indonesian Chinese very well. I remember going to Hong Kong with the first Director of EDB, Mr Mayer,[13] and Mr Lien Ying Chow.[14] I tell you; I never forget these people. Mr Lien Ying Chow was a Teochew. So, he called on his Teochew compatriot in Hong Kong who was in an industry making clocks. I can't remember the name of the company now. So, this fellow, what he did was talk, talk, talk, talk, talk. In the end he turned around and said, "No. Singapore can never industrialise. Don't waste my time."

Of course, they were hungry for work. So, the Hong Kong industries had no confidence in Singapore. But I am glad to say in the end, if you talk about industrial structure, Singapore has a far more industrial structure than Hong Kong ever had. Today it is Shenzhen — still low-cost industries. Whereas here, we have ship-repairing, petrochemical, high-end electronics. Much, much better. Hong Kong never concentrated on education. Now they realised it. It's too late now.

IQ **In the old days when you heard such comments made by all these people, did you feel a bit demoralised?**

NTD That's one thing. I must tell you that we never did. We just wiped the dust off our feet and walked away. That kind of attitude. We never thought of giving up. I can tell you that. We never gave up.

I remember one American company came. Sometimes you have got to learn to say no. So, this guy, what he wanted was a grant from us. You know, this company actually went bankrupt. I am glad to say that he went bankrupt. He wanted us to give him a sum of money in order to set up his company here. Entirely at our risk. A grant.

So, I told him: "In Singapore, no such thing as a grant. I can give you tax incentive. I can give you training, train some people for you, but no grant."

He said, "In that case, I am going to Ireland."

The Irish were very stupid. They were so hungry for work that the Irish government gave him a grant. He started a factory there making machines for lifting cargo around, the small machines. In the end, after three years in Ireland, despite all the grant, he failed. He went bankrupt.

---

[13] E. J. Mayer, Israel's director of industrial planning in the Ministry of Commerce and Industry, whom Goh Keng Swee hired in 1961 as the first Managing Director of the EDB.
[14] Founder of the Overseas Union Bank (OUB).

I judged then, as Chairman of EDB, that if a man can have the audacity to tell me that he is not going to risk any of his money and that I should give him money for his factory, that means his factory is at an end. He has got no hope in his industry.

However hungry we are for work, we have to learn to say no. We cannot buy a factory. We cannot buy an industry. We must have enough merit in order to get the industry. That means our labour. Basically, it's labour. Our labour must be low-cost enough and secondly, our infrastructure must be top class, besides law and order and political stability. That's all preconditioned. But these are the two things — cost and production. Because we don't have the market. They have the market. Cost and production is the key.

Singapore must remember this now. Our labour costs are going up very rapidly. Secondly, our dollar is strengthening like mad. I really fear for our industry. I don't want to be critical of economic policy because it's none of my business now. But we are caught in our own blind corner. The moment we say we are going to impose levies on foreign work permit holders, we are really protecting the Singapore worker. We only protect if there is plentiful supply. But we are protecting when there is not enough supply. You'll fail your economics exam if you make such a policy. Unfortunately, we did. Our Ministers think that too many foreign work permit holders will bring about social disharmony, blah, blah, blah. I don't buy that.

Now are wages are rising rapidly. On top of that, because we managed our finances so well, our dollar is a much-desired currency. So, they are pushing our dollar up. Even Japan, you know, the yen. Even such a strong economy and loyal people, they can't stand it.

I remember Mr Lee Kuan Yew used to tell us: "The world doesn't owe us a living."

That's very true. But today we behave as if — sometimes I think so — the world owes us a living. We talk about the Singapore premium. All that is rubbish. I am a dissident in economic policy today. From an activist to a dissident!

Dr Goh used to tell me, "In a city-state like Singapore, if you make a wrong economic decision, in six months' time you'll suffer for it. In China or India, if you make a wrong economic decision, maybe in six years' time you don't even see the effect."

We have been adopting this policy since the last recession in 1985. When I was Chairman of EDB, I used to tell the university and polytechnics, "You produce for me one engineer, I can give you one job. You produce me one diploma holder, I give you one job." I think if we have stuck to my policy, we can deliver. But today, NTU [Nanyang Technological University], NUS [National University of Singapore] and the four polytechnics are producing a lot of graduates. When these people come out, I am not very sure whether we are able to deliver the jobs. I am beginning to have doubts. In any industry the top layer depends on a large base. Once the base is relocated out of Singapore, why is there a need for an accountant or an engineer if you don't have the production workers at the base?

When I told PM [Lee Kuan Yew] all that, he always told me: "You are a pessimist."

I don't think I am a pessimist because I have seen it. We used to practise virtue and therefore, we were rewarded. Today, sometimes we are not practising virtue. Other people are practising virtue. They are welcoming all these industries. They are keeping their currency low.

IQ   **Our wages have actually increased tremendously. I would agree with that.**

NTD   Yes, wages. Nobody owes us a living.

IQ   **In the early days, did your Division actually have overseas representation in places like ...**

NTD   EDB, we set up our offices quite early — New York, London, Frankfurt, Tokyo. In the early days, Chan Chin Bock (and I agree with him) said, "Investment promotion is not a matter of nice advertisements in the *International Herald Tribune* or the *New York Times*. It's not a matter of having all these nice conferences with the Henry Kissingers[15] of the world. Which we are prone to doing now. Investment promotion is real hard work."

Chin Bock used to tell me, "In America, you must make hundred phone calls before you can get 10 American chaps to say, 'Yes, come and see us.' And when you can see these 10 chaps, you are damn lucky if one or two will take the trouble to visit Singapore to see for themselves. Of that one or two, you are damn lucky if one out of five says, 'Yes, I am putting the money in.'"

It's personal conviction. Like I describe to you the Japanese MITI fellow giving me an oral examination. Decisions are made by people. You have got to see the President, you have got to see the Deputy President.

In Europe, the Germans are very proud. The German doesn't waste time. They say, "You want to see me, I have no time. You put on a piece of paper, fax to me, the reasons why I should see you."

---

[15] Henry Kissinger, the US Secretary of State and National Security Advisor in the 1970s.

Then you fax it to his secretary. If he thinks that you have some sense, he may give you an interview. But mostly he just turns you away.

Yes, it's real hard work. But today, I think we tend to do a lot of PR [public relations] which is not bad. PR only creates the atmosphere. But if you want to get investments, you want to get people to put their money down, you must really go and see them. Maybe I am getting old or very hidebound.

Even the style of marketing we have changed. We cannot avoid hard work. It's quite easy to hold a conference. You just hire a PR firm and that fellow will do it for you. But in the end, what is the use? So, I think we have to have personal persuasion.

IQ

What was the selling point of Singapore then in the early days?

NTD

In the early days, it was very simple. One hour of your labour would cost you so many US dollars, so many German marks. In Singapore, our people have diligence, have some education. We can produce it for you for one-tenth the amount. We have no market. You have the market, you have the technology. But we have got the people. And they came. As our costs go up, as our people become better trained, better educated. But you must have the initial mass.

That's why I get fed up with the academics in the university. High-tech, pick and choose. I tell you, in life you don't pick and choose. You take the rough with the smooth in economic development. It's only in the comparative process that maybe you get some goal being defined. Today, when I read all these papers, you know, Singapore is no longer cheap, therefore we cannot attract industries. Who are we to say which industry can survive in Singapore and which cannot survive?

So, I get angry with MAS [Monetary Authority of Singapore] particularly. Those guys there believe that the more we strengthen our dollar, the more we will force the restructuring of Singapore. But they are not running the companies. Your dollar can only strengthen by the productivity increase in any particular year. When our dollar rises against the US dollar — I don't know by how many percentage points — in a matter of months, we will not be able to stomach it. Even Japan cannot stomach it. Even they cannot restructure fast enough.

Those of us who faced the music then, I think we are no longer in charge. Therefore, the younger chaps, those who are new, find all sorts of fanciful and sophisticated arguments. Very nice to read on paper. But in reality, go try and implement your programme. But anyway, maybe I am too pessimistic. I don't know. I wish the Prime Minister luck.

Intraco,[16] and civil servants in business

NTD   I joined Intraco which was really two hectic years. I really learned what is it like to be in business. As a civil servant, a businessman treats you with great respect. But when you are in business yourself, they treat you as if you are dirt. That is the time when you really got to learn to take a lot of insults.

IQ   **You come from a civil service background. How do you actually learn the business dynamics?**

NTD   We didn't know a thing about business. Maybe [Sim] Kee Boon and I were over-confident. Dr Goh wanted to use force, that all Japanese products in Singapore should be sold through Intraco. It means a monopoly on distribution. So, we told Dr Goh, "No, no. That's not the way we start business. That's the worst way of starting business."

So, Dr Goh said, "Oh, in that case, you go and concentrate on Russia. It's different."

So, we struggled and struggled. I would say that we had the help of some businessmen. But even then, I would say when it comes to business, no holds barred. We had a Director on our company. We wanted to supply canned food to Vietnam. So, he asked us to quote a certain price for him. He, in turn, behind our back, quoted a lower price. We learned hard.

At one stage, I remember distinctly our contractor because Hong Leong was squeezing them on the cement price. So, they came running to Intraco and said, "Why don't you import cement. We guarantee that we will buy from you and give you a nice commission."

So, we said, "Yes, okay. How many tons do you want?"

So, we collected enough for one shipload. So, we imported cement. When I arrived at the wharf, Hong Leong dropped their price. So, all these bloody rascals went

---

[16] Intraco, Singapore's international trading company, that started from operations within the EDB, was incorporated in 1968 with the purpose of boosting Singapore's industrialisation programme by identifying and trading with overseas markets for local products. Intraco was listed on the Singapore Stock Exchange in 1972.

back to Hong Leong and left us with thousands of bags of cement, which in the end turned into stone. I tell you, no morality in business. No holds barred.

In the end they said, "We have to go back to Hong Leong because Hong Leong told us, 'If you don't take cement from us, we won't sell you steel.' Can you sell us steel?"

Anyway, we survived by taking orders for garments and all the rest of it. Then we did some timber business. Actually Intraco struggled for a long time. I was there only for two years. Kee Boon, I think, stayed on a bit longer.

IQ   Those two years were full-time?

NTD   Yes, full-time. We were just on secondment full-time. I think it was even worse than doing EDB work. I remember trying to sell toilet paper in Port Moresby of all places. But it was a really useful period. You really feel the harshness of business. Being a government company, we could not even use normal business tactics like offering illegal commission to the buyers. We couldn't.

Tai Ping Carpet. You know the carpet factory? When Mandarin Hotel was being built, they tried to sell carpets to Lien Ying Chow.[17] So Tai Ping told us: "If you can sell carpets for us, we'll give you a commission. You can speak to Mr Lien." Mr Lien was on our Board. But then this lady, quite a nice lady, added: "But I don't think you will succeed."

True enough, we never succeeded. The reason is: we, being Intraco, would have wanted to sell directly to Mandarin Hotel. But she, in the private sector, sold to Mr Lien's private company. The private company then sold to Mandarin Hotel. So, she said, "You do not know the ropes of business."

This really opened our eyes. It stood up as a good stead as an administrator — how business people use tactics to get business.

IQ   Did Intraco eventually venture into the Eastern European market?

NTD   Yes, we did. We even had a shoe factory here making shoes for the Russians. Also folded up. But I would say Intraco, only in the last few years, began to stabilise

---

[17] Lien Ying Chow owned the Mandarin Hotel at Orchard Road.

because they've got a few good agencies. We bid for the Hyundai car, for the Pony Agency, without knowing at the same time that our Ambassador to Japan, Wee Mon Cheng, was also trying to bid for the agency. So, in the end, neither of us got it.

I wouldn't stay in business because as Mr Pillay said, "If you want to be in business, you must be prepared for the other guy to spit in your face and you keep on smiling." He said, "As a civil servant, we can't take it." Although he is running a large business [Singapore Airlines], that's a different kind of business. And I am doing DBS [Development Bank of Singapore] Bank. That's a different kind of business. But if you go into "real business," you just try.

Pirate taxis, buses, MRT

IQ **How did your Ministry handle problems like pirate taxis and buses?**

NTD In fact, looking back, I would say that the pirate taxis served a very useful purpose. I don't think you all remember. When the bus services were inadequate, along Bras Basah Road people were lining up and you could just hop into one of those taxis. But I think they served a need. Of course, pirate taxis, in a way, posed unfair competition to the regular taxis because they did not pay the proper taxes and so on. But they did serve a purpose, providing competition to the regular taxis.

But in the end, I think gradually we shrunk the problem. I think the pirate taxi problem was solved when we started Comfort.[18] Previously, the number of taxis was controlled by the Yellow Top owners. We helped the NTUC to start Comfort, where the taxi-driver, being a driver all his life, in the end became an owner driver. That was a very successful scheme. The Finance Ministry provided Comfort with the first loan. At that time, they had no collateral. We provided them with a loan. They, in turn, then sold the taxis by instalments to the taxi-drivers.

So, once you get a proper fleet of taxis, well-managed, then I think the pirate taxi problem was solved. Of course, there was strict enforcement. You must always provide an alternative. If your regular taxi service is bad, the bus services are bad,

---

[18] Comfort (the acronym of Co-operative Commonwealth for Transport Ltd.) was established by the NTUC in 1970 as a transport co-operative. Today, it is part of the multi-national transport corporation Comfort-DelGro.

then pirate taxis will emerge. It's all a matter of economics. But the moment you have a regular taxi service and a better bus service, then I think the pirate taxis, with some enforcement, the problem will be solved. In a way the pirate taxi industry was also an absorber of unemployment. You must remember that in the early days, throughout the whole of the 1960s, there was quite a bit of unemployment in Singapore. So, they became pirate taxi drivers.

IQ   **The urban legend was that the pirate taxi drivers, some of them were actually gangsters.**

NTD   Yes. In fact, the pirate taxi drivers, I think most of them were very hardworking people. Even Comfort found that they had to learn, because every week, these guys are supposed to pay the hire for the taxi. Some of them went and gambled and they didn't turn up. So, I think one of the successful part of Comfort is the enforcement squad. In fact, we had our own strongarm enforcement squad. If a taxi driver doesn't turn up to pay his weekly payment, the very next day the strongarm squad will go and catch him on the road and get him to pay. Or else we would seize his taxi. That's the only way.

Maybe they lived from hand to mouth. But some of them had bad habits — gambling, Turf Club and drinking. So, they won't pay up. So, they know that if they don't pay up on the fixed day of the week, the next day the taxi will be gone. We will take it back. You must be very tough. In fact, the trade union was very tough. You don't assault them. The really strongarm chaps have to go around enforcing payments.

In fact, STC [Singapore Traction Company] was riddled with corruption. I don't know whether you remember. Maybe you are too young. The bus conductors used to pocket the fare. I think STC, although owned by a public company, was run by expatriate policemen from Palestine.

My most vivid experience in the Ministry of Communications was to close down the STC because they were just running the fleet down. So finally, we decided it was better to close them down and to get the Chinese bus companies to provide the service into the city. That was a good exercise for me in executing policies. At least one or two thousand people were employed by STC. Suddenly for them to be out of job was quite a shock to them. There could have been riots. So, we had to make arrangements for them to be absorbed by the Chinese companies, which were then allowed the routes to come into the city. So, the transition was very well handled.

224 • SPEAKING TRUTH TO POWER

IQ   **The amalgamation of the bus companies like Hock Lee and ...**

NTD   I think we amalgamated the North, South, East, West.[19] From about eight or 10, we amalgamated them into four. They came from all the four corners of Singapore into the city. Subsequently, we reduced all four into one, which I thought in retrospect is a mistake. You must always have two bus companies to operate.

IQ   **We have TIBS.[20]**

NTD   TIBS was after SBS came into being. Then the government realised it was a mistake to rely just on SBS in the same way as we relied on STC. So, we have TIBS as a supplementary service. Now actually it's the other bus company already.

But the Chinese companies, I would say, were not paragons of virtue. They were very short-sighted. The way they ran the bus companies was like this: if there were the shareholders, say six of them, every evening they would wait at the depot, and all the takings were then divided among the six of them.

Yes, something like that. It was the way they did business. And then the next day, say a tyre is punctured, to buy the new tyre, all six of us would come out with their share. There was no depreciation policy, nothing. They didn't believe in scheduling, although they are supposed to schedule bus services.

The Punggol Bus, I remember when I was a boy, would wait until the bus was loaded before they started the journey. Which made sense. It is no use running an empty bus. But that is not the way to run a regular bus service. I think the Chinese bus companies were short-term people. What they could get out of it, they did. STC failed because of high cost and was caught.

---

[19] During Ngiam's tenure as Permanent Secretary for Communications, the 10 "Chinese bus companies" (bus companies which had been owned and run by Singaporeans of Hinghwa (Henghua) and Hockchia (Fuqing) origins for many decades hitherto) and the British-owned Singapore Traction Company were amalgamated into four entities, each of which was widely known by the area of Singapore they serviced (the north, south, east and west of Singapore). In 1973, these four entities were merged into one to become Singapore Bus Service (SBS).

[20] Trans-Island Bus Services (TIBS), which was then acquired by SMRT in 2004.

IQ   **But how did the government then manage to persuade all these Chinese towkays to amalgamate?**

NTD   We had to use some persuasion or threat of removing their licence. I think they were quite strong characters — the Tay Koh Yat Bus Company, Green Bus, Hock Lee, and Changi Bus. I think all of them had some gangsterism in them. Although I have got no proof, I suspect.

I think that is an example of really a good grassroots leadership. Because on the morning that I had to close down STC, we enlisted the help of the union leader in STC. I can't remember his name. He was Chinese and spoke Malay very well. He was able to go down and tell all his fellow workers, "Look, you don't throw stones. We will organise for you to get into the other Chinese bus companies." I think he handled it very well. That's why I have my respect for the grassroots natural leadership. That's our standing example.

Mr Goh Yong Hong was our Police Commissioner. I was the Permanent Secretary for Communications. Both of us could not have swung the transition, the changeover, without the help of this union leader. A very effective man, he could speak all the languages. He was one of them. He could persuade them. So, we really held our breath. By one morning they left the STC employment and then they moved, so to speak, across the road and joined the Chinese bus companies.

In a way I don't know whether I am right, or my successor is right. They should not have amalgamated the four bus companies into one. I think it was a mistake. We should always have at least two companies. I think four or five years after SBS came into being, they started TIBS.

IQ   **The negotiation to re-employ the STC workers in the other Chinese bus companies — who were involved in the negotiation?**

NTD   Actually the union was the one that arranged it. We did tell the Chinese bus companies, "You are taking over the routes and you must take over the people too." I think they were quite cooperative. They didn't pick and choose. They absorbed most of them. Of course, some of them were too old. Then they just retired. It was quite a shock to them.

I think the companies thought that they could just get rid of all the problems and then have a windfall, which we prevented. Because they owned this depot next to Rex Theatre — Mackenzie Road. Today it is a used car depot. They thought that they could convert that into an office building. But we refused. They failed as owners and managers. Why should we have rewarded them?

So, the old STC was closed down. It was very rough justice. I think under today's context, we could not have done that. Those were the early days. If we think that we are right, we just did away with the niceties. Today they would take us to court.

IQ **When you were in the Communications Ministry, was the debate on the Mass Rapid Transit [MRT] going on?**

NTD I was very much involved in the Mass Rapid Transit studies because we had the consultants. Of course, I was very much in favour of the Mass Rapid Transit. But as we all know, Dr Goh was against it. So, the Finance Ministry was against it. But the Minister for Communications[21] and everybody else were for it. We really had to fight our way through on this one. We really had a public debate because the sum involved in those days was tremendous — $5 billion. So, I think SM [then PM, Lee Kuan Yew] wanted to be dead sure that we were right in investing this sum of money.

But I told SM, "Look, there is no way that you can solve the transport problem without this Mass Rapid Transit because land is limited. How many more roads can you build for the buses to run through, if you depend on the bus system?"

In fact, Mr Howe was also telling him the same thing. Mr Howe Yoon Chong was very much involved in this. "Unless you are prepared to drive off all other vehicles from our roads, then maybe a bus system will work. But if you are not prepared, then I think the Mass Rapid Transit system has to be brought in."

In any case, ours is both a bus as well as a MRT system until today. But it cannot be a total bus system. Impossible.

But Dr Goh's view was that it was a very lumpy investment and if we were wrong, we could be very wrong. He thought that by adding buses, you add one bus at a time. If you were wrong, then you could just write off one bus. But I disagreed with Dr Goh. I told him that this MRT is a way of providing access to the whole of Singapore, and our land prices were bound to appreciate. It was like opening up Singapore. Just like in a huge country, a railway system opens up the whole country. Similarly, the MRT is also a means of opening up the whole of Singapore. You can have quick transport.

So I looked at it as an economic development project. But Dr Goh looked at it as just a pure traffic project. You can ask him if you interview him. He nearly

---

[21] Ong Teng Cheong.

overturned it. MINCOM [the Ministry of Communications] put up a paper laying out the benefits of all this. So, he said, "Okay, what are you aiming at? You want to bring the MRT into the city. How many more new jobs can you accommodate in the city with the MRT?"

I think we gave some figure. Mr Lim Leong Geok gave some figure. Then he said, "Okay, $5 billion divided by this number. You mean to tell me that you're going to spend a hundred or two hundred thousand dollars just to be able to bring one more worker into the city?"

He nearly torpedoed it. It was a sort of minimalist approach. Whereas my approach was the other way around. With the MRT we would open up the whole of Singapore. Land values would go up. You could locate offices and factories in various places. You can locate shopping centres in various places. In fact, you can disperse the concentration in the city to the outlying areas.

IQ   To the suburban areas.

NTD   Suburban areas, yes. Economists are very dangerous people. Dr Goh is an economist. I am also an economist. It's how you interpret the situation. He looked at it from a very narrow point of view. Anyway, thank goodness, the pro-MRT camp won and the anti-MRT camp lost.

IQ   Was SM in support of this?

NTD   SM was sitting on the fence. Dr Goh enlisted the support of Mr Pillay to challenge me. Mr Pillay was asked to shoot it down. We had a study done. That was why we brought in the Harvard team.[22] The sole aim was to shoot down MINCOM and everybody else who were in favour.

---

[22] A team of transport economists from Harvard University was brought in by the government in 1980 to review the plans for the MRT system, and they recommended an all-bus system instead. In a televised debate that same year, presided over by Prime Minister Lee Kuan Yew, the Harvard team was pitted against another group of consultants who were recommending the MRT system to be built. In 1982, the government decided in favour of the MRT system.

EDB and human capital

NTD After just over two years in MINCOM, then Mr Hon recalled me back to the Finance Ministry, the Economic Development Division. The EDB was actually, I would say, the predecessor of MTI. Actually, it was the Ministry of the Economy, although we were in the Finance Ministry, Economic Development Division.

In 1974, I became Chairman of EDB. By about 1972, hardly five or six years after we launched our export-oriented industrial programme, we had already more or less achieved full employment. I would say our economic planning was from cheap, low-tech, labour-intensive industries. We were trying to upgrade to higher skills. (Even the word "high-tech" wasn't around yet; that came later.)

To do that, we had to really make a breakthrough in education. My role as Chairman of EDB was really, not only as a salesman, but really to push the education and training programme. I had a big fight in those early days with the late Dr Kwan Sai Keong.[23] Are you related to him?

IQ No.

NTD Again, SM stood in the middle. So, the Chairman of EDB was fighting with the Vice-Chancellor. Dr Kwan thought that the university education was only for the elite. You must really be a top brain to benefit from a university education. So, he wanted a smaller university but a very high-powered university. Whereas as Chairman of EDB, I was telling SM, I said, "Look, we don't need geniuses to industrialise. What we need is just competent, well-trained people. More engineers."

So, there was a big debate. I thought we should expand the engineering faculty. I had to write several papers. In that sense, I think Dr Winsemius was instrumental in really helping us. He saw the need for technical manpower. The university, I thought, was playing a very unfair game. We asked him from our side, "Look, okay, to get to university, how many points do you need for 'A' Levels?"

So, he said, "Okay, this is the cut-off point."

But as the results improved, they raised the barrier so that the numbers remained the same. Endless fights, you know. We were really quite frustrated. But in the end, I

---

[23] Vice-Chancellor of the University of Singapore (1975–1980).

think Mr Lee Kuan Yew saw our point. If you really want Singapore to go into high-tech, then an engineering education was the key — technical education.

So EDB, I would say, was really, in a way, taking the initiative in education policy. We really pushed for expansion of the engineering faculty. Then technical training at the polytechnic level and at the ITE [Institute of Technical Education] level.

Our philosophy is very simple. If you have got the skill and you don't overprice yourself, you are bound to get a job from the world. It's really our economic strategy. We are only sellers of labour. So, to sell your labour, first you must have the skill that the customer demands. Secondly, your wage cost must not be out of line with a similarly skilled person in another country.

IQ

But in 1979, I think the NWC [National Wage Council] adopted a high-wage policy.

NTD

I'll come to that. I used to tell SM — not as a slogan, but as a simple way of looking at it — I told him that every year we had to produce 1,000 engineers, 10,000 diploma holders, and maybe twenty or thirty thousand ITE types of labour. I used to tell all my colleagues: "If you produce for me one engineer, I'll produce for you one engineering job."

There was no doubt in my mind that if we could train our people, there would be jobs for our people, provided your wage rate is not out of line. I think EDB was very successful in the early years because we welcomed foreign investments, unlike other countries which tried to keep out foreign investments. They were nationalistic. Of course, today the whole thing has changed now. Today, everybody welcomes foreign investments.

Because of the NWC, we have a guided wage policy. We were quite conservative. We always erred on the lower side of wages. We set our wage level at a level which was actually less than what the market was prepared to pay. Therefore, there was an excessive demand for our labour. Therefore, it led to job-hopping and all the rest of it, shortages of labour, which are actually not good for an industrialising country. There should be no shortage of labour and there should be no job-hopping. Only if you stay long enough in a job, then you pick up the skills. You don't do that when you go around job-hopping.

So, I think our wage level was, in a way, below what we could have gotten. So, in 1979, we started the wage correction policy. I must say that the government accepted that policy with recommendation from Dr Winsemius and myself. But I think they only took one side of the equation. Then we suggested to the government: "We don't want to put the lid on wages. We lift the lid and let wages rise in accordance with market demand."

The other side of the equation which we wanted was: "We should also allow a free flow of foreign labour from outside." That means the Singapore worker had to be prepared to compete on the same basis with a foreigner who has the same skill as he. So, the supply must also be free. I think the government could not accept the other half of the equation, which was the free flow of foreign labour.

IQ   **They put a levy.**

NTD   They put a levy. We were trying to protect the Singapore labour. It makes no sense because you're already short of labour. Why should you protect the Singapore labour? The NTUC was scared that if they did not impose a restraint on foreign labour, then Singapore wages would not rise, which I think is a negative way of looking at things. But unfortunately, the government accepted NTUC's advice against our advice. Our advice was that if you got the skill, there would always be a demand. The employer, between employing a Singaporean and an outsider, will definitely employ a Singaporean. So there was no need for us to, so to speak, artificially engineer for wages to go up, which we did. In fact, by imposing quotas for foreign work permit labour, we were artificially forcing wages up.

I thought there was always a danger of overshooting, which happened. In 1985, we overshot. Our wage rate, including CPF payment, was above what the world was prepared to pay for our labour. Of course, at that time, the neighbouring countries were also not doing very well. But I think the lesson to learn from the 1985 recession was: we overpriced ourselves.

So, in 1995, 10 years later today, I also ask the same question: Have we overpriced ourselves? This is a very serious question which I think MTI ought really to study very carefully. Definitely in 1985, we overpriced ourselves. If you look at the GDP, the share of labour went up very rapidly and the share of capital went down.

We don't seem to have learnt our lesson. That is my great concern today. We recovered rapidly. Again, you can say that the trade unions were very responsible when we reduced the employer CPF. That really amounts to a cut in the labour cost. If we had faced up to competition from the beginning, there would have been no recession in 1985. That means the government mustn't overpay the Singaporean.

I think the economic dilemma today is: What is the right pay for the Singaporean? I have a feeling that all these retrenchments are taking place because we have overpaid ourselves at certain levels. I hope it will never happen. Even the white-collar people. We may have overpaid ourselves. You look at university teachers, administrative officers in the Civil Service, managers in the companies, we may have overpaid ourselves.

The MNCs have no nationalistic attachment to any country. The moment their costs are out of line, if they can hire an engineer, say, in China at half the price that they hire somebody in Singapore, they would move their factory there. They have got no compunction.

The only resource we have is human resource. Which means labour. Labour means wage cost, including CPF and everything else. Through our neglect, if we overpay ourselves, I think the punishment will be very swift.

IQ   **When our wages actually increased, how do we prevent our Singapore products from being overpriced?**

NTD   It must overprice because wages increase. Our dollar became stronger and stronger. Of course, our dollar is strong because our fiscal policy is very prudent. We always achieve a balanced budget or a budget surplus. Today I think we are suffering from that. Rising wages coupled with the strong Singapore dollar means that our price in US dollars for a product is higher than that, say, in South Korea, Taiwan, China, India, whatever. Of course, in certain products, we are still very strong. But I think we have got to watch out.

So, the wage correction policy was actually introduced. I would say the government only implemented the easier half of it. They didn't bite the bullet on the other half of it. I think we are suffering from that wrong turn in the road.

IQ   **From hindsight, did our high wage policy also yield expected results of actually attracting high value-added investments?**

NTD   Actually I have been out of touch with EDB a little bit. If you really look at the electronics industry today, I would say that the companies were already here in the seventies and early eighties. There is no new company that is coming here. It is just an expansion of some of them and then relocation of some of them.

I think the high value-added industries will come only when our R&D [research and development] pays dividends. I think it is still very early to say whether our R&D programmes are going to pay any dividends or not. Maybe our R&D is too academic, too government managed. That one I am not very sure. We are spending quite a bit on R&D today through NSTB [National Science and Technology Board],[24] universities, the whole lot. But I don't see any dividends yet from R&D.

In the last 15 years, I can only think of two really new companies. One is the Petrochemical Corporation of Singapore which I told you about earlier, and the other one maybe is Singapore Technologies, the semi-conductor company, in the last five years. But other than that, our industries have remained the same. The shipyards have been there all along. Singapore Airlines has been there, NOL [Neptune Orient Lines], the banks. So, the new penetration really is the petrol chemical plant which spawned off a lot of other downstream projects. But it is the same thing.

I think the greatest challenge to us today is that the other countries are not practising virtues of good government. The whole environment has changed. Previously, they used to have import substitution industries. Today, everybody is going for export-oriented industries. Previously, they used to reject foreign investments. Today, everybody welcomes foreign investments. Previously, they didn't concentrate on education and training. Today, everybody is throwing money into education and training. Almost everybody.

The so-called Singapore premium is being reduced. In the past, you could say that Singapore wages could be higher than, say, the wages in our competing countries, because of the political stability, better infrastructure, better trained workforce. The premium is still there, but it is being narrowed. Tax incentives. Everybody gives tax incentives. We are at the turning point.

Services industries, in my view, cannot replace manufacturing, which is really, I would say, the foundation. Even the financial sector. Our ACU (Asian Currency Unit) lead has long been eroded already. Everybody is now encouraging fund management. All the same type of activities.

So in competing with the financial sector, you compete on the basis of cost production, the cost of your managers and your accountants, of your

---

[24] Renamed the Agency for Science, Technology and Research (A*STAR) in 2002.

bankers as against the cost of managers, accountants and bankers in Hong Kong, tomorrow maybe Shanghai, or even Kuala Lumpur, and then rentals. Telecommunication network, everybody can pull out. You know what I mean? Satellites.

Services industries, I would say, can relocate far more easily than manufacturing. Manufacturing, you really sink it onto the ground. Service industries, you just hire an office space, telephones, and then there you go off. So, all these merchant banks can come and go.

Sentosa

IQ   **Mr Ngiam, you were also Chairman of the Sentosa Development Corporation.**

NTD   That was really, I would say, like a distraction for me. I think Sentosa couldn't take off because we were half-hearted about it. We were not prepared to sink in the money in order to have a so-called critical mass. When I was in MTI, together with STPB [Singapore Tourism Promotion Board], we put up a $1 billion tourism development programme. Out of that, I think about three or four hundred million dollars was meant for Sentosa. The moment we committed spending this $1 billion, maybe 40 per cent on Sentosa, mainly for the causeway [from mainland Singapore to Sentosa] actually, Sentosa took off. The hotels started coming in. Then all the other attractions started coming in.

I think Sentosa is a case of either you don't start it, or if you want it, you must do it very well. We cannot be half-hearted about it. I think our great mistake about Sentosa in the earlier years was that we were half-hearted. We were not prepared to put in the necessary capital. When I became Permanent Secretary of Trade and Industry, I fought and said, "No, we must give the money."

Then it took off. But on the other hand, we also depended on good leadership. I think Mr Alan Choe is a very imaginative man with a lot of energy. The moment we appointed him as the Chairman of Sentosa, gave him the money, and he really applied himself to it. In fact, if you ask foreign visitors to Singapore, "What do you remember of Singapore?" they will tell you it's Sentosa.

Permanent Secretary at the Prime Minister's Office, and Cabinet Meetings

IQ **You were appointed as the Permanent Secretary to the Prime Minister Office (PS (PMO)).**

NTD For a while I used to work with Mr Howe who was the Head of Civil Service. I used to be like a tough deputy, doing very partially the job of what Mr Lim Siong Guan is doing today. I was PS (PMO) because SM wanted me to sit in Cabinet meetings. Until last October, I stopped. I was sitting in Cabinet meetings for almost 12 or 15 years with Mr Sim [Kee Boon] who was Head of Civil Service, and then later together with Dr Chew [Andrew Chew Guan Khuan].

The Head of Civil Service and PS (PMO) always attended Cabinet meetings. The whole idea was to give us a good overview of what the government was thinking of. You had no executive functions, but they really thought that we should have a good overview so that in our respective ministries, I could brief the Permanent Secretaries on what the government really wants done. Today, Mr Lee Ek Tieng and Mr Lim Siong Guan are now sitting there.

I had no operational duties in PMO but more at the policy level. Coordination of policy or dissemination of policy — that was the role. It was a very, I would say, low-profile kind of role. It was a very useful role.

IQ **From your observations by sitting in the Cabinet meetings for the last 12 to 15 years, do you observe any change in the style?**

NTD I don't know whether I could speak a word. I would say I found the earlier years far more interesting than the later years. In the earlier years, I would say, there were three or four heavyweights in Cabinet — SM, Goh Keng Swee, Rajaratnam and Hon Sui Sen. In those early days, SM used to have a discussion. But when they left, then SM regarded Mr Goh and his colleagues as a younger team. So, there was less debate.

But on the other hand, he changed it a little bit. In the early days, everything he wanted to discuss, he'd discuss in the Cabinet meeting proper. But when Mr Goh and the younger people came in, the Cabinet Secretary Wong Chooi Sen and the two of us just attended the formal part of Cabinet. It means that the Cabinet papers were already produced, decisions more or less arrived at. We were just there to witness what decisions they were making, so to speak. But after the Cabinet meeting proper, then

SM will, I would say like a tutor, discuss politics. So, he divided it into two parts. But in the early days, there was only one. There were sometimes very honest differences of views — Dr Goh on economics, Mr Rajaratnam on politics, Hon Sui Sen on finance. Very interesting. They regarded each other more as equals.

The government's budgeting system

IQ   **As the Permanent Secretary in Finance (Budget) since 1987 ...**

NTD   After all the years in the frontline, Budget in fact is a sort of a backroom job. I wanted to decentralise the whole budgeting system, but with accountability. Secondly, I have also, through the budgeting system, tried to make the Permanent Secretary and Deputy Secretary more and more managerial. Actually, they should manage their own resources and produce the results for themselves. Previously, I would have said that first and foremost, we did not give them the authority and therefore, they were not responsible for their results.

So, the first step I took was that I introduced the block budgeting system. I told each Permanent Secretary: "This is the pie that I have, the GDP growth. Out of that, we will tax maybe 20 per cent of GDP. This is the sum of money. Each Ministry will get a certain share of this pie. What you do with your share is essentially your business. I am not going to tell you what to do with your share of the pie. As far as movement of people around, it's up to you. You want to transfer from Department A to Department B, that is your job. But you keep the overall figure the same."

So, I tried to inject some freedom of action for them. In a way, I was quite disappointed because most of them still took the attitude that "if Finance says yes, okay; if Finance says no, then we go and argue." They did not exercise the freedom which I gave them. So, in a way, I would say, I am not fully satisfied. Now I move to the final stage of budget reform, which is budgeting for results, which I am introducing from this year.

Previously, their attitude was: "Okay, you give me $100, then I'll get so many things done for you for $100."

But from today actually, I am asking them: "You tell me what you're going to do first? What is your output? Then I will give you enough money to produce the output. At the end of the year, we will then audit whether or not, having got the money, you produced the output that you promised to deliver?"

And I told them that the customer really is their own Minister, the politician. He is the customer. He is going to say: "Okay, this is what I want you to do in the coming year. I am ordering this unit of service from you."

So, Finance Ministry will say: "Okay, if that is what your customer wants and the Cabinet agrees, then we will work out the unit cost."

Take the universities. "You want to produce so many students a year. We know this is the unit cost. If your enrolment goes up, we provide you with more money. If your enrolment goes down, then less money. But within that sum of money, you want to spend it on computers, higher salaries for the teachers or what, well, we won't say anything. At the end of the year, we will audit you, and you give us the output."

That's accountability. Today, they just argue with me for the sum of money. Then having got the money, they just do what they like. But they never come back and tell me whether or not they have achieved what they set out to do. But from now on, every year we have to scrutinise.

I am having a trial run now, starting in July. I told them: "Okay, last year you spent so much money. You know actually how much, 100 million, 200 million dollars. For that amount of money, can you please just list out very approximately what is your performance and what is it that you have achieved?"

Recently I had a meeting with MFA [Ministry of Foreign Affairs]. Quite interesting. MFA thought that their product was very intangible. No, not quite. They were able to say: "We attended so many policy meetings. We prepared so many visits for the PM [Goh Chok Tong], SM [Lee Kuan Yew] or whoever. We received so many visitors. We have to tackle so many crises in relationship and all that. This is the sum of money that was spent to produce that."

Then I told them: "Okay, what I want you to do now is this. Now you've got SIGMA, the accounting system. You know how much it costs you to host, say, a Commonwealth Finance Ministers' meeting here in Singapore. Or how much does it cost for you to prepare SM in one of his foreign missions, or the PM and so on."

Even MFA could come out with a good listing of what they did last year and what is it they are going to do in 1995 and 1996. In other words, the Permanent Secretary has to be more pro-active, become like a company CEO. So, I told them: "Actually, Parliament is the shareholder. Your customer is your Minister. Parliament is the shareholder. The Budget Division is like your auditor and accountant."

It's a new experiment. We are on a joint exploration. But I think it will lead to a lot of good because I want the civil servants, the senior officers, not only to be a staff man writing policy papers, blah, blah, blah, but to be a manager. At the end of the day, having spent a lifetime as a Permanent Secretary or whatever position as civil servant, do you consider yourself a professional? It's a serious question we must ask ourselves. Are you a professional? Are we professionals? Or are we just talented amateurs? I haven't answered that question myself.

IQ **Professional administrator?**

NTD Yes, professional administrator. Are we? Whereas if you are the President of a bank, I would say, "Okay, you are a professional." If I want to start another bank, then I look at you. We are prepared to pay you whatever amount of money. I have maybe 70 per cent certainty that you are going to deliver certain things to me. But as a Permanent Secretary, suppose when you retire, a business organisation takes you over. Where is your professionalism?

Tommy Koh

Singapore's representative at the United Nations

Date of interviews: June 1998
Interviewer: Irene Quah

Professor Tommy Koh (b. 1937) is known for his many roles and contributions to Singapore, key among them being his time at the United Nations (UN).

Koh studied law at the University of Malaya in Singapore, Harvard University and the University of Cambridge. During his tenure as a law lecturer at the University of Singapore, Koh was appointed Singapore's Permanent Representative to the UN in 1968 at the young age of 30. His stints at the UN — punctuated by his term as Dean of the Faculty of Law at the University of Singapore from 1971 to 1974 — culminated in his presidency of the Third UN Conference on the Law of the Sea (UNCLOS), which resulted in a seminal international treaty which defines ocean boundaries, as well as the rights and responsibilities of states with regard to the marine environment. In 1984, Koh became Singapore's ambassador to the US.

After returning to Singapore in 1990, Koh served in many capacities, including as the first Executive Director of the Asia-Europe Foundation, the Director of the Institute of Policy Studies, and the Chairman of the National Arts Council. He is also known for his role as part of the team representing Singapore at the International Court of Justice in 2008 in the Pedra Branca dispute case with Malaysia, for which Koh was conferred with the Order of Nila Utama (First Class) by the Singapore government.

In these interviews, Koh shared about how he was approached by then Prime Minister Lee Kuan Yew to be Singapore's Permanent Representative to the UN, and how he tried to convince Lee to set up a Foreign Service. Koh also discussed his experience in presiding over UNCLOS, as well as Singapore's role in the UN following Vietnam's invasion of Cambodia in 1978 to 1979.

Appointment as Permanent Representative to the UN

IQ We now move on to your diplomatic experience. You did mention in our last session that you spent 1965 to 1968 teaching at the university.

TK Yes.

IQ Then one day you had a call from SM [Senior Minister Lee Kuan Yew, then Prime Minister] who offered the job as the Singapore Permanent Representative to the UN. Could you recall the actual event of that?

TK Yes, it was at City Hall, his office was at City Hall then. We had known each other since I was a first-year law student. We were not strangers to each other. We were not close. But he had known me from my first year at the Law School as he had come to give us a talk. I was very impressed by him as I have always been. In fact, I had asked him a very stupid question which he answered very gently at that time [laughs]. Because of my activist role in the Socialist Club and the Student Union, I had also met him because I had invited him to speak on campus.

But from 1965 to 1968, I had never met him one to one. So it was a bit of a surprise to get a request to see him, which I went for. I thought "Boy! He was going to say, 'Why have you been saying and writing all these nasty things about my government and about me?'" So I was really quite surprised when he said, "You know, we need to find somebody for the UN," and his colleagues and he had come to the conclusion that I was the best person they could think of. I said, "It cannot be." I was only 30, I had no diplomatic experience. "How can I be your Perm Rep to the UN?"

But then our nation was young then. We were only three years old. We had no foreign service. So I guess the government was quite desperately looking around for people and he then said, "Why don't you take a week off and think about it?" Then he called me back. In the mean time, I really agonised over whether to accept.

First, because I felt I was inadequate for the job. Second, I was newly-married, and my wife was still in the final year of medical school. So it meant leaving her behind. I was very reluctant to accept but she urged me to take it. She said, "It's okay, I will join you seven months later if you think this is an experience that will be helpful to your law teaching career. Why not accept the appointment."

IQ   **So she stayed back to finish her medical studies?**

TK   Yes, she stayed back for seven months and then she came to join me.

IQ   **So did you have any prior preparations before actually going to the UN?**

TK   No [laughs]. I still remember the Foreign Ministry, in City Hall, was just a suite of a few rooms with Mr Rajaratnam, as the Minister. Was it Stanley Steward, his Permanent Secretary at the time? And just a few fellows. We had no UN division, no desk officer in-charge of UN. So they knew as little about UN as I. So they were in no position to help me.

IQ   **So there was nothing, no brief, no ...**

TK   So there was nothing.

IQ   **Nothing?**

TK   I was just told that "Your job is to go and listen and learn and to report back and help us to understand better how the UN works, to make friends for Singapore." Very general guidelines were given. I was completely unprepared for what I found when I arrived.

First, nobody even told me in Singapore that I was the Chairman of the Asian Group. When I arrived, Wong Lin Ken was delighted to turn over the baton to me so that he could go back to Washington. He said, "Oh, Tommy, congratulations! By the way, I didn't tell you, you are the Chairman of the Asian Group and next Monday, you have to chair a meeting of the group." I said, "What? Why didn't you tell me? I would have delayed my arrival!"

Then on Monday, I turned up at the UN, which I had not been to since my internship, to chair the Asian Group, most of whose members were twice my age or older. And they were all wondering, "Who is this young kid who is chairing the meeting?" And I still remember that one seasoned ambassador tried to pull a fast one on me. Before the meeting started, he came and said, "Oh, Ambassador Koh, we have one request.

My country is a candidate for a certain office. Can you please announce our candidature and ask the group to endorse our candidature?" At least, I was not stupid to say, "Yes, yes, I will do for you." I said, "No, I will call on you. Why don't you make your own announcement?" And sure enough when they did it, the ambassador of another country jammed it up [laughs].

But it was a very exciting entry. I had a busy month as Chairman of the Asian Group. Then the following month, September, I was the Chairman of our Afro-Asian group which, at that time, was an influential group. It's since faded away. In my capacity as Chairman, I had to convene several meetings of the group, to hear heads of state and government who wanted to address the group. Then it coincided also with the Warsaw Pact countries' invasion of Czechoslovakia.

So I had a really interesting entry into the real world. The acting Perm Rep of Czechoslovakia came to call on me to plead for my good support. He said, "Look! The Warsaw Pact has invaded my country against our will. It's suppressing our aspirations for independence."

IQ **As you mentioned Singapore had just gained independence in 1965, so how important was the UN as a forum for Singapore then?**

TK One, we still had a concern which we don't have now. It was our legitimacy. There was a communist-inspired campaign to say that Singapore was not truly independent, that it was some kind of neo-colonial machination. There was a concern about the world accepting us as a sovereign and independent state. My first job was to ensure that we were accepted by the world as a sovereign and independent state, which I think I did accomplish during my first three years.

My second job was to be the "ears" and "eyes" of Singapore and try to understand how the UN works, and through the UN, to keep track of contemporary developments around the world. I tried to make as many friends as possible for Singapore and to project a good image of Singapore.

IQ **How big was your mission in the UN?**

TK Oh, very small. When I first started, when I arrived in 1968, there were just two of us — myself and Tan Siak Leng who was a Singaporean working in the UN Secretariat, and whom we encouraged to leave the Secretariat in order to join the mission.

I had as my second deputy, See Chak Mun — our current ambassador in Geneva. Chak Mun was cross-posted from Washington. So there were just two of us — a two-man mission [laughs]. But we were both learning.

We were happy and we got along quite well. We were just happy to be representing Singapore at the UN and learning something new everyday about the world, about the UN. So we had a good time together. That was a team, just the two of us.

Making friends for Singapore

IQ   **You mentioned that in your first three years [at the UN], you made a lot of friends, and your other task was to project a good image of Singapore.**

TK   But the most important was to overcome whatever doubts and reservations the world had about the legitimacy of Singapore as an independent sovereign state. That was number one.

IQ   **Was there any memorable encounters of the diplomatic circuit in the UN which you can recall?**

TK   The UN had and always has had very charismatic individuals and even eccentric ones. And it was no different during my first three years. I had met some of these individuals. They had always stayed in my memories. But in terms of learning about diplomacy, international politics, I would say the Warsaw Pact invasion of Czechoslovakia in August 1968 was a climactic event for me, because it showed that the world was still ruled by force rather than by law. In 1968, the Soviet Ambassador to the UN was a man called Yakov Malik who had no compunction about telling the most awful lies to the whole world.

First, he denied that his country had invaded Czechoslovakia. And then when this was undeniable, because you could see it was in the public domain with photos and so on, then he said, "Oh, we were invited in." I was not impressed. I think that episode made me very anti-Machiavelli, because Machiavelli, in his advice to the Prince, had said that one must lie and dissemble in order to succeed. The world is full of gullible people and you can always deceive them. I feel that in this modern world, Machavelli's advice was bad advice and that when Yakov Malik told all those lies, he reduced his own credibility to zero. And none of us was deceived. So I think it reinforced my belief that one should be honest and one should not tell lies even in your country's national interest [laughs]. And especially not to tell lies when the evidence against you is so accessible. But that was a big thing in 1968.

Other than that, I don't remember the big events. But I had a very happy time. I made many friends and got to know, for the first time, Africans and Arabs, people with cultures I had never met before. I also made many good friends among the Latin Americans. I tried really hard to understand the different cultures, history, so that I could be better friends to them.

IQ **So as the newcomer to the UN circuit, how did you go about cultivating the friendship?**

TK I was very hardworking ...

IQ **Because they were all from different nationalities?**

TK Yes, but it was a club. UN was a club and is a club, the Perm Reps of the UN constitute a club. It's like belonging to a club. You see each other every day and after a while, friendships formed and if you are bright, people would take note of you and invite you to functions. If you have no value, people wouldn't invite you.

So I found that I was quite popular and was invited to many functions by the Europeans, the Arabs and Latinos. So I made a lot of friends. But maybe because I was exceptionally young, I also appealed to people with maternal or paternal instincts, which was good. So I had a lot of "uncles" and "aunts" who sort of took me under their wings and were particularly kind to me, including U Thant — the UN Secretary-General — who was a wonderful man from Myanmar, then known as Burma. U Thant treated me like his nephew. He was very kind to me and his Chef de Cabinet who was from India — C.V. Narasimhan — was very kind to me. So a lot of the older guys felt that because I was young, I was from a young country, they went out of their ways to be nice to me and when I needed advice, they were accessible.

I remember U Thant even invited me home for dinner. And his Burmese Perm Rep, U Soe Tin, was like an uncle to me. I went to see him recently, by the way, in Myanmar. He's still alive, in his 80s. When I went to Yangon in December last year with my older son. I invited him to dinner.

IQ **So the support staff at the UN, did they only remain at one, or did they increase in number?**

TK In the first years, I had a third person who was looking after the administration of the mission and so on. Just the three of us.

Setting up a career foreign service

IQ **So upon the return of your tour of duty in 1971, you had urged strongly for the setting up of a career foreign service by the Singapore government?**

TK Yes.

IQ **You were quoted as saying that diplomacy was "too serious a business to leave to amateurs."**

TK Lee Kuan Yew was very sceptical. It took me a long time to convince him. I remember having long discussions with him at lunch. It took me a while to convince him. Our Civil Service believes that if you are a bright kid you will get inducted into the Admin Service. You can do any job. I can be at Ministry of Health today, tomorrow I can run MOF [the Ministry of Finance], the day after I can be in Defence. So why not the Foreign Service, right? It's a very logical extension of the belief that a bright boy or girl will very quickly learn the work of any department or Ministry or agency. But I have always believed that in the Foreign Ministry, we are dealing with a body of specialised knowledge. Sure, you can learn it all. But you need an esprit de corps, it's like Mindef, you are like warriors of peace. You need an esprit de corps, you need continuity, you need an institutional memory, and there are skills that you have to cultivate, and you can't just do it overnight.

The other obstacles I had to overcome was Mr Lee's belief at the time that no bright boy or girl would join the Foreign Service because it was so small. That a bright boy or girl would rather join the Admin Service because they could serve in huge ministries like Defence and Finance and MND [the Ministry of National Development].

But, in the end, I managed to convince him that there were some people who would be attracted to a career in the Foreign Service because it caters to their interests. That not everybody thinks in the same way as he does, in terms how I can advance my career to my maximum potential, or how I can earn the highest salary in the public service. So there are many of us like me, I am not interested in my rank or the pay I get, it's the satisfaction I get from the work I do. And I told him once that there is such a thing as psychic income. He laughed. He said, "No such thing." He is very cynical. I said, "There's such a thing as psychic income." And I said, "It's very important for you to recognise that in addition to the pay cheque we get, there's such a thing as psychic income." I said, "Why would people opt to be a teacher, right? A very bright boy and girl can get a better paying job elsewhere, higher social prestige and so on."

IQ   **When you first became a diplomat, from what you recall, what was the status of joining the Foreign Service? At that point of time, we were a very young nation, so a lot of priority was placed on, say, our economic survival. An economist would have enjoyed higher status than, say, a Foreign Service officer or an army officer?**

TK   I don't know, I can't answer that. At that time, university professors were more admired than now, I think. But there were very few ambassadors at the time. So the few of us who made it were a rare breed. So there was more prestige attached to being an ambassador in 1968 than, I would say, 30 years later, because there were very few of us. But I don't know, it just never crossed my mind. It's not on my agenda. I mean, I am not interested in prestige or money. So I was asked to do it and as a good son of Singapore, I said, "Okay, I will do it."

IQ   **Why did you think that with the creation of a career foreign service, the professionalism and efficiency of the Foreign Service would be improved?**

TK   Why? Because I had observed how other countries work, that I could see that even small countries like New Zealand have a world class Foreign Service. And we learned a lot from them, we asked them to teach our people, we borrowed their papers as a model for our officers to emulate. When SM needed briefing, I remember at one time on China, one of the people who briefed him was Bryce Harland, a New Zealand diplomat. The British had one of the best Foreign Services in the world. So you could see some countries have a really world-class Foreign Service and not just big countries, even small countries.

IQ **In your view, what makes a good diplomat?**

TK Oh, boy! How to answer that?

IQ **Or what kind of quality would the person ...**

TK Hard to generalise. You know, I have met good diplomats who are very sociable and good diplomats who are not very sociable. I have met good diplomats who are of a rather cynical caste of mind. Most of the Singapore diplomats are, by the way. I have met good diplomats who are very idealistic like me. I have met diplomats who have a great power imagination and others who have got a great sense of realism. So very hard to generalise, I would say.

First, I think that there's no escaping that you need to have a good mind. If you don't have a good mind, then no matter what your other qualities of personality are, charm and so on, I would not regard you as a good diplomat. A good mind. Second, an interest in the world and, through hard work, be willing to keep with the developments around the world. So that you are very knowledgeable. Third, I think, a person who likes other people. I think it helps in diplomacy; you like people because people will reciprocate your good will, and like you.

Fourth, I would say, a person who has an open mind who therefore can interact with other countries, other peoples, other cultures with as little prejudice as possible, who are willing to judge other people in their own context rather than imposing your frame of reference on them.

And finally I would say that a good diplomat should have qualities of integrity and professionalism. I don't admire diplomats, no matter successful they are, who are scheming and dishonest. Some of them are successful. I have met at the UN people who were very successful, much admired by my colleagues, but I don't admire them. Why? Because they fall short of some of my own criteria — honesty and integrity being two important ones.

So, very hard to answer your question because I cannot say that if you lack certain qualities, you will not be successful, because I have seen men who are successful. But even evil people can succeed. This is a very unfair world, right? So it does not follow that if you are a good person, you will succeed in life. And it does not follow unfortunately that if you are an evil person, you will not succeed in life. This is the wicked world in which we lived.

248 • SPEAKING TRUTH TO POWER

IQ **What has the government done to improve the quality of our Foreign Service officers?**

TK I think the pay is good. The pay, the conditions of work, the sense of esprit de corps are there. The satisfaction that we get from accomplishing great tasks on behalf of our country is there. I think the unhappiness now relates to what is perceived by the young ones as the unfair and unreasonable induction right at the top, of people from outside the Foreign Service.

As a result, some young ones have resigned. They said, "What's the point of my staying? I could never rise to be a Deputy Secretary or Perm Sec." It's clear that the government's agenda is that they will bring people in from the Admin Service to fill these top jobs. In my view, it is wrong, it's unnecessary and it is very demoralising to the Service. So I don't understand why the Cabinet is doing it, but it is doing it.

Law school dean, and back to the UN

IQ **In 1974, you were re-appointed as Singapore's Permanent Representative to the UN. Could you relate to us the circumstances of the re-appointment?**

TK Yes, but I would like to first go back to the interregnum of three years when I was back here [in Singapore], because they were three wonderful years. On my way home, my Law Faculty colleagues punished me for being absent for three years by making me Dean. Because in those days, they elected their Dean, it was not appointed. Which I thought was not fair to me, because I had been away for three years and suddenly when I arrived, [the then Dean Thio] Su Mien said, "Oh, Tommy, I am so happy to congratulate you. You are my successor. They have elected you Dean." I said, "Why! Here am I, just coming back and trying to catch up with the progress of the law during the three years I was away." Now, I found that I had to administer the faculty. I wanted also to set the pace. So during the three years as Dean, I taught as many courses as I assigned to my colleagues, and I published as much as anybody else, because I wanted to be a good leader, and to be a leader by example. But as I looked back on the three years, they were very good years because I had a very young and brilliant team.

And in a way, I regretted going away in 1974 because the team disappeared. It was essential that I was there to hold it together. When I went away, the team disintegrated. People left and it was a shame. But it was a good time. Because I was very young, I was very close to the students. I felt that I was incrementally building a better Law School both in terms of the quality of teaching and research; the very close rapport that existed between teachers and students; and the reputation that we were gaining overseas, as a good Law School.

In my three years, I also did some regionalisation which was ahead of my time. I entered into exchange schemes with Indonesian law schools in Jakarta, Bandung, and Surabaya, exchanging staff, teaching materials and so on. Which all disappeared when I left in 1974. I liked the academic life. I was very happy on campus.

So when Lee Kuan Yew asked me in 1974 [to return to the UN as Singapore's Permanent Representative], I said, "No." But the third time he asked me, I told my wife I had to go. I think I could not say no to my Prime Minister the third time. She was very reluctant to leave because our second son was born in 1972. She wanted to bring up the two boys here because she's more foresightful than I. She foresaw that there would be problems for our kids if they grew up abroad, and she didn't want to leave till they were grown. So she said, "Why can't you tell Mr Lee to send us back to UN twenty years later." I said, "Gee, I can't tell him that." She didn't want to leave because she said it would create problems for our kids. Which was true, it came true.

IQ **Did she start her medical practice after she came back?**

TK She was going to. She wanted to first complete the family, but after Aun was born, she thought once Aun was a little older, she wanted to return to medicine. But that plan also got aborted, because the second time we went abroad was for so long. We were away for 16 years.

They were also very wonderful years. I think I am incorrigible, right? [Laughs] Every period of my life, I tell you is wonderful [laughs]. I was very happy at the UN, in the following ten years, because I had this great challenge of bringing the Law of the Sea Conference to a successful conclusion. By that time, I also had a higher state of knowledge about the UN and how it works. I became better known to my colleagues, and I was much sought after by my colleagues. So you sort of became part of the elite of the club.

I enjoyed my years at the UN very much. I also had this major confrontation with Vietnam over Cambodia, which was the second challenge I had. And the third challenge I had at the UN was to prevent the Soviet Union from hijacking the Non-Aligned Movement, which almost came true in 1979. So I had major battles and challenges to fight. And then to fight against protectionism, in civil aviation by Australia, by the West in trade. I was sent all over the place. I was sent by the government to UNCTAD V [Fifth session of the United Nations Conference on Trade and Development] in Manila to beat up the

Australians which we succeeded in doing. I had to persuade the UN General Assembly to adopt a resolution opposing protectionism in all its forms because, at one time, we felt very threatened by what we saw was an increasing tide of protectionism. So it took me some doing, some persuasion, and a lot of lobbying to get that through.

But the campaign against Vietnam on Cambodia was a very major campaign that would absorb over ten years of my life. It began in December 1978 and really didn't end till October 1991, when we signed Paris Agreement. So I have devoted a big chunk of my life to Cambodia.

IQ   **In 1971, after you came back, who succeeded you?**

TK   Jayakumar. At first, the government wouldn't let me come home until I found a successor. So I said, "What about my good friend from the Law Faculty — Jayakumar?" At first, the SM opposed my choice. He said, "How can I send this man to the UN? He never opens his mouth. Are you sure he can talk?" [Laughs] I said, "Yes, he can talk but he is a very quiet person. He is very competent and he will be all right." Like me, Jayakumar had also worked at the UN. After Yale, he had worked as an intern in the UN in the Human Rights Division. So at least he had some knowledge.

IQ   **And you were made the key spokesman for the developing nations, then later the principal draftsman for sensitive articles of the UN Conference in the Law of the Sea?**

TK   Not for the developing countries, because I was viewed more and more as a good honest broker by various groups and countries. So I think I have gained a reputation as being a competent lawyer and negotiator, but also as somebody who was able to rise above his own cause to be an honest broker between competing interests.

IQ   **But nevertheless, you were the chief spokesman.**

TK   No, that was not true, I was a spokesman. But I have never wanted to be just a spokesman for the developing countries. I wanted my cause to have a very secure base. I wanted the developing countries to look up to me. And I never betrayed their interests. But, I wanted to transcend that and to be viewed by the developed world as someone they could trust. Someone who could negotiate compromises that would accommodate their legitimate interests as well as those of the developing countries. I didn't want to be just viewed as a spokesman for developing countries. As I began to take on more of the role of chairman of negotiating groups and negotiations, then my role as a spokesperson for the developing countries was diminished in a commensurate way, because I could not be viewed by the North as being partisan. But I always made sure that my constituency was strong. I was one of the few Chairmen of big conferences at the UN who would regularly request meetings with the African group, the Asian group, the Latin American group, the Group of 77, because I wanted to be sure that their perceptions of me were that I was from the South, that I understood their interests; that while my job as chairman of a conference required that I rise above the partisan interests of my constituency, I would never betray them.

So I went out of my way. I would ask to brief them, to speak to them and there were times when I had to make compromises that would appear to them to not be in their best interests. Rather than run away from them, I asked to speak to them. I went in and explained patiently why I had to make the difficult choices that I had to. And I must say they were always very kind to me. People always gave me a good hearing. Once they listened, they knew I was trustworthy.

The other thing they knew was that I was not a running dog for anybody. So I never conducted any secret negotiations. Whatever I did, I did it out in the open. Be transparent. And, when I had to hold a closed door small group negotiation, I would explain to the entirety of the conference why I was going to do that. In the Earth Summit, I had to do that at one critical point. I told them, "I am sorry. I cannot have a negotiating process that involves 175 countries. It's not possible. We will run out of time in 24 hours. If you want me to deliver, then you give me a mandate to have a closed door negotiation that involves only 16 countries." And I told them, "You developing countries, you choose your eight representatives. And you, the developed countries, you choose your eight representatives." And I said, "No observers, no gallery to play to." They gave me the mandate, so there was no resentment against me. So when I met behind closed doors with no observers, and if somebody wanted to gate-crash, I threw them out.

One of my African friends was holding secret negotiations and I was a member of his group. But you know things would eventually leak. I believed that you shouldn't do anything in secret because it would leak. Although we spent weeks in this secret negotiating group and we produced what I thought were very good compromises, they were rebuffed — not because the product was no good, but because the process was not acceptable. So I learned a very valuable lesson from that. Never do things like that.

252 • SPEAKING TRUTH TO POWER

As President of the Third UN Conference on the Law of the Sea (1980–1982)

TK   Before I returned [to Singapore after my first stint at the UN], I wrote to the Senior Minister to point out that the UN was about to launch a historic lawmaking exercise relating to the sea. Since the sea was so important to Singapore's livelihood and national interest, I felt that this was one exercise which we should get into, because of the importance of the port, the sea lanes and so on.

    I think it convinced him and the Cabinet that if Singapore did not play a proactive role in this exercise, we would not be able to protect our interest in the freedom of navigation, in ensuring that our interest as a port state was properly taken into account. And this led to Jayakumar, Chao Hick Tin, S. Tiwari and myself playing a major role in the whole Law of the Sea Conference.

    When I came home in 1971, Jayakumar took over from me, and he served in the Preparatory Committee for the Conference on the Law of the Sea. And then I went back in 1974, just in time for the conference to begin and spent eight years of my life helping to negotiate the historic treaty.

    But, my being selected later on to become President of the Law of the Sea Conference was completely fortuitous. It was because the President died. The Asian Group had two brilliant candidates from Sri Lanka and Fiji who had equal support in the group, and neither would concede to the other. In the end, the Asian Group, through [then Indonesian Foreign Minister] Mochtar Kusumaatmadja, brokered a deal whereby he managed to persuade both my Asian brothers to stand down, and for the Group to appeal to me to be the compromise candidate. That's why I became the President of the Conference.

IQ   **What was your reaction on being asked to serve as its President?**

TK   I felt that Satya Nandan of Fiji had contributed so much to the Conference and that the honour should have gone to him, but unfortunately he was blocked by Chris Pinto of Sri Lanka. The first thing I did was to bring the family together. So I included both Chris Pinto and Satya Nandan in my collegium. I sort of created a leadership group and assigned to each of them some negotiating responsibility. I think it's partly a reflection of my own nature. And partly the wisdom I have learned from watching others.

    So I created unity in Asian Group. I then wanted to create unity in the Conference so I had, in fact, daily meetings of the Chairmen of all the regional groups, interest groups. I don't believe in keeping everything to myself, so I devolved responsibility to able men and women to help me conduct negotiations. I included all of them in what I called the collegium. We met every day. It was my routine every day, as I am a very early riser, so I punished all my colleagues by making them turn up early for work. I would have a daily meeting at nine o'clock with my collegium. Then at 9.30, a meeting of the Chairmen of all the regional interest groups; and then I would meet the Secretariat. The other thing I did was unlike some Chairman who excluded the Secretariat I used the Secretariat because I talent-spotted good people in the Secretariat and said, "I want you to work with me."

But I knew I faced very formidable challenges. And in my last year there, it was very stressful because whatever was not resolved, the conference wanted me to take them over personally. So in that final year, I found that I was conducting so many simultaneous negotiations on so many things. It was really stressful and I was not sure if I could do it. But because of the tremendous support I got from the Conference, because I had enlisted very able people to help me, with the help of the Secretariat, we succeeded in the end.

But it was a close call. This was true in the Law of the Sea and also in the Earth Summit. Having learned all these lessons from the Law of the Sea, when I was asked 10 years later to chair the Preparatory Committee for the Earth Summit and then the main negotiation in Rio [de Janeiro] itself, I was able to modify, adapt the lessons that I had learned from the Law of the Sea to chairing this even bigger negotiation. But when you are the chairman of the negotiation, at the end of the day, fate really lies in your hands. Whether you succeed or fail depends very much on whether you deliver or you don't deliver. So right to the end, you never know. And you could make or break.

In Rio, I didn't know even at the final stage, we met without a break. We started in the morning, adjourned for lunch. Started at 3 o'clock, adjourned for dinner. Started at 8 pm again and went through the night. At 4 am in the morning, I was still not sure I was going to make it or not. It was only at 6 o'clock in the morning that I felt I was close to the end. By that time, I think I could scale Mount Everest — "Go for it!" And I really pushed it through. But that was a very long night and there were so much drama during that night. At no moment was anybody sure whether it was going to succeed or fail. And even the members of the Secretariat sitting next to me, behind me, were not sure, you know. When it was all over, they thought I had schemed the whole thing, that I had planned everything to end at 6 o'clock sharp.

I told my friend, "You must be kidding, you know." I said, "I have no idea if the night was going to end successfully or in utter failure. How could I possibly predict our end of the conference at 6 am sharp?" I said it was just good fortune.

254 • SPEAKING TRUTH TO POWER

IQ **What was the impact of the refusal by the US and some of the Western countries which actually did not sign the treaty?**

TK Well, a few of the allies followed them by not signing at the time — the UK, Germany, to keep them company, to maintain this facade of solidarity. But it didn't bother me because I knew history would vindicate me. And I knew at the end of the day, the Americans would come to the conclusion when a more sensible administration took over, that it would be in the national interest of the United States — because we had secured for them all the national security interests they wanted in terms of passage rights, on the surface of the sea, underwater passage right for the submarines and so on. And in terms of protecting their fishing interests, as they have such huge coast on both sides. So I felt that history would vindicate me, and I was not bothered.

And I knew that the Germans had a vested interest in coming on board at the last moment, because the tribunal was going to be based in Hamburg. So I knew, okay, they could stay out but at the end of the day, they would lose their right to host the Law of the Sea Tribunal. So I knew the Germans would be on board.

IQ **One hundred and nineteen nations signed the UN Convention on the Law of the Sea. What personal satisfaction did you gain in steering the UN members through the critical final stages?**

TK I think my friends were more proud of me than I was of myself, actually. I just felt that I was given a job to do, and I had put my heart and soul to doing a good job. That's it. In fact I did something extraordinary. When the treaty was finished, Javier Pérez de Cuéllar [the then UN Secretary-General] offered me the top post at the UN to look after the Law of the Sea and legal matters. I turned him down. He couldn't understand, he said, "Why?" And I said, "Well, I didn't want the world to think that I wanted to be President of the Conference so that I could get a job in the international system afterwards."

So I declined and I nominated Satya Nandan. I did him one big favour. I got Satya Nandan this job in the UN as Under-Secretary-General. And then when the treaty came into force, the government of Jamaica invited me to Jamaica for the big ceremony. I didn't go. Germany invited me to Hamburg to witness the opening of the Sea Tribunal. I also didn't go because I didn't want to seek glory. I mean, if you get the job done, history will vindicate you, people will remember you. So why go to all these?

Just as when I completed the Earth Summit, [Boutros] Boutros-Ghali [the UN Secretary-General after Pérez de Cuéllar] also offered me a job at the UN as the Under-Secretary-General for Sustainable Development. So when I said no to him, he was very angry with me. He asked, "What you have got against me?" I said, "I got nothing against you." "Why are you not accepting this job?" I said, "You know, you go and speak to Javier Pérez de Cuéllar. He offered a similar job on the Law of the Sea and I turned him down also." He said, "Why?" I said, "Since I chaired this Conference, I don't want to go on to a job. Otherwise there would be a perception that I chaired the conference in order to get this job." He said, "Nobody suspects that of you." I said, "No, no, I don't want the job. I don't need the job." I said, "Why don't you give it to one of my good friends?" So I gave him a list of people. He did appoint one of them — Nitin Desai from India.

IQ **What's the importance of the UN Convention on the Law of the Sea for a small place like Singapore?**

TK Well, I think it is important to all states, in the sense that it settles a law. There was a period in the 1960s and even the 1970s when the law was in a flux. Nobody knew for certain what was the extent of the territorial sea we could claim. Nobody knew what their fishing rights were. Nobody knew what are the limits of their continental shelf were if it contained oil and gas. Therefore, very important to countries. Nobody was very clear about the rights of ships. When they went through straits like the Straits of Malacca, through an archipelago like Indonesia, what the status of the water of these straits and archipelagos were.

So there are many conflicts between states because the law was uncertain. So my great satisfaction is that I played a modest part in helping to settle the law and write a new constitution for the oceans. This was important to all countries, not just to Singapore. But Singapore is one of the beneficiaries of the treaty because it settles the law on international straits, it settles the law on passage rights through archipelagos. It settles the law on port states, the rights of port states, and I think it has achieved, in my view, an equitable balance between the rights of the coastal states and the rights of the international community.

So in that sense, the treaty has been good for Singapore and good for the world, and that's exactly the kind of opportunities I have always looked for in my life — which is to do the right thing for my country, and to also do something good for the world. Both the Law of the Sea and the Earth Summit gave me opportunities to do that.

IQ   **I do recall that one of the issues not covered in the 1982 Convention relates to competing claims to sovereignty over disputed islands or territories?**

TK   Well, it could not be, because these claims are bilateral or multilateral in nature. The treaty cannot settle these claims. They have to be negotiated and if negotiations fail, they must be adjudicated, arbitrated or mediated. So that was not something I could do. So at the end, near the closing date of the Conference, I chaired the negotiation between groups of states like Turkey on one side and Greece on the other, that had disputes over islands or maritime boundaries and wrote a compromise which both sides could accept. But which can't settle their specific disputes. Because specific disputes have to be settled through direct negotiations.

But there were some other unfinished business, one of which was that the Conference was not able to agree on the rules that would govern fish stocks like tuna, which are highly migratory, travelling long distances through many people's fishing zones. Or fish stocks like salmon, whereby its life cycle could straddle two or more jurisdictions. At the Earth Summit, I had the opportunity to return to this unfinished business and to recommend that we hold a separate conference to deal with these remaining issues. And then I got Satya Nandan to chair the Conference. And he succeeded. He produced a new Convention on highly migratory species and straddling stocks of fish. So that loophole has been closed as a result of the Earth Summit and the subsequent Conference that Satya chaired.

Now, my next ambition for the sea which would probably take generations to achieve is to deal with the principal source of marine pollution — which is not ship-based but land-based, which presents an almost impossible task. To persuade all the countries of the world to take action in their respective territories, to stop discharging noxious substances like chemicals and untreated sewage to the sea. This is the biggest remaining threat to the safety and health of the sea, and it is an almost impossible challenge because there isn't the political will on the part of many countries to do it. Also, many countries are too poor and don't have the means to clean up, or clean the sewage before they dump it into the sea.

And I guess for millennia, men have treated the sea as our garbage dump and our public toilet. So to change that mindset, to say that is not the way to deal with the sea, is difficult. If you poison the sea, then more and more countries will be assaulted by the red tide, like Hong Kong was recently. And fish, which is the primary source of protein to human kind, will become increasingly contaminated or over-fished. And one day, we may find that we can't eat fish from the sea because of the contamination, which would be terrible tragedy for humankind. But it is an assiduous task, it's a task which I have to leave to succeeding generations, I think [laughs].

Vietnam's invasion of Cambodia, and ASEAN

IQ   **Maybe we would like to discuss on Singapore's role in UN on the Vietnamese invasion of Cambodia. You mentioned that a good ten years of your work in the UN was devoted on this issue. Could you tell us what was the reason for Singapore taking such a high profile regarding the Vietnamese conflict?**

TK   Historically, if you remember the second half of the 1970s, Saigon fell in April 1975, then Cambodia fell, Laos fell. There was a sense of crisis in Southeast Asia. It seemed as though North Vietnam was an aggressive power. It suffered, I think, at the time from triumphalism. And they were making threatening noises towards Thailand and others.

So there was a great and genuine fear that this great war machine could actually roll over the borders and threaten Thailand. Cambodia acted as buffer state between Vietnam and Thailand. So when the Vietnamese invaded Cambodia in December 1978, that buffer was gone, and Vietnamese troops were at the border of Thailand. This created a sense of anxiety in Thailand. And therefore we had to help Thailand, and we took the issue to the UN as a team.

We were part of a team, but because of our proactive nature — Singaporeans are proactive, hardworking — we are often asked by our ASEAN partners to do the dirty work for the team. I remember one of my bosses, Dhanabalan, used to scold me and said, "Tommy, why do you always do all this work for them?" So I always tell him that work is power, that we are a small member of the family. And to the extent that the bigger members of the family delegate the work to us and we do it well, we earned credit for the whole family, and for ourselves.

So because of our effective diplomacy in the UN, it enabled Singapore diplomats to become recognised by the world for their excellence. It was fortuitous, in a sense. And then we stayed with it and we had great enduring power. We stayed with it from December 1978, all the way until the Cold War ended and Vietnam changed, decided to leave Cambodia; and then there was the Paris Conference in 1989 which was inconclusive, and then 1991 when the issue was settled. So we stayed with it from December 1978 right up to October 1991.

IQ   **Singapore had played an active role in rounding up international support for the resolution condemning the invasion, with other UN delegates on the Non-Aligned Movement, and was eventually passed by a large vote in the General Assembly.**

TK   Yes.

258 • SPEAKING TRUTH TO POWER

IQ   **How was this achieved?**

TK   By a combination of persuasive arguments and sheer hard work. Because you really had to go from delegation with delegation to explain your case, and to convince them why it is in their national interest to support you. And so with the small countries in the Third World, one of our arguments which resonated with them is that if you are a small country and you have a big neighbour, you certainly don't want the big country to invade your territory on the excuse that you have an evil government, but then you become its colony. We persuaded the majority not to support the doctrine of humanitarian intervention, which has some legal basis in international law. It works against small countries. And the UN Charter is very strong on territorial integrity, non-interference and so on.

So for a combination of persuasive argument and the sheer hard work of going to talk to people, one on one, going back again and persuading them. But it was not a foregone victory. In 1979, when the issue first came up in the UN General Assembly, I was there. This was soon after the Non-Aligned Movement Summit in Havana, where the Cambodia delegation was thrown out unilaterally by Cuba.

So whether we could have succeeded in the UN in retaining the seat for Cambodia, and not be replaced by the Vietnamese-appointed government, was unknown. We don't really know because the opposition was so formidable that time. The Soviet Union, Vietnam, India ... India was the part of the team on the other side. And all the radical members in the Non-Aligned group were arrayed against us.

It was touch-and-go, actually, that first year — 1979. We fought very hard and prevailed. The majority was not big. It only became bigger with each passing year. But if you look up the record, our victory was quite small but very significant, because we took on the whole Soviet camp. We took on Vietnam and her friends like India and others, and prevailed. Once we did that, then the following year became easier.

And then with each succeeding year, we managed to persuade some of Vietnam's supporters to either move from Vietnam's camp to neutrality, or to move from neutrality to our side.

IQ   **How was that actually achieved?**

TK   I guess that's how diplomats earn their bread and butter. It's their job [laughs]. Go and persuade others that actually on merit, you have a better case than Vietnam, and that you are not a Chinese stooge, that you actually have a plan which will help the Cambodians get rid, sequentially, of the Vietnamese, and then the evil Khmer Rouge.

That was very important. If ASEAN's agenda was merely to oppose Vietnam, we could not have made the number of converts that we did. But what we did was that we actually developed a plan, which was adopted by the International Conference and Cambodia, held I think in 1981 at the UN, which showed the world that we also had a positive agenda. And the positive agenda was to not only persuade Vietnam to leave Cambodia, but to prevent the Khmer Rouge from coming back to power again, and to enable the Cambodian people to have a new dawn. So without that positive agenda, we would have made fewer converts.

IQ **At that point of time, why did ASEAN choose to take the Cambodian issue to the UN instead of dealing with Cambodia as an issue involving ASEAN and Vietnam alone?**

TK Vietnam would not come to our meetings. We had no alternative forum and the Non-Aligned Forum was being manipulated by Cuba against us. The only forum which offered us a level playing field was the UN. It's the only universal forum. So we took it there.

IQ **What were the reactions from our ASEAN member states on the diplomatic prominence which Singapore subsequently assumed on the issue?**

TK That was no problem, I mean. We worked very well as brothers and sisters. No, later on, we wisely said to our partners, "Look! It will not be fair if we were to do most of the work. So can we divide the member states into groups, and then each of us be responsible for a certain number of countries, and it is your responsibility to deliver the votes of those assigned to you. So we shared our workload.

We got along so well and we were not acting for own cause alone. It was a common cause. We were not a front-line state. Thailand was the front-line state. So I think they were grateful to us for having worked so hard, for a cause that was not immediate to Singapore.

IQ **So there was actually close cooperation between Singapore with the other ASEAN member states?**

TK Oh, yes, we met every day at the UN. We met every day, we plotted together, we devised all our strategies, developed our papers.

260 • SPEAKING TRUTH TO POWER

IQ   **Having served as Singapore's permanent representative to the UN from 1968 to 1971 and from 1974 to 1984 ...**

TK   Yes.

IQ   **Has it in any way affected your view of the world?**

TK   Oh, I am sure it has. Some would say that it has been a very bad thing to do, because it's made me too much of a citizen of the world. And still other people will say multilateral diplomacy is very different from bilateral diplomacy, and that bilateral diplomacy comes closer to reality.

I have no regrets, actually. I mean, I have done both. I had 13 years in UN and six years in Washington. I enjoyed my work both at the UN and in Washington. My agenda was different, and I found that many of the skills I developed at the UN were applicable in a different setting, with a different agenda. But the UN made me much more of a citizen of the world because you cannot live in this club and interact every day with men and women from so many nations, cultures, languages, without becoming sensitised. Becoming aware that we live in one global community and that the world is becoming more and more interdependent, interlinked has also developed, I think, a great deal of understanding and tolerance for other people.

And the UN taught me certain diplomatic skills, I would say, the skills of advocacy which I would have learned in law anyway. But it is different in diplomacy — the skill of drafting, the skill of negotiation and the skill of chairing meetings. Because by good fortune, I was beginning to get opportunities to chair meetings, so I was learning on the job, developing a new set of skills of chairing meetings.

As Ambassador to the US

IQ   **When you were moved from the UN in New York to the Singapore embassy in Washington DC, what new challenges did you see in your new assignment?**

TK   Before I arrived in Washington DC, I had gone to visit my predecessor who was my teacher in Law School. Punch Coomarasamy and I are very close, because we have known each other since I was a kid. And he is like an uncle to me.

Punch has never served in a multilateral posting. All his postings are bilateral — India, Australia, the United States. His mindset is therefore different from mine. His mindset is that of someone indoctrinated by the wisdom of the realist school in international politics, which teaches you that a country's influence in the world is roughly commensurate with your size.

So before I arrived in Washington, my good friend said to me, "Tommy, when you arrive in Washington, don't expect to be treated in the same way as you are now being treated at the UN, where people regard you as one of the movers and shakers. Because Singapore's position on the totem pole of the US is somewhere towards the bottom."

So I listened with respect to my teacher. But as I said, I didn't accept this, I don't accept that size is destiny. I said, "Before I leave Washington, I am going to make it one of the ten most influential missions in Washington."

So my first challenge was how to overcome the handicap of size and acquire that influence. But I was very fortunate because I was in Washington during what I would call the golden years of US-Singapore relations, with Reagan first in the White House and then later with [George H. W.] Bush.

Fortune smiled on me, I would say. I am very blessed because when I was permanent representative to the UN, the United States mission [to the UN] used to ask me each year whether I would be prepared to meet the two senators and the four congressmen that they appointed each year to their delegation to the UN. Most people don't bother. They wonder why they should bother cultivating these characters, because they just come for a few weeks and then they disappeared, and you would never meet them again.

But with my Boy Scout good nature, I hosted a lunch for them each year and invited my ASEAN brothers and sisters to meet them. And so I had a lot of friends in the US Senate and the House of Representatives. Because of this, the goodwill was generated and they remembered me. So when I was in Washington, these senators and congressmen extended their hand of friendship, you know. They said, "Whenever you want to see me, just call." So that door was open to me.

And then, you know, President Reagan, Vice-President Bush and [Secretary of State George] Shultz had such high opinion of Senior Minister, that I managed to have access to them. I was granted a degree of access not granted even to big powers. I could see Secretary Shultz. Normally if you are an ASEAN ambassador, the highest you can go is the Assistant Secretary of Statefor East Asian and Pacific Affairs [at the US State Department]. I had access to the White House. I had gone to the White House to see Reagan and also to see Bush. I had access to the National Security Council. So I was granted an unusual degree of access.

And then also, I found that it is not true that size is destiny, because your influence depends not just on how big your country is in the world, but how good you are. So I told my colleagues in the mission, "Look, if we work hard and if we could develop a special expertise on trade, I want the Singapore mission to be the most well-informed of all the ASEAN missions on US trade policy. That I want somebody in my team to be on the 'Hill' regularly. 'Hill' meaning the US Congress. So if there is anything in the works on trade policy, we would be the first to know.

So over time, our reputation was that if you wanted to know anything about US trade policy, ask Singapore. And at our monthly ASEAN meetings, they always looked to Singapore to brief them. We were happy to do that. Again I explained to my colleagues, like my deputy Lee Yoke Kwang who is here and Cecilia Khoo who's gone to PSD [Public Service Division], I think, that work is power. So I said, "Look, this is the lesson I learned at the UN — we are a small country; one way we can leverage ourselves and acquire a degree of influence that is beyond our size is to be knowledgeable and to be well-informed." And so we were. For example, I remember one day the [New York-based organisation] Asia Society asked whether I was prepared to debate the lobbyists for the textile and garment industry in America. Actually, they should have asked the ambassador of China or India or Pakistan — whoever are the big exporters of garment — but they asked me. Not because we are major garment exporter, but because I was very proactive. I was very pro-active in the Asia Society, in the think tanks and the universities. So I was very happy to debate this guy. Because I felt I was arguing for a just cause, for free trade, and against that kind of protectionist US trade policy in this particular sector.

So when you do a good job, and my colleagues did do a good job, your reputation begins to grow. And I would say that I don't know whether I have succeeded, but I would say that when I left in 1990 — and I don't want to be boastful — I would think that our position is certainly not where Punch thought it was on that totem pole of the US.

It was an unusual thing, when I was leaving. [US Secretary of State James] Baker actually had a farewell dinner for me at the State Department, and many people attended this dinner. And I was asked to speak briefly. This was an unusual mark of respect. Most of the time, they don't even give you a lunch. So fortune smiled on me, but also because I am a naive person who doesn't accept the received wisdom of the realists that you must know your place. Too many of our diplomats suffered from this syndrome — that you must know your place.

Actually, why should I accept that size is destiny? I always tell my colleagues. "Singapore is a very unusual small country. You are representing the 15th largest trading power in the world. We may be tiny, in terms of territorial size, we may be 150th in the world. But we are 15th in the world — our trading power. And you could also look at the other achievements of Singapore in the economic field, communications and so on."

Tommy Koh • **263**

IQ **You mentioned that the multilateral diplomacy is different ...**

TK From bilateral diplomacy.

IQ **So how do you actually go about it, as far as the conduct of diplomacy is concerned, to familiarise oneself with the American system?**

TK Well, I had the great fortune to having studied in America and lived in America for so long before I went to Washington. So it was a country that I already knew fairly well. A country that I had travelled extensively in. A country where I had networks of friends all over. So I had that advantage. If I were coming cold to America, not having studied there, not having worked in New York, having no friends, not familiar with the political process, then I would be lost.

Many of my African colleagues were lost. People were transferred from New York with me to Washington. I asked one ambassador of Tanzania, a very dear friend, I said, "What's your agenda in Washington?" He said, "I have no agenda." I said, "This is crazy! How can you have no agenda?!" He said, "I am lost here. Nobody is interested in my country." So I said, "You have to be proactive. You must define what you want to achieve as ambassador of Tanzania here. You then go and look for allies that will help you achieve your goals." I said, "Washington is so open, you know." The wonderful thing about America is such an open society, you see. And that if you have a point of view that is valid or has merit, if you have a good cause, you can find supporters. So whether it be on Cambodia, free trade or whatever, I found that it was possible to win over this cumbersome machinery called the United States Congress and to actually persuade them to pass the legislation that we wanted, or to oppose the bills that would be inimical to our national interest.

But we worked very hard. First, you have to understand how the system works, how the committee structures work. Find out who the influential members of the committee are, who the staffers are. Then I spent a lot of time visiting the US Congress. Every week, I would go up to the Hill, have lunch with the staffers. I worked very hard with the various agencies, because I know that in American politics, you can't expect the State Department to deliver. They can't. They were not as well organised as we are. So you have to organise them for themselves.

I used to joke with the Americans and said, "Look, you should pay me." Every month, I would have a working lunch with the Assistant Secretaries of the Department of State — Pentagon, the defence department, the CIA [Central Intelligence Agency], the White House and the NSC [National Security Council]. So we became good friends, and I was very fortunate that during my years in Washington, there was relatively little turf-fighting between them. So I was able to get these four important agencies to have a common point of view, and for me to explain what our point of view was. So hard work, understanding of the system, cultivating the right people. And I even cultivated the Civil Society of America, because they were very helpful in my work. I told my wife, "Let's divide the work. You cultivate two medical charities because you are a medical doctor, you can relate to them. And let me cultivate the Asia Society and the National Symphony Orchestra. And through them, I was able to get an entrée to important Americans.

So both in work and in play, we were able to gain access to people, develop a network of support for Singapore. So in the end, Washington was not as intimidating as most people think it is. I found that it was actually a very friendly and welcoming place.

IQ **One of the issues which cropped up during your term of ambassador was the decision by the Reagan administration to graduate Singapore from the generalised system of preferences (GSP) together with other NIC (newly industrialised countries) like South Korea, Hong Kong, Taiwan and so on. So how did we go about doing that?**

TK There were actually three very difficult issues I had to manage during my time. Although I said it was a golden period, it was not trouble-free. The most difficulty was not GSP but Hendrickson — when we asked Hendrickson to leave and they in turn asked Robert Chua to leave.[1]

Then second would be our perception that the Americans backtracked from the commitment given to us, not to graduate us until we bumped against a GDP per capita ceiling. And a third — another row we had with them was the sanctions which their Fish and Wildlife Services imposed against the import of aquarium fish from Singapore. Because of our decision not to become a party to a Convention to protect endangered species of flora and fauna called CITES [Convention on International Trade in Endangered Species of Wild Fauna and Flora]. So we had three fights with them. So it wasn't always hugs and kisses.

---

[1] In May 1988, the Singapore government expelled E. Mason "Hank" Hendrickson, first secretary of the political section of the US Embassy in Singapore, accusing him of interfering in Singapore politics by cultivating a group of lawyers to contest in elections against the PAP. In retaliation, the US State Department expelled Robert Chua, a diplomat in the Singapore embassy in Washington DC of equivalent rank to Hendrickson.

IQ **Maybe we would like to touch on Hendrickson. As you mentioned, we requested the US government withdraw Hendrickson, and they in turn requested that we withdraw one of our diplomats from Washington.**

TK Yes, right.

IQ **What was your reaction then?**

TK My reaction was to try to explain why we were asking Hendrickson to leave Singapore — to control the damage to our bilateral relations. So I was very proactive in the explanation part. I was not afraid. I offered to speak to various platforms on the reasons why we had a dispute over Hendrickson.

I wrote to the *Washington Post* to explain our point of view, and they published my letter. And then once the act was done, Hendrickson had left Singapore, Robert had been recalled, they tried to contain the damage and to get on with things. I think that Secretary Shultz was very upset because he had to defend his team. The United States and us never agreed on the facts, because they said Hendrickson was not guilty of the acts which we alleged. So there was a dispute about whether he had transgressed the line of propriety or not, and that was never resolved. We offered to refer the dispute to third party procedure, which they declined.

I felt that that was a good proposal to make, because it showed the American people that we were not afraid to refer this dispute between the two of us to a third party procedure, which may actually have found us at fault. And the fact that the United States was not prepared to accept a third party procedure put them on the defensive.

Winston Choo
The first Chief of Defence Force

Date of interviews: September 2002 and July 2009

Interviewers: Mok Chok San and Jason Lim

Lieutenant-General (Retired) Winston Choo (b. 1941) was appointed the Director of General Staff — the head of the Singapore Armed Forces — in 1974, and then became Singapore's first Lieutenant-General and first Chief of Defence Force, when his position was renamed in 1990.

Choo joined the military in 1959, after graduating from the Anglo-Chinese School. He received his officer cadet training at Federation Military College in Port Dickson, Malaya, and was commissioned a Second Lieutenant in 1961. When he was in 1st Battalion Singapore Infantry Regiment (1 SIR), he was deployed to Borneo in 1963 during the Confrontation between Indonesia and Malaysia.

He was recalled to the Singapore Armed Forces (SAF) in 1965 after serving as the first military aide-de-camp to President Yusof bin Ishak. After attending the US Army Command and General Staff course at Fort Leavenworth, Kansas, Choo returned to Singapore to command 1 SIR. In 1974, he became Director of General Staff, and was promoted to become the youngest Brigadier in the SAF at the age of 35 later that year.

He was the first professional soldier in the SAF to attain the rank of Major-General in 1976, and then the rank of Lieutenant-General in 1988. In 1990, Choo became Singapore's first Chief of Defence Force, retiring from the SAF two years later. Since then, he has served as Singapore's high commissioner to Australia, Fiji, South Africa, and as ambassador to Israel.

In these interviews, Choo talked about the action he witnessed when he was deployed to Borneo in 1963 during the period of Confrontation with Indonesia, and the situation in the armed forces during the time of Singapore's separation from Malaysia. He also shared extensively about his experience of working with Goh Keng Swee, when Goh was Minister for Defence, in building up the SAF.

Joining the military

MCS   **You joined the Singapore Military Forces after you finished your HSC [high school certificate]. How old were you then?**

WC   Well, when I joined, this is about November, October of 1959. And I was in the throes of my "A" level exams, so I was about 17 years old. I went for interviews halfway through or between papers.

MCS   **How was the officer cadet training like during that time?**

WC   Well, we went to Federation Military College (FMC), which was designed like Sandhurst[1] in those days — a two-year course. So what FMC did was to replicate what was done in Sandhurst. Most of the instructors, both the officer instructors and the warrant officer instructors, were British-seconded officers.

But there was a portion they called education or continuing education, which was requiring us to do "A" levels. So in my case, I already had two "A" level credits from school, and while I was in College, I sat for the "A" levels again.

And then, you had the military portion and it was conducted over a period of two years. So in the first year you were a junior cadet, in the second year you were a senior cadet.

MCS   **How different was this military portion as compared to our SAF Cadet Course?**

WC   Oh, different because, you see, FMC (now known as RMC, the Royal Military College of Malaysia) was designed for career officers. And so they could afford two years, whereas for us today, the courses we conduct in OCS (Officer Cadet School) are

---

[1] The Royal Military Academy Sandhurst is the British Army's initial officer training centre.

designed for National Service, which they do full-time for two and a half years. So, if we do a two-year programme, it would mean that effectively they got six months to serve before their ORD [Operationally Ready Date]; that's what they call it nowadays.

Well, the OCS Course concentrated purely on the military and operational aspects, whereas the Sandhurst type of course — because of the time available — they could spend time on things like Military History, Military Law, Military Accounts and a host of other things that are intended to prepare you to be a regimental officer upon your commissioning. Whereas our OCS is designed for you to become a Platoon Commander straightaway, full stop, because that's all the time that we have.

MCS **So, which was the unit you first got posted to?**

WC When I was commissioned in 1961, 9 December 1961, I think, that was the date if I am not wrong … there was only one battalion at that time, 1 SIR [Singapore Infantry Regiment]. So, I was commissioned and then sent to 1 SIR. In 1961 we were a self-governing state but we were still a British colony, in the sense that Defence and Foreign Affairs were still handled by the British.

So, my commissioning certificate was signed by the Yang di-Pertuan Negara, the Head of State, although it was the Queen's representative in the sense that … the Queen was still the sovereign.

MCS **How was the life of a PC [Platoon Commander] like then?**

WC Well, you see, when we first went to 1 SIR, the concentration in the early days of 1 SIR was really on internal security. So, a lot of time was spent in training on internal security, and then in jungle warfare. The soldiers were all regulars. So, when I was commissioned in 1961, I was 20 years old. My platoon sergeant, Nelson Sng — you know, Sng Cheng Chye who's retired now — he was the RSM [Regimental Sergeant Major] of the SAF while he was still serving.

The Indonesian Confrontation[2]

MCS **Maybe I can now change the topic to the insurgency and the Confrontation period. Were you involved in any fire fight[3] situation where your life was in danger?**

WC Well, my battalion went to Sabah during Confrontation. We were based on Sebatik Island which is part of that chain of islands which is now still an issue between Malaysia and Indonesia. You know, the Ligitan and Sipadan Islands.[4] So, it is that chain of islands, Sebatik being one of those. But Sebatik is nearer the Sabah coastline. So, half of Sebatik is Indonesian, the southern half, while the northern half is Malaysian. So, we were there. I mean, that was a real operational situation, in the sense that it was a shooting war. It is not unusual for us to be shelled with a mortar. And when you went on the patrols, you sometimes met the Indonesian forces and then there would be a fire fight.

The Indonesian volunteers that came — either they got parachuted in or they came by boats — and we were involved in a sweep to capture them. And my battalion was more fortunate than the second battalion, the 2 SIR, which had an incident [in the jungles of Kota Tinggi, Johor].

This platoon was a composite platoon led by a sergeant where they were encamped for the night, but they did not do all the necessary security and protective duties. The Indonesians came and wiped the whole lot up, and shot them up very brutally, you know. And their bodies were scattered all over the jungle. And so it was almost a vendetta after that, and the battalion went out and got every one of the Indonesians that did it. And I am afraid that there were no prisoners either. So, I mean, it was that kind of situation. When in Sabah, we [1 SIR in Sabah] were living every day not being sure whether tomorrow was going to be there. I mean, it's a war situation; it's an operational situation, were we afraid? Yes, we were afraid, but after some time you got used to such a situation. Manning the trenches was a drill, it was something that we did as an accepted thing, and when you are shelled,

---

[2] Because of Indonesia's opposition to the creation of the Federation of Malaysia to include Singapore, North Borneo (now Sabah) and Sarawak, Indonesia launched a series of cross-border raids into Malaysian territory on the island of Borneo, in a policy of *Konfrontasi* (Confrontation).

[3] A military term referring to a shoot out with an enemy force.

[4] The Internal Court of Justice awarded Ligitan and Sipadan Islands to Malaysia in December 2002, shortly after this interview with Winston Choo took place.

you go right to the bottom of the trench. You would be walking around with loaded weapons everywhere you go.

MCS **Did some of these experiences change the way you look at leadership and conduct of war?**

WC No, I think the conduct of war is different. I mean, the conduct of war is dependent on the actual type of operations we go into. Leadership has never changed then as it is today; leadership is the ability to have the soldier or the people you are commanding work with you. And whether it is in a nuclear war, a 21st century conventional operation or back in the days of a limited war like the Confrontation, it is important that the Section Commander, the Platoon Commander, the Company Commander and the Battalion Commander are able to work with their men.

And I've seen all kinds of people, you know, and even the best of the British; three of our companies were commanded by British colonel officers when we were in Sabah. Right? So, even the British officers, they may not necessarily show themselves off to be good leaders, you know.

Separation from Malaysia

MCS **Maybe now we go on to this question of the Separation. What was your reaction when suddenly you found Singapore separated from Malaysia?**

WC Okay, 1965; I was the BSO — Battalion Signals Officer, and at the same time 2nd Command of HQ Company. When it was announced that we were separated, it came up on television, I think. SM [Senior Minister] then PM [Lee Kuan Yew]. Yes, we were shocked. Bear in mind the composition of our battalion — my Battalion Commander was a Malaysian, you know, at that time. The Company Commanders were a mix of Singaporeans as well as British. My GSO [General Staff Officer], or S3 [Training and Operation Officer] now as you call it (back then you called him Adjutant) was a British officer.

And in 1965, we had been part of the Malaysian Armed Forces for two years. Things were happening which we ourselves as originally Singaporean officers were not necessarily happy about. Like how they changed our name from Singapore Infantry Regiment to Malaysian Infantry Regiment; from SIR to MIR. And then the Malay name was Persatuan Infantry Malaysia, so the abbreviation was PIM. And we were obviously not happy about the change of name.[5] There was no need for the change of name in our opinion. So, we looked upon it as a move to remove our identity.

There was this disquiet amongst ourselves about this. Mind you, even the British officers who had been with us since before 1963, and who had gone through the Malaysian Emergency era, were not necessarily pleased with some of these changes. And frankly also, we saw the cards were on the table — for those of us who were non-Malays, our chances of actually doing well were not going to be very good. I mean, that was no secret.

So, we were not necessarily very happy being part of the Malaysian Armed Forces. That was the scenario of people like us in the military at the time of the separation.

So, when Separation was announced, the first reaction was shock, and then there was elation and exuberance. And funny enough, the people that were actually celebrating this with them were the British officers besides ourselves, you know. I remember a British officer went to the mess, and the first thing he did was to remove the Yang di-Pertuan Agong's[6] photograph from the mess. But we had to be again sensitive to the fact that we had Malaysian officers and a Malaysian Commanding Officer.

After that, sensibility prevailed and people started to settle down and waited to see what came next.

Origins of the SAF

MCS So, let's move now on to the SAF; the origins of the SAF. When SAF was formed in 1967, which were the countries we approached to help us form the army?

WC I think, there is enough material out there on this.

---

[5] Presumably because PIM, when read, would sound like "pimp".
[6] The Malaysian King.

MCS **Is it?**

WC You must bear in mind when that happened, I was a very junior officer. Actually, shortly after that in September or late August, I was moved to the Istana to become ADC [Aide-de-Camp] to President Yusof Ishak. So, obviously I was out of the loop from understanding what were the considerations, who were approached. But, I think, if you read SM's memoirs, you would know.

We approached the British, we approached the Australians and, I think, the Indians, the Egyptians and the Israelis. But as it turned out, I think, the Israelis were the ones that came up with the most possibly favourable plan for us to build an armed force, and that was where we went. And I don't know, I can't delve into the minds of Dr Goh Keng Swee and Lee Kuan Yew, who were actually involved in these things, as to the considerations. But I am quite sure, or I would venture a guess to say, the similarities of the situation of Israel and Singapore really did not matter.

MCS **But then later on, when you rose up to more senior positions, did you observe how the Malaysians and Indonesians reacted to this fact that Singapore was actually asking Israel to help with the SAF?**

WC No, Singapore by then had already asked.

MCS **Yes, that's right.**

WC We already had Israeli advisors here disguised as Mexicans. We were calling them all kind of things, but it was no secret … it was an open secret, right? So, later on in my conversations with my Malaysian friends, my Malaysian counterparts, and the Indonesians, outwardly, politely, they said, "Oh, it's fine," but inwardly, obviously, they knew that we had chosen as advisors people who were serious about soldiering, serious about preparing a military force that was credible. Because Israel, as shown by their own actions right from their Independence War through the Six-Day War, through the Yom Kippur War and so on, that using National Servicemen, they had still been able to take on larger countries around them.

So in the backs of their minds, they considered the fact that Israeli advisors were here, that the Singapore Armed Forces was actually being formed through the advice of very professional and serious military people. If you ask me whether it was good or bad, I think it was good. Because even if — though that's not the case — we don't turn up anywhere near like the IDF, the Israeli Defence Force, the fact that they were training us was in itself one hell of a deterrent.

MCS **But as the CDF [Chief of Defence Force], how did you explain to the Malaysian and Indonesian counterparts Singapore's SAF build up, which seemed very aggressive?**

WC No, we have never had to explain that, because I think we have never been apologetic about what we were doing. It's only very recently that we started to show openly the things we have, the things we do. But in the early days, everything was kept under wraps, so it wasn't public knowledge that we had this equipment, we had that weapon. It was only during one National Day — because that was the time when again, I think, the Malaysians were posturing — that we rolled out our tanks.[7]

MCS **That was in 1991 is it?**

WC I can't remember which year that was. Actually those tanks had just landed in our docks, painted up and all that, then General Colin Theseira was the Column Commander for the tanks. But other than that kind of thing, we had never overtly or intentionally or openly boasted. And for very good reasons, you know. Because we were not really ready, so why create unnecessary friction. Even without us having to create the friction, it was already there.

---

[7] A joint Malaysian-Indonesian military exercise, codenamed Malindo Darsasa 3AB, took place in August 1991. Part of the exercise was an airborne assault by paratroopers in southern Johor codenamed Pukul Habis ("Total Wipeout") that was scheduled for 9 August, Singapore's National Day. The SAF triggered an open mobilisation in response.

MCS But in the early years, did the Malaysians and Indonesians do anything to make it difficult for us to build up the SAF?

WC I don't think they made it difficult for us to build up, because there was a limit to what they could do, and they knew that. But obviously they didn't give us training areas; Malaysia never gave us training areas, so that's why we had to go to Taiwan, Brunei, Australia and New Zealand. I mean, we are the only armed force in the world that can tell people to join the army to see the world, because we are training everywhere.

So, they didn't have to. We had our own obstacles without them creating it, but in the later stages where, at least the Indonesians felt, that there was no reason for them to stop us. General Benny[8] himself told me and he spoke openly to the Temasek Society. He said that he did not see the SAF as a threat, which is true. Indonesia is so big. There is no reason for Singapore to take aggressive military action in Indonesia. No, he didn't see that, but on the other hand, his point was that a strong SAF would be good for Indonesia. And indeed, I worked with him to open up the air range in Siabu, and things like that.

And then he said two things that are in my mind: that the distance from Jakarta to Singapore is nearer than Jakarta to the extremes portions of Indonesia. So, what happens in Singapore would have a greater impact on Jakarta than what happens in some other areas of Indonesia. Number two, he saw that the SAF was growing professionally, and by opening up the areas to us, he saw it as an opportunity for the air force in Indonesia to learn from our air force. So, it was a mutual benefit.

Early encounters with Goh Keng Swee

JL At what point of your career did you work with Dr Goh?

WC I think I first met Dr Goh, or got to know of Dr Goh, when I was ADC to President Yusof Ishak in the Istana, at the time when Singapore had just broken away from Malaysia.

---

[8] Leonardus Benjamin Moerdani, known as Benny Moerdani, was Commander-in-Chief of the Indonesian National Armed Forces from 1983 to 1988, effectively Winston Choo's counterpart, and then became Minister of Defence and Security.

And the biggest impact to my life was Dr Goh's call for me to come back to the SAF halfway through my term as ADC to President Yusof. He was building up the SAF and he was short of certain categories of officers, and I was a Communications or Signals Officer. So he asked that I come back to the Ministry of Defence. But to cut a long story short, there was a lot of argument over whether I should come back or not, between President Yusof and PM Lee Kuan Yew at that time. Of course, Dr Goh was never the front for this. He told PM and PM told President that I should go back. So eventually, I went back.

And Dr Goh called me up and said, "You are better off soldiering than pushing chairs and opening car doors." These were the terms he used. So he met with me and briefed me exactly what he had in mind, on why I was brought back. Because we were starting the formation of the signals organisation of the SAF, and as you know, communications is vital if you want to run a credible armed force or an army. So he told me, "You come back," and by then, there was a police officer who was Head of the Communications of the Police. He was a Deputy Superintendent of Police — Michael Too, who was there. And I was to start off the first Signals battalion and to work under Michael Too, who was Chief Communications (Electronics). And he told me that "We will send you to England." This was Dr Goh. He planned ahead. "We will send you to England to do a communication and electronics course with the Royal Signals, and you will come back and eventually, you will take over as Chief Signals Officer." That was the kind of thing that he did. So that was my first encounter with Dr Goh.

JL   **What were your feelings as you stepped in and met Dr Goh for the first time?**

WC   With all the stories one heard about him, and though I had seen him in the Istana on various occasions, Dr Goh was not somebody that would say "Hi" to you and be friendly. He normally looked down, didn't look up. You know, very grouchy. So when I was going to see him in his office, I was short of trying to wet my pants. That was the kind of feeling one got. But sitting in a chair across from him, across the table, he came across as very, very ... I wouldn't say friendly, but upfront. He was not lecturing you or talking down to you. He would just call me and lay out his thoughts: "Winston, let me tell you why you had to come back." It was that kind of a tone he used — why it was important, what the plans were. So he laid it out nicely. Eventually, I felt ... I won't say relaxed, but at least not so apprehensive.

Becoming Director of General Staff[9]

JL   **So you only had to report to Dr Goh directly when you were Director of General Staff [DGS]?**

WC   Short of becoming CDF [Chief of Defence Force] or DGS. The year, I cannot remember — 1969, 1970s, I think. I had gone to Staff College.

JL   **At Fort Canning?**

WC   Fort Canning. Somewhere along that stage, he called me up to his office. Again, I was wondering "What was this about?" And he practically told me my future, almost. He said that "From here, you are going to command 4 SIR because you haven't had a battalion command. You were only commanding a Signals unit. 4 SIR command, short term. Then you go to Command and General Staff College, United States. You come back, you do a posting in MINDEF [Ministry of Defence] in the General Staff. Then you become DGS."

Can you imagine? At that stage, I was 29 or 30 years old, that kind of age. I looked rather blankly at him when he said all these kind of things. And I think the people who were privy to these movements were Director of Manpower then, Chia Cheong Fook, and of course Pang Tee Pow who was the Permanent Secretary, and the chief Israeli adviser that was here at that time — Jack [Yaakov] Elazari [...] I think there were about five people or so who were privy to this.

My reaction was: "But I am young." I told him, "If I become DGS in about three years' time or whatever, you have just shortened my career!" Because, how long can I be DGS? (Then the title was Director, General Staff.) Three years, four years, five years? Which bring me to about 35, 36 years old. Then what happens? I joined the army as a career, a lifetime career. He looked at me and he said, "Don't worry. You just go and do." He was that kind of a person. "Yes sir." And I walked out, still dazed.

---

[9]At that time around 1970, the title of the head of the SAF was Director of General Staff (DGS), and was held by a Brigadier. After Winston Choo assumed the position of DGS in 1974, the position became that of Chief of General Staff (CGS), and Choo was promoted to Major-General. In 1990, Choo's position was renamed Chief of Defence Force (CDF), and he was promoted to Lieutenant-General.

278 • SPEAKING TRUTH TO POWER

JL   **Did you ever wonder why you were selected to be DGS?**

WC   I don't know. Actually, I spoke to the Israeli adviser and Pang Tee Pow. First, the Israeli adviser said to me, "Well, he was looking around for somebody who's got some degree of intelligence and some sense of educational achievement." (Laughs) And somebody who had come from the professional ranks of the armed forces, and not like my predecessor, Kirpa Ram Vij, who was from the civil service and had become a volunteer.

      I said, "But I am not a university graduate." At that time, I had only two "A" level certificates — one from Singapore in ACS [Anglo-Chinese School]. The other when I went to military college, I did another "A" level, which was compulsory. For SAF, that was enough at that time. "You must have caught his eyes somewhere as having a person with some degree of leadership capabilities." But Pang Tee Pow came back to me and said, "He thinks you can be a good chief." Just it. (Laughs)

      In those days, what he [Dr Goh] thought was done. So you asked me, "Why?" I don't know. I can only give you these little anecdotes of what people told me. But as it turned out, I survived 18 years as Chief.

JL   **You started reporting directly to Dr Goh at what stage?**

WC   When I came back from the US ... well, before then, he used to check on me. When I was CO [Commanding Officer] for 4 SIR, I did some exercises. It was a brigade exercise — two brigade exercises controlled by 3rd Brigade, and I think by which time, the news had leaked that I was the future chief. And of course, there were lots of people much more senior than me. The controller of the exercise, the Brigade Commander from 3rd Brigade, was taking it out on me, making life difficult for me throughout the exercise.

JL   **What rank were you then?**

WC   I was Lieutenant-Colonel. And this officer was also a Lieutenant-Colonel and Brigade Commander of 3rd Brigade. I was given a tough time. So I took it in my stride. But funny as it may seem, Dr Goh called me up two three weeks after the exercise and he said, "What is this? I heard Peter Lim gave you a tough time, is it?" Therefore, he must have had his ears on the ground. That was how he found out. So he said, "Never mind. That's the way it must be. You keep it up. It's okay." He told me. He was that kind of person.

You asked me whether I reported to him. This was not reporting per se, but he was calling you up more than you reporting to him. But my actual reporting to him took place again when I came back from Staff College, United States around 1972. I was called up. He said, "You will go to 1 SIR for a while, because I want you to go to 2nd Brigade, and because you must do the various levels of command. But 2nd Brigade is not quite available yet. So you go to 1 SIR as the CO of 1 SIR." So I went to 1 SIR, and then 2nd Brigade position became available. "You go to 2nd Brigade. Maybe six months to half a year in 2nd Brigade, then you come to MINDEF." He told me, "You come to MINDEF, become Head, Training. Then Head, Organisation and Plans, then DGS [Director General Staff]." "Yes Sir." So I went through the process.

Then when I went to MINDEF as Head, Training, that was when I saw him more often. Like I said, he did not speak to my DGS. The things that he wanted to know about training or things like that, he would call me up directly. He said, "I think we should find places for our commandos to train, as there is no possibility in Singapore. Why won't we try Thailand?" So we made some contacts and all that. Tham Chee Onn, who was in the commandos (not the CO of commandos) and I went to Thailand in 1973, made contacts. I think the contacts were established through our SID [Security and Intelligence Division]. Made contact, and we went to Lopburi which is the Special Forces' [46th U.S. Army Special Forces] camp, to make the arrangements. And there was no precedent for training overseas and payment, that kind of thing. And Chi Owyang, who was then our Ambassador to Thailand ...

JL   **But Dr Goh accepted that.**

WC   He accepted that. He was a very practical man. So he got his information that way. He spoke to people. Oh, Singapore is a small place. Let me put it that way.

280 • SPEAKING TRUTH TO POWER

Working with Goh Keng Swee

JL   **So as first Director of General Staff [DGS], was it part of your work that you had to report to Dr Goh about any major issues?**

WC   There was no set schedule of reporting. He called you whenever he wanted to know about something, or he wanted you to do something. Otherwise, you would meet him normally at the weekly MINDEF HQ meetings where you would present a paper and discuss things. Of course, in the process, other things are discussed. And you got your instructions through these meetings. But reporting to him mostly was dependent upon whether you had something to tell him, or whether he had something to tell you. Most of the time, it would be the other way — that he had something to tell you.

Because I was in the old MINDEF in Tanglin, it took me about a good four minutes to walk to his office because of the distance. And it was like walking the stations of cross[10] when he called you.

"What the hell does he want this time?" You would try to guess. You walked in there, you saw his PA [Personal Assistant]. The first thing you asked her was: "Miss Tan, the mood, how?" She said, "Okay, okay. He is quite happy."

So you went in down there. His room was not brightly lit. So he used a magnifying glass sometimes because his eyesight was not very good. He used a magnifying glass as though he were a stamp collector. Then suddenly he would look up, "Ah, Winston. Let me show you this." It would be a range finder. "That is a range finder." He said, "I am going to use this for the golf course. Then I can know how far ..." And I said, "That is illegal, you are not allowed to use it when you are playing golf. Your golfing partners will not be happy." He looked, looked, looked and then he opened his office door. It looked out to the Botanical Gardens. You know, the golf course [that used to be around there]. You could see the range. Then we just talked about golf, and I would go back.

So you got that kind of thing. Or sometimes, he called you up, "You know this thing is not on." I said, "What?" "You saw the report about the food poisoning in a particular camp? (I can't remember which one.) I think you have to have the CO [Commanding Officer] removed." Just like that.

I said, "Okay. Fine, let me go and find out." And you went out and checked and came back and told him, "Actually, it was not the CO's fault." "So you think he should

---

[10] The Stations of the Cross is a 14-step Catholic devotion that remembers Jesus Christ's last day on earth.

stay?" "You removed him." "There must be a reason to remove him if he is guilty." "All right, all right." He was like that. "You got a case, sack him!" "Can I recommend that we demote him?" "Okay, demote him."

It was that kind of dealing when you dealt with him. If you explained, he was fine. You wanted to know his style — whether he liked criticism. You could disagree with him to an extent. You didn't criticise him, not in an open forum. Even to disagree, you had better know your facts before you disagreed. What I normally did was when he said he wanted to get it done this way, you didn't object or you didn't react immediately. Then you went back to see him and say, "Dr Goh about this, this, this ... You are saying that we should go and do certain things in a certain way. I have thought about it, and I think that the repercussions would be such and such. Could I suggest and recommend we do it some other way?" Then you went into a discussion with him. If he agreed with you, go ahead.

There had been occasions when he disagreed with me. So I accepted it because I had done my part as his subordinate, as a staff to him, to point out all the facts. Then he makes ... he thinks it is a risk worth taking. Then you went all the way with him. But you wouldn't engage him or criticise him openly, because I think any man will be like that. But more so for Dr Goh, maybe because he did not suffer fools gladly and in the same manner. He didn't like to be shown up to be not right. But neither was he such a person that he would not accept reasoning. I found on many occasions that I could reason things out with him, when he wanted to do something that I thought was not right at that time.

JL **These MINDEF HQ meetings, could you tell us something, say, about the atmosphere of the meetings, or how he chaired the meetings?**

WC He would come in, he would sit down. There would be a proper agenda, and we would go through the agenda, and the minutes of the previous meeting. It was conducted like a board meeting in the civilian sense of the word. We would go through the agenda, the matters arising, and then the minutes, the matters arising, and then the topics to be amended or to be presented, or things for information, and so on. It was a small room. It was a very narrow room because those were the old British senior officers' quarters, bedrooms converted into a room. And then there were all the Directors: General Staff, Logistics, Manpower and the two Perm Secs. So there would be about 10 or 12 people in that room. Air Force, Navy.

And we used to smoke. I used to remember. I mean the biggest smoker there was the late Ong Kah Kok.[11] Dr Goh smoked sometimes, because he smoked my cigarettes. (Laughs) It was terrible, by today's standards where smoking is most unacceptable. But I tell you, if you opened the door [of the meeting room], you could see the smoke coming down. And there was another thing that was always there, and that would be the Polar Cafe curry puffs. There had always to be enough for one each, but Dr Goh would have two. So you didn't take more than one (laughs).

The meetings were very business-like. Of course, it was also very human; it was interspersed with jokes, laughter, that kind of thing. So one did not fear going to MINDEF HQ meetings although one did not come out of meeting feeling terrible. There were some people who had been criticised and so on, but normally, it was the meeting where business was conducted and things followed up thereafter.

JL   **During these meetings, could you tell from the body language of Dr Goh whether he was happy with certain developments, or unhappy, fed up?**

WC   Oh yes, you could see from his body language, which was so pronounced. When he shifted about his chair and he looked down, not looking up at you, you knew he was unhappy about something. And normally from the context of what went on, you knew what he was unhappy about. Oh, he was very readable in terms of body language. At least I found it to be so. And I am sure that the people, my colleagues who were there, would also be able to tell.

Learning from the Americans, Japanese and the "Winsemius of the SAF"

JL   **What was your understanding of Dr Goh's vision for the future of the SAF during your interactions with him?**

WC   I think what he wanted was to have an armed forces that was credible, that was respected, not only in the region but internationally. And it had to have the right equipment, the right people and the right training. So that was the emphasis that

---

[11] The then Director of Logistics at the Ministry of Defence.

was always given. If you had to have equipment, we had to try to get the best that we could afford to buy. People, you had to get the right people, train them, give them the education. That's why we send them around to various colleges, to various countries and all that. Expose them and bring back to Singapore along with knowledge of all the good things about various armies, and then create and evolve a culture for the SAF, such that it became a credible deterrent. That had always been his vision and he never deviated from that.

So what you see in the SAF today is an extension of what Dr Goh had envisioned the SAF to be. Now, we have the 3G [third generation] SAF. All that is an extension of his vision and he would not have spared expense. For instance, we needed to know things to expand our knowledge, our professionalism; immediately after the Vietnam War, he said, "Let's go and learn what the Americans did not do right." And he sent a whole team; I led a whole team to Fort Bragg, North Carolina,[12] and we spent about three weeks talking to various people. We also arranged meetings with the Pentagon, talking to them for three weeks or so about their experience in Vietnam — what went wrong. And we came back and we documented it here.

Then through the Security Intelligence's connections, we arranged to meet with the Japanese generals of the Second World War — Sugita[13] and a few others. We were closeted in the Dai-ichi Hotel in Tokyo, and a group of us who went through the Japanese mission and military operations in this part of the world to get their considerations, and so on. It was all Dr Goh's doing.

Later on, he felt that we need a Winsemius [Albert Winsemius][14] in the SAF, the equivalent of Winsemius. So through SID again, through S. R. Nathan,[15] we got Siegfried Shultz who was a Lieutenant-General from the German Army. He was a young lieutenant towards the closing stages of the Second World War. And he came here and was an adviser to us for a long time. He was only to advise on the Army, not the SAF as a whole, although we had advisers for the Air Force, the Navy and so on. But he [Dr Goh] felt that because we had so much Israeli influence, he would say, "Let's see whether we could get a different perspective." And Shultz was with us close to 10, 12 years. The great man has passed away now. I used to work with him. We found that he was very useful. If you wanted things done, you would write the papers

---

[12] A US military installation, the largest of its kind in the world.

[13] Ichiji Sugita was a general of the Japanese Imperial Army who was a principal participant in the surrender of Singapore by the British during World War II.

[14] The Dutch economist who was the instrumental adviser behind Singapore's successes in economic development and industrialisation.

[15] The Director of the SID who later became the President of Singapore in 1999.

for Shultz to sign and it normally got approved. That's how we started the General Staff in the SAF.

I argued with Shultz; we needed a General Staff. And from there, we took it one step further and had a Joint Staff, and all of this was through the support and assistance of the adviser of somebody like General Shultz. And Dr Goh would listen to him.

Dr Goh wanted the best for the SAF. He wanted the best of advice, usually saying, "Let's go and seek it. Let's go and pay for it to get the advice."

CPSIA information can be obtained
at www.ICGtesting.com
Printed in the USA
BVHW041637130320
574934BV00008B/35